OTHER BOOKS BY ELIZABETH WAYLAND BARBER

Archaeological Decipherment
Prehistoric Textiles

WOMEN'S WORK:

THE FIRST 20,000 YEARS

WOMEN'S WORK:
THE FIRST 20,000 YEARS

Women, Cloth, and Society
in Early Times

Elizabeth Wayland Barber

W. W. NORTON & COMPANY

NEW YORK LONDON

First published as a Norton paperback 1995

The text of this book is composed in Sabon, with
the display set in Bernhard Modern Bold.
Manufacturing by the Courier Companies, Inc.
Book design by JAM Design.

Library of Congress Cataloging-in-Publication Data
Barber, E.J.W., 1940–
Women's work : the first 20,000 years : women, cloth, and society
in early times / Elizabeth Wayland Barber.
p.   cm.
Includes bibliographical references (p.   ) and index.
1. Textile fabrics, Prehistoric.   2. Women, Prehistoric.
3. Textile fabrics, Ancient.   4. Women—History.   I. Title.
GN799.T43B37   1994
305.4´3´09—dc20   93-47924

ISBN 0-393-31348-4

W. W. Norton & Company, Inc., 500 Fifth Avenue, New York, N.Y. 10110
W. W. Norton & Company Ltd., 10 Coptic Street, London WC1A 1PU

2 3 4 5 6 7 8 9 0

To Paul,
whose idea it was

Contents

CONTENTS

Preface

My mother liked to weave and sew, so I grew up with interesting textiles all around, learning to sew and weave for myself at an early age. I was constantly being made aware of the form, color, and texture of cloth. Textiles have a particular crossing structure that dictates what sorts of patterns will be easy and obvious to weave or, conversely, hard to weave. Thus later, when I began to study Classical and Bronze Age Mediterranean archaeology at college, I soon noticed decorations on durable things like pottery and walls that looked as if they had been copied from typical weaving patterns. But when I suggested this idea to archaeologists, they responded that nobody could have known how to weave such complicated textiles so early. The answer was hard to refute, on the face of it, because very few textiles have come down to us from before medieval times, outside of Egypt, where people generally wore plain white linen.

Unconvinced, I decided to spend two weeks hunting for data on the degree of sophistication of the weaving technology, to see at least whether people *could* have made ornate textiles back then. I expected to write my findings into a small article, maybe ten pages, suggesting that scholars ought to consider at least the possibility of early textile industries.

But when I began to look, data for ancient textiles lay everywhere, waiting to be picked up. By the end of the two weeks I realized that it would take me at least a summer or two to chase down and organize the leads I had turned up and that I could be writing a 60-page monograph. By the end of two more summers I knew I was headed for a 200-page book. That "little book" turned into a research project that consumed seventeen years and yielded a 450-page tome covering many times the planned geographical area and time span. It finally appeared in 1991 as *Prehistoric Textiles,* from Princeton University Press.

For that book I had restricted myself to the history and development of the craft: a big enough topic, as it turned out. Along the way I kept running across wonderful bits of information about the women—virtually always women—who produced these textiles and about the values that different societies put on the products and their makers. When I talked about my work, people seemed especially eager for these vignettes, stories that told of women's lives thousands of years ago. They urged me to write a second book on the economic and social history of ancient textiles, in effect on the women who made the cloth and clothing.

Then a friend asked me to read her unfinished translation of the memoirs of Nadezhda Durova, a woman who had spent ten years disguised as a man serving in the czar's cavalry during the Napoleonic Wars. Far from giving a catalog of campaigns, battle arrays, and tactics, Durova spent the entire war recording how people lived from day to day: how she and her fellow soldiers interacted with horses, geese, each other, the weather, and the local folk with whom they were billeted. I am not normally fond of reading history, but this was different. I could hardly wait for each new installment. As I realized that the source of my fascination was the glimpses into real people's lives, I began to understand in a new way what my early material contained. (This book has now appeared as *The Cavalry Maiden,* translated by Mary Fleming Zirin [Bloomington: Indiana University Press, 1988].)

Thus I have tried to explore and pull together what real facts we can deduce about early women, their lives, their work, and their values, chiefly from the technological record of the one major product of women that has been well studied as yet—textiles. I have also paid some attention to what language can tell us. Messages perish as they are uttered, but language itself is remarkably durable. Sometimes it preserves useful clues to a more abstract and thought-oriented part of the human past than material artifacts do.

Perhaps the most important thing that has been omitted from this book, however, is fiction. Romantics may enjoy Hollywood tales of Ooga and Oona grunting around the fire of a squat and hairy, stoop-shouldered Palaeolithic ruffian, after he has dragged them in by the hair from the next cave. Idealists may savor the rosy utopian visions of "life before war" in a Neolithic age ruled by women totally connected to the pulse of Mother Earth. These stories are fun. But what, I ask, was life *really* like? What hard *evidence* do we have for what we might want to know about women's lives? No evidence means no real knowledge.

Stacked against our endless questions, what we know remains small, and no matter how clever we become at tracking down evidence, if we want reality, we are stuck with what fragmentary facts we happen to have. I have not invented answers just to fill in, the way a screenwriter must. But we know much more than has gotten into the general literature about women's history. The reader will find in these pages glimpses of real women of all sorts—peasants, entrepreneurs, queens, slaves, honest souls, and crooks—good and bad, high and low. For all the strangeness of their cultures, they seem refreshingly like us.

WOMEN'S WORK:

THE FIRST 20,000 YEARS

Introduction

"Four, three, two, one—good. One more bunch to go; then we've got to get dinner on."

I yanked the loose knot out of the last bundle of pea green warp threads and began passing the ends through the rows of tiny loops in the middle of the loom to my sister to tie up on the far side. The threads of the warp are those lying lengthwise in the finished cloth, and the most tedious part of making a new cloth comes in stringing these onto the loom, one at a time. Once you begin to weave in the cross-threads—the weft—you can see the new cloth forming inch by inch under your fingers, and you feel a sense of accomplishment. But the warp just looks like thread, thread, and more thread. At this moment I was balancing the pattern diagram on my knee, counting out which little loop each thread had to pass through on its way from my side of the loom to hers.

For nearly eight hours we had been working on the warp, between and around the interruptions. In the morning we had wound off the requisite number of green and chocolate brown threads of fine worsted wool, stripe by color stripe, onto the great frame of warping pegs—pegs that hold the threads in order while measuring them all to the same length. By lunchtime we were ready to transfer the warp to the loom, tying one end of the long, thick bundle of yarn to the beam on one side. Then began the tedious task of threading the ends through the control loops (heddles) in the middle on their way to the far beam. It would have been simpler if we had intended to use the plainest sort of weave. But because we were setting up to weave a pattern—the fine diagonal pattern called twill that is used typically today in men's suit material (see fig. 0.2)—it was taking far longer.

"Why am I doing this?" I thought ruefully, glancing at the time. "We've spent the entire day and aren't even ready to start weaving yet! If I spent this much time every day writing, my book would be finished in no time." One forgets that laying in the weft—the actual "weaving"—is only half the job of making a cloth, the second half. First comes the equally lengthy task of making, organizing, and mounting onto the loom the foundation set of threads, the warp. And that is where a helper really speeds the work: a friend to receive and fasten the other end of each long warp thread, saving all the time and energy of walking back and forth, back and forth, from one end of the loom to the other. It is also much more entertaining to have a friend to chat with while the handwork proceeds.

In fact, my sister and I were actors in a scene that, with only minor differences, has been repeated for millennia: two women helping each other set up a weaving project. The looms, the fibers, the patterns may differ, but the relation of the women to their work and to each other is much the same.

Unlike women of past ages, however, we were not making cloth for our households. (When our mother entered a weaving school in Denmark fifty years ago, she was told to begin with a dozen plain dish towels—a useful way to gain skill on the loom and start one's trousseau all at once.) Nor were we weaving for sale, for piety, or for artistry—the other common reasons. We were weaving a thread-for-thread replica of a piece of plaid cloth lost in a salt mine in the Austrian Alps some three thousand years ago (figs. 0.1 and 0.2).

It was the salt that had preserved the handsome green and

Figure 0.1. Plaid woolen cloth and fur "tam-o'-shanters" from ca. 800 B.C., found in the salt mines at Hallstatt, Austria (see map, fig. 3.1) and displayed in the Natural History Museum, Vienna. The makers of these objects were the ancestors of the Celts, now living in such places as Scotland and still famous for plaid twills and tams. (The original scrap of cloth is lying at lower left on a replica.)

Figure 0.2. Detail of author's replica of the Hallstatt twill in fig. 0.1, showing the offset pairing of threads typical of twill pattern. The original warp ran vertically, constructed in groups of four threads of green and brown. The weft ran horizontally, and the weaver judged the width of those stripes by eye as she wove.

brown colors as well as the cloth itself, and it was the color that caught my eye in the Natural History Museum in Vienna—that and the particular objects surrounding the piece (fig. 0.1). The torn fragment of cloth, about the size of one's hand laid flat, nestled on a newly rewoven strip of identical cloth in such a way that the plaid stripes matched. Thus the visitor's eye could follow the pattern outward in both directions and comprehend what this ancient cloth must have looked like when it was new. And it looked for all the world like a simple plaid twill from some Scottish kilt. Furthermore, above and beside it were hung two furry leather caps, also from prehistoric shafts in the Hallstatt salt mines, of the exact same shape as a Scottish tam-o'-shanter or a beret from Brittany in western France, another outpost of Celtic culture.

Between 1200 and 600 B.C., the era when this cloth was apparently woven, the ancestors of the Celts were living in what is now Austria, Hungary, and southern Germany. Many of these people were miners, digging out of the mountains both metal ores and salt. (Salt was very precious for preserving food before the days of refrigerators. Those who could supply it grew rich.) By 400 B.C. the early Celts were beginning to fan out westward across Europe into France, Britain, and Spain, where they live today, carrying a culture directly descended from that of the Hallstatt miners. In a very real sense I *was* looking at the original tam and at the ancestor of the Scottish plaid tweed or twill, all produced by the immediate ancestors of the Celts. (*Twill*, like *tweed*, comes from the word *two* and refers to a distinctive method of pattern weaving in which the threads are paired [fig. 0.2].) These habits of cloth and clothing that we associate today with Celts began in prehistoric times and traveled with them through space and time. I had been studying the scant remains of ancient cloth for almost a decade, and if one thing had become clear, it was that the traditions of cloth and clothing in most parts of the world were remarkably ancient. This display case eloquently said it all.

"I'd love to have a scarf like that," I announced on the spot. So here I was, two months later, sitting at home, trying to reproduce it from the diagrams in the scholarly publication. It had taken much hunting through weaver supply catalogs to find wool yarn of precisely the right colors and thickness, yarn that had also been combed and not carded. (Combing the unspun fibers to lie parallel results in a strong, hard thread. Carding, on the other hand, makes the fiber lie all which way—just like teasing one's hair—and gives a soft, fluffy thread like our knitting yarn. Most wool yarn now available is of this latter sort, but the process wasn't invented till the Middle Ages.) If I was going to go to all this trouble, I wanted the replica to be as near exact as I could make it. Of course, if I had begun by raising and shearing a sheep, cleaning and dyeing the wool, then combing, spinning, and plying it, the long day spent warping would seem quite a small expenditure!

After dinner I began to weave, while my family sat nearby chatting. It took me half an hour to weave the wide swatch of plain green that preceded the first brown stripe. Having put all the intricacies of the twill patterning into the warp, by the way in which we had tied it onto the loom, the weaving was now straightforward, and it went fast. I reached the first color stripes and added a shuttle of brown thread: four brown rows, four green, four brown, four green . . . I was eager to see what the plaid would look like, and I cursed gently as first one shuttle, then the other fell to the floor while I worked. The stripes were so narrow that it didn't seem worth tying off the finished color each time, so I put up with the nuisance. Another four brown, four green—another shuttle hit the floor.

Suddenly light dawned on me.

It had taken us so long to put the warp through the tiny control loops on the loom because the pattern, simple as it looked, had actually been quite complicated. That was because both the color stripes and woven pattern stripes were so uneven in width: sixteen, nineteen, twenty, eighteen. No two stripes that direction had exactly the same number of threads, and getting them all exactly correct had required great care. Now I was cursing at the stripes running crosswise—the weft stripes—because they were in little tiny sets of four, an even number.

I had done the replica backward! If my weft had been warp, its sets of four threads would correspond to what I knew to be the structure of the warp on the ancient loom, as well as to the twill pattern. Thus the cloth would have been *easy* to warp up. Conversely, if my warp had been weft, the slight differences in the number of threads per stripe would make perfect sense; the weaver had not been counting but judging by eye how far to weave before changing to the next stripe.

Far from being unhappy at my mistake, I was delighted. Most fragments of prehistoric cloth from the Hallstatt salt mines—and there are more than a hundred extant—are torn on all four edges, so it is not possible to tell which direction they were woven the way one usually does, simply by looking for the type of closed edges found only at the sides. But by trying to imitate the product, I discovered not only which way *this* shred was woven and some criteria for analyzing other pieces but also several interesting details about how Hallstatt weavers worked. The cloth ends up looking much the same either way, and the time had been doubly well spent. It was another lesson to me that the process of re-creating ancient artifacts step by step can shed light on the lives and habits of the original craftworkers that no amount of armchair theorizing can give.

It is no longer possible to know most of the details of prehistoric women's lives. Far too much has been lost with the passage of time. Even in early historical times—in Egypt, Mesopotamia, Greece—very little of the ancient literary record was devoted to women, so we have few sources to consult. Indeed, the lack of clear sources has led to a good deal of guessing, even wishful thinking, in books about how women lived in early times (when the topic has not been omitted altogether). Here among the textiles, on the other hand, we can find some of the hard evidence we need, since textiles were one of women's primary concerns. We know, for example, that women sometimes helped each other with their weaving projects, exactly as in the modern scene above, because we sometimes find the wefts in ancient cloth crossed in the middle of the textile. This can only have been caused by two people handing spools of weft back and forth to each other as they wove simultaneously on different parts of the same cloth. It is a tiny detail, but interesting precisely because of its realness. We also know, now, that prehistoric women sometimes wove their patterns by eye rather than strictly counting.

Of course, being perishable, the textiles themselves are not easy to learn about—just like most of the rest of women's products (such as food and the recipes for preparing it). Therefore, to recover the reality of women's history, we must develop excellent techniques (see Chapter 12), using not just the obvious data but learning to ferret out every helpful detail. Practical experiments like reweaving some of the surviving ancient cloths are a case in point. Among the thousands of archaeologists who have written about pottery or architecture, how many have actually tried to make a pot or build a building? Precious few; but with so much data available for study in these fields, scholars felt flooded with information already, and such radical steps hardly seemed necessary. Our case is different; we must use every discoverable clue.

The available material is most revealing when treated chronologically, starting with the Stone Age and moving through the Bronze Age into the Iron Age. We can watch how the craft of clothmaking develops and how women's roles change with the change of technology and its relation to society. But when I say "chronologically," I mean in a conceptual way rather than strictly in terms of years. It could hardly be otherwise. At 3400 B.C., as the Near East was edging into the Bronze Age, central Europe remained at a Neolithic stage of economy, while the Arctic north was Mesolithic and many other parts of the world still lay deep in the Palaeolithic (fig. 0.3). To chart technological stages so heavily skewed from place to place against a scale of absolute time is difficult. Understanding the basis of the categorization is perhaps of greater help to a reader not acquainted with the system.

When systematic archaeology began to emerge in the nineteenth century, long before modern methods of absolute dating were available, Danish scholars suggested dividing the pre-Roman arti-facts into three successive groups, based on the dominant material for tools: stone only (oldest), bronze (in the middle), and iron (youngest). This system worked pretty well, but it soon became clear that the Stone Age was enormously long and needed a further division based on whether the stone tools were always chipped *(Old Stone Age, or Palaeolithic)* or sometimes ground down to a smooth finish *(New Stone Age, or Neolithic)*. As methods of recovering ancient remains became more refined, scholars noticed that polished stone tools correlated with the advent of agriculture. The grinding of tools was not unrelated to the grinding of grain. And gradually, as more and more material accrued, finer divisions were installed as needed. The simplest system was to divide into Early, Middle, and Late; Late into I, II, and III; Late III into A, B, and C; and so on. (A pot might thus be assigned to Early Bronze IIA.) But sometimes other terms fell to hand.

Thus the last levels of the Palaeolithic era are those uppermost at Palaeolithic sites (which themselves go back over a million years), and these uppermost layers correspond to a sudden blos-soming of all sorts of arts and crafts in Europe after about 40,000 B.C. The era thus represented came to be known as the *Upper Palaeolithic* and was found to extend to at least 10,000 B.C.—later in some places. Its cutoff point is taken to be the advent of domes-tic plants and animals, which mark the beginning of the *Neolithic*. In Europe the domesticated stocks were imported from the Near East in an ever-widening circle. Because the far northern climate was too harsh for easy agriculture, however, people there contin-ued to live a Palaeolithic life-style for millennia, augmented with a few handy Neolithic ideas borrowed from the south (such as actively herding the wild reindeer, rather than just hunting them). This intermediate type of culture soon got nicknamed the *Meso-lithic*. I have chosen to treat the Upper Palaeolithic and Mesolithic

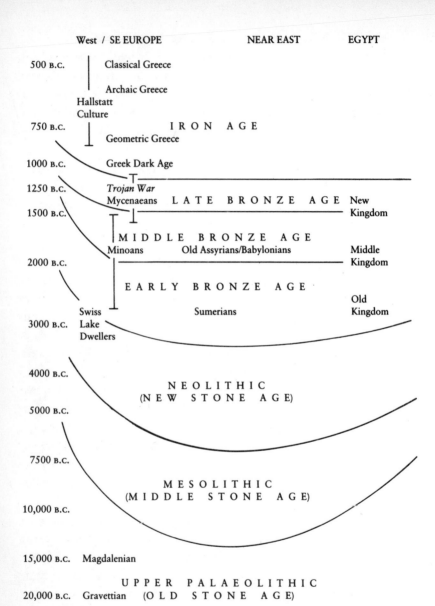

	West / SE EUROPE	NEAR EAST	EGYPT

500 B.C. — Classical Greece

Archaic Greece

Hallstatt
Culture

750 B.C. — I R O N   A G E
Geometric Greece

1000 B.C. — Greek Dark Age

1250 B.C. — *Trojan War*
Mycenaeans   L A T E   B R O N Z E   A G E   New

1500 B.C. — Kingdom

M I D D L E   B R O N Z E   A G E

Minoans   Old Assyrians/Babylonians   Middle

2000 B.C. — Kingdom

E A R L Y   B R O N Z E   A G E

Old
Swiss   Sumerians   Kingdom
3000 B.C. — Lake
Dwellers

4000 B.C.

N E O L I T H I C
(N E W   S T O N E   A G E)

5000 B.C.

7500 B.C.

M E S O L I T H I C
(M I D D L E   S T O N E   A G E)

10,000 B.C.

15,000 B.C.   Magdalenian

U P P E R   P A L A E O L I T H I C
20,000 B.C.   Gravettian   (O L D   S T O N E   A G E)

Figure 0.3. Chart of the main chronological periods covered in this book. The scale is logarithmic.

together (in Chapter 2), followed by the Neolithic (Chapter 3). The development of metalworking and of efficient metal tools marks the start of the *Bronze Age* (although again in the seminal areas there are transitional phases with various names: Copper Age, Chalcolithic, Aeneolithic). In the Near East the beginning of the Bronze Age shortly before 3000 B.C. is accompanied (or triggered) by radical changes in living conditions: Cities spring up everywhere and writing is invented. Again, the innovations are not unrelated to each other.

Bronze Age technology and urbanization quickly spread to southeastern Europe, but some aspects of life there continued with one foot in the Neolithic, an interesting hybridization that allowed textiles to flourish (Chapter 4). The mainstream of Bronze Age life developed full speed ahead in Meşopotamia (Chapter 7) and Egypt (Chapter 8), eventually reaching Greece in its full form in the Late Bronze Age, midway through the second millennium B.C. (Chapter 9), only to be cut off around 1200 B.C. by waves of destructive migrations emanating ultimately from the steppes of central Asia. After the dust settles and the smoke clears away, we find the Mediterranean countries in possession of some new ways of living and of a new and much harder metal, iron—in an era suitably called the *Iron Age* (Chapter 11). It takes another two to four hundred years, however, for the complex technology of ironworking to make its way all the way across Europe, during which time "Bronze Age" labels in some parts of Europe correspond in absolute years to "Iron Age" labels in other parts.

By the mid-first millennium B.C., when iron was reaching the far west and when this book ends, southern Europe and the Near East had already experienced vast cultural developments and redevelopments, whereas most other areas had not yet gotten on their feet (China, northern India, and Central America excepted). The chapters that follow concentrate on this geographical area of early development and for the most part omit the rest. Of course, the same methods developed here can be applied to those other times and places to recover more of their histories.

1

⋘

A Tradition
with a Reason

For millennia women have sat together spinning, weaving, and sewing. Why should textiles have become *their* craft par excellence, rather than the work of men? Was it always thus, and if so, why?

Twenty years ago Judith Brown wrote a little five-page "Note on the Division of Labor by Sex" that holds a simple key to these questions. She was interested in how much women contributed to obtaining the food for a preindustrial community. But in answering that question, she came upon a model of much wider applicability. She found that the issue of whether or not the community *relies* upon women as the chief providers of a given type of labor depends upon "the compatibility of this pursuit with the demands of child care." If only because of the exigencies of breast feeding (which until recently was typically continued for two or three years per child), "nowhere in the world is the rearing of children primarily the responsibility of men. . . ." Thus, if the productive labor of women is not to be lost to the society during the childbearing years, the jobs regularly assigned to women must be carefully chosen to be "compatible with simultaneous child watching." From empirical observation Brown gleans that "such activities have the following characteristics: they do not require rapt concentration and are relatively dull and repetitive; they are easily interruptable [I see a rueful smile on every care giver's face!] and easily resumed once interrupted; they do not place the child in potential danger; and they do not require the participant to range very far from home."[1]

Just such are the crafts of spinning, weaving, and sewing: repetitive, easy to pick up at any point, reasonably child-safe, and easily done at home. (Contrast the idea of swinging a pick in a dark, cramped, and dusty mine shaft with a baby on one's back or being interrupted by a child's crisis while trying to pour molten metal into a set of molds.) The only other occupation that fits the criteria even half so well is that of preparing the daily food. Food and clothing: These are what societies worldwide have come to see as the core of women's work (although other tasks may be added to the load, depending upon the circumstances of the particular society).

Readers of this book live in a different world. The Industrial Revolution has moved basic textile work out of the home and into large (inherently dangerous) factories; we buy our clothing ready-made. It is a rare person in our cities who has ever spun thread or woven cloth, although a quick look into a fabric store will show that many women still sew. As a result, most of us are unaware of how time-consuming the task of making the cloth for a family used to be.

In Denmark fifty years ago young women bought their yarns ready-made but still expected to weave the basic cloth for their households. If they went to a weaving school rather than being taught at home, they began with a dozen plain cotton dish towels.

---

[1] Notice Brown's stipulation that this particular division of labor revolves around *reliance*, not around *ability* (other than the ability to breast-feed), within a community in which specialization is desirable. Thus females are quite able to hunt, and often do (as she points out); males are quite able to cook and sew, and often do, among the cultures of the world. The question is whether the society can afford to rely on the women as a group for all of the hunting or all of the sewing. The answer to "hunting" (and smithing, and deep-sea fishing) is no. The answer to "sewing" (and cooking, and weaving) is yes.

My mother, being a foreigner not in need of a trousseau, and with less than a year at her disposal to study Danish weaving, consented to weave half of *one* towel to get started. The next assignment was to weave three waffle-weave bath mats. (Indeed, the three were nicely gauged to last a lifetime. The second wore out when I was in college, and we still have the third.) Next came the weaving of woolen scarves and blankets, linen tablecloths, and so forth. Most complicated were the elaborate aprons for Sunday best.

Thirty years ago in rural Greece, much had changed but not all. People wore store-bought, factory-made clothing of cotton for daily wear, at least in summer. But traditional festive outfits and all the household woolens were still made from scratch. It takes several hours to spin with a hand spindle the amount of yarn one can weave up in an hour, so women spun as they watched the children, girls spun as they watched the sheep, both spun as they trudged or rode muleback from one village to another on errands (fig. 1.1). The tools and materials were light and portable, and the double use of the time made both the spinning and the trudging or watching more interesting. In fact, if we reckon up the cleaning, spinning, dyeing, weaving, and embroidering of the wool, the villagers appeared to spend at least as many labor hours on making cloth as on producing the food to be eaten—and these people bought half their clothing ready-made!

Records show that, before the invention of the steam engine and the great factory machines that it could run, this sort of distribution of time and labor was quite normal. Most of the hours of the woman's day, and occasionally of the man's, were spent on textile-related activities. (In Europe men typically helped tend and shear the sheep, plant and harvest the flax, and market any extra textiles available for cash income.)

"So why is it, if women were so enslaved by textile work for all those centuries, that the spinning jenny and power loom were invented by a man and not a woman?" A young woman accosted me with this question after a lecture recently.

"Th[e] reason," to quote George Foster, writing about problems

Figure 1.1. Seventeenth century woodcut of women in the Balkans spin-ning while traveling. Spinning was such a time-consuming yet simple and necessary job that women frequently spun thread while doing other things.

in pottery making, "lies in the nature of the productive process itself which places a premium on strict adherence to tried and proven ways as a means of avoiding economic catastrophe." Put another way, women of all but the top social and economic classes were so busy just trying to get through what had to be done each day that they didn't have excess time or materials to experiment with new ways of doing things. (My husband bought and learned to use a new word-processing program two years before I began to use it, for exactly these reasons. I was in the middle of writing a book using the old system and couldn't afford to take the time out both to learn the new one and to convert everything. I was already too deep into "production.") Elise Boulding elaborates: "[T]he general situation of little margin for error leading to con-servatism might apply to the whole range of activities carried out by women. Because they had so much to do, slight variations in care of farm or dairy products or pottery could lead to food spoilage, production failure, and a consequent increase in already heavy burdens." The rich women, on the other hand, didn't have the incentive to invent laborsaving machinery since the work was done for them.

And so for millennia women devoted their lives to making the cloth and clothing while they tended the children and the cooking pot. Or at least that was the case in the broad zone of temperate climates, where cloth was spun and woven (rather than made of skins, as in the Arctic) and where the weather was too cold for part or all of the year to go without a warming wrap (as one could in the tropics). Consequently it was in the temperate zone that the Industrial Revolution eventually began.

The Industrial Revolution was a time of steam engines. Along with the locomotive to solve transportation problems, the first major applications of the new engines were mechanizations of the making of cloth: the power loom, the spinning jenny, the cotton gin. The consequences of yanking women and children out of the home to tend these huge, dangerous, and implacable machines in the mills caused the devastating social problems which writers like Charles Dickens, Charlotte Brontë, and Elizabeth Gaskell (all of whom knew each other) portrayed so vividly. Such a factory is the antithesis of being "compatible with child rearing" on every point in Judith Brown's list.

Western industrial society has evolved so far that most of us don't recognize Dickens's picture now (although it still does exist in some parts of the world). We are looking forward into a new age, when women who so desire can rear their children quietly at home while they pursue a career on their child-safe, relatively interruptable-and-resumable home computers, linked to the world not by muleback or the steam locomotive, or even a car, but by the telephone and the modem. For their part, the handloom, the needle, and the other fiber crafts can still form satisfying hobbies, as they, too, remain compatible with child watching.

Spinning and weaving were such common household activities for millennia that everyone undoubtedly knew how they worked, whether ever performing the actions or not. But now that factory machines have taken over these jobs, most Americans have engaged in weaving only as a childhood game—such as weaving little potholders out of the stretchy loops in a kit—and have never encountered spinning. A brief description of these basic processes is thus in order.

Weaving cloth requires thread of some sort, and thread is made from fibers, so we must begin with the fibers.

Imagine yourself with a handful of coarse fibers, or better yet, go get some. Not cotton: cotton hairs are extremely short and fine so you can't see how they behave. (They are also not easy to spin for these reasons.) Imagine instead a hank of wool just as it comes off the back of a sheep or goat; you may have seen it stuck to the fence of a cage at the zoo. Or take the long, coarse fibers from a rotted plant stem or from a piece of old frayed rope or twine. (Rope used to be made chiefly from hemp, the species to which marijuana belongs, but now it is usually made from synthetics, which are slippery and therefore hard to work with.)

To make thread out of these fibers, you must twist them together longways a few at a time. Although each individual fiber is weak, twisting a number of them together can make a thread that is quite strong. An easy way to do this is to take a small bunch of fibers and roll one end down your thigh with the flat of your hand while holding the other end tight (fig. 1.2). Thus one end gets twisted with respect to the other end, locking the fibers together in the process.

If the fibers you begin with are also very long, that may be all you have to do. Hemp, for instance, grows twelve feet high, so you can make a twelve-foot string by doing nothing more than adding twist to the natural fibers. Flax, which gives the fine material we call *linen* when it is processed, grows to four feet, while silk fibers, which are unwound from the cocoon of a special species of

34

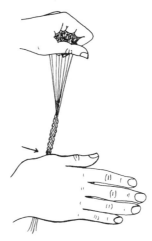

Figure 1.2. Fibers will lock into a strong thread when twisted tightly together. A simple way to make a short thread is to hold the ends of some fibers in the left hand and roll the other end of the bundle down one's thigh with the flat of the right hand.

moth, may be as much as a thousand yards long (and incredibly thin). But most fibers are not that long. Wool is at best only a few inches in length and usually much shorter; cotton is shorter still. So we need some way to make thread longer than any one single fiber, extending it as long as we please.

To accomplish that, imagine overlapping the end of one bundle of fibers over the ends of the previous group before adding the twist that locks them together. But you can see that we will get lumpy spots at the overlap and thin spots in between. (Some ancient thread is actually made that way.) What we really need is a way to keep a constant trickle of overlapping fibers flowing into the thread as we make it, instead of adding them in discrete bunches. To do this, we need some preparation and a simple tool, the spindle.

First, the fibers you draw from must be loose and not tangled together so you can get the exact amount you need at all times. Otherwise you will suddenly find you have pulled a big clot of them all at once—or worse, gotten too few somewhere, so the thread gets too thin and breaks.

There are two basic ways of arranging the fibers for spinning, as you loosen them: laying them parallel to each other or encouraging them to lie every which way in a fluffy mass (this is practical only with fairly short fibers). You can make them sit parallel by combing them, much the way you comb your hair to get the tangles out. Then you get a very strong thread (called *worsted*) that is also very hard to the touch, because it has no fluffiness. The fibers all are packed in close, lying right next to one another as they twist. Men's wool suits today are usually made of worsted thread, for long wear.

If you want softness, however, you can use *carding* paddles to loosen the tangles in the fibers without actually combing them. These flat boards with handles have lots of little bent teeth to pull the fibers apart so they lie in all directions. (The name comes from the Latin word for a thistle, *carduus,* because in ancient times the teeth of thistles were set into boards for fluffing fiber.) The process of carding is much like teasing your hair to make it fluffy. The problem with yarn from carded fiber, however, is that it is rather weak and breaks easily. Modern knitting yarns are almost invariably carded, and they can afford to be because the knitted loops make the cloth stretchy enough to offset the relative weakness of the yarn. Sweaters knitted from these carded yarns feel soft and even spongy.

Once you have your fibers prepared, you are ready to spin. The crudest way, and probably the oldest, is the one we have mentioned: taking a small bunch of fibers and rolling one end down your thigh with the flat of your hand while holding on to the other end. But to get a constant stream of fibers flowing into the thread as you make it, you need one hand to hold the prepared fibers, another to add them to the thread, a third to keep twisting (the core operation), and a fourth to hold the finished thread—because if you let go of the new yarn at this stage, it will instantly ball up in a snarl like an angry rubber band and then start coming apart. Time for some tools: We don't *have* four hands.

A *spindle* is basically just a stick, usually about a foot long.

When the end of the new thread has been attached to the tip of the stick, turning the stick will force the end of the thread to turn, too, adding twist to the fibers to make the thread. But when some thread has been finished, it can be wound around the stick to keep it from tangling while still more is being spun. Thus the tool that twists is at the same time the tool that holds. That reduces the needed hands to three.

How to get it down to two? One hand must always be used for the crucial job of adding the fibers at a controlled rate into the new thread, while somehow the spindle must be kept turning and the fiber supply must be held near.

One solution is to lay the fiber supply down on the ground, turn the spindle with one hand, and use the other to flick the fibers a few at a time into the growing thread. This is how ancient Meso-potamian women did it, as well as rural women today in the Sudan. (It is practical if and only if the fibers are quite short—less than a couple of inches long.)

The other solution is to hold the fibers and drop the spindle—after giving it a quick flick to start it spinning like a top (fig. 1.3). It hangs in the air like a yo-yo, whirling merrily on its thread, while the spinner uses one hand to hold the unspun fiber and the other to control the feeding of the fibers into the twist. When the new thread gets so long that the spindle reaches the ground, you have to stop and wind everything up on the spindle shaft and then start the spindle twirling again in the air. This is the way European peasants spin, and apparently always have. It has the advantage of being entirely portable since nothing has to be laid down. In fact, I have seen Greek village women spinning quite handily while riding sidesaddle on muleback. In order to be able to carry a big supply of raw material, one can bind the prepared fiber to a long stick or board, called a *distaff* (from an old word *dis-*, meaning "fuzz, fiber," plus *staff*, a fuzz-stick).

Back in the Neolithic era people discovered that to reduce wob-ble as the spindle turns and to prolong the spin it is helpful to add a little flywheel—a small disk called a *spindle whorl*. Spindles are usually wooden; whorls are most often of clay. But one can use an

Figure 1.3. Woman spinning with a drop spindle, depicted on a Greek vase of ca. 490 B.C.

apple, a potato, or a rock for the whorl if nothing else is available. Contrary to popular assumption, it doesn't have to be perfectly round as long as the spindle shaft goes through the very middle of it.

Spinning this way is slow, but far faster than rolling the thread on the thigh with no spindle. Early in the Middle Ages, however, a new invention appeared: the spinning wheel. Just who invented it is still unknown, although an old Chinese device for winding thread may have been the inspiration. The foot-powered spinning wheel allowed people to spin about four times faster than with the dropped spindle, so it was much in demand. But the principle is exactly the same as with a hand spindle: Pull fibers, twist them, and wind up the thread. Finally in the late eighteenth century, early in the Industrial Revolution, a man named James Hargreaves invented a mechanical spinning machine (later nicknamed the spinning jenny) because he was distressed at how hard his wife and daughters had to work to spin their increasingly large quotas of thread for the new power looms. The women in his family were delighted, but his neighbors became fiercely jealous of the "unfair" competition and ran him out of town after wrecking his first machine.

To keep the thread from untwisting when it is taken off the filled spindle, the most efficient remedy is to *ply* the thread. The word comes from French *plier,* meaning "to bend," because if you take a spun thread, bend it in half, and let go, the two halves will briefly twist around *each other* and leave you with a nice thread of twice the thickness that will no longer try to come undone. Try it. (The same can be accomplished by twisting two separate threads together in the opposite direction from that in which they were spun. This is the normal way to do it.)

Spinning, incidentally, is a very restful activity. That is a good thing, because it takes an enormous amount of time to make thread by hand. Like knitting, it is pleasantly rhythmic and can be done sitting down, with no physical exertion, just patience.

Once enough thread has been made, weaving the cloth can begin. Weaving consists of interlacing two sets of threads at right angles to each other. But because thread is very floppy, like spaghetti (unlike the materials that mats and baskets are made of), it is almost impossible to weave the one set of threads through the other without one group's being held down tight—that is, putting tension on one set of threads. The set that is pulled tight is called the *warp,* and the frame that holds the warp fast is known as the *loom.* The second set of threads, which needs to be interlaced into the first, is called the *weft* (an old past tense of the verb *weave*— that is, "what has been woven in"). The enterprising reader can take a few short lengths of string, lay half of them out parallel on a table, and try weaving the other half into them at right angles. The problems will become clear immediately.

In the simplest weave, called *plain weave,* each thread of either set goes over one and then under one thread of the opposite set (fig. 1.4). You can see cloth of this sort in any household; simple items like sheets, pillowcases, and handkerchiefs are still made this way. (If you have never thought before about the structure of cloth, take a close look at a sheet or handkerchief right now.) It is also possible to weave various patterns into the cloth by having the weft go over and under different numbers of warp.

To make these structures—to weave—somehow one has to push the weft under some of the warp threads but over others on the loom. One can do this the tedious way, using a needle to take the weft over or under one little thread at a time, row after row. (This technique is known as *darning* and is still used as a way to mend socks by those who don't just throw holey socks away.) Or one can try to lift at one swoop all the warp threads that have to be gone under, leaving in place all the ones that the weft must go over (fig. 1.5). This massive lifting forms a little passageway called a *shed* (in a vertical loom it looks like the double-pitched roof of a toolshed slanting off to either side), and through this passage the weaver can insert a whole line of weft at once.

How to raise the selected warp threads so nothing gets tangled up? That is not an easy problem. The normal way is to pass each thread through a separate little loop, a *heddle* (fig. 1.5), in the middle of the loom, and the heddles in turn are tied to bars above the warp (the *heddle bars*). The warp threads can then be controlled by raising the loops in large groups by means of the bars, much the way the sustain pedal on a grand piano raises a whole row of dampers at once, although the dampers (like heddles) can also be raised one at a time.

Figure 1.4. In the simplest weave (plain weave or tabby), each thread passes alternately over one and then under one thread of the threads at right angles to it.

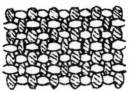

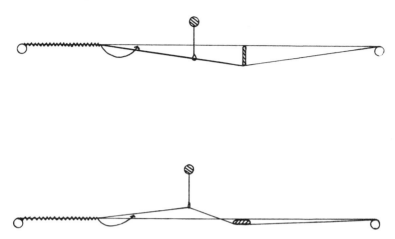

Figure 1.5. Diagram of how the warp threads, stretched between two beams (hollow circles), are separated into two alternating sheds (openings) to allow the weft to be inserted. Top: The weft (arrow) is passed through the shed formed by using a shed bar (hatched oblong) to depress every second thread—i.e., half the warp. Bottom: The weft (arrow) goes through the opposite shed formed by raising the same half of the warp with heddle loops attached to a heddle bar (hatched circle). To orient this diagram for a vertical loom, rotate it ninety degrees (clockwise for a warp-weighted loom, counterclockwise for a tapestry loom).

In fact, it seems to have taken several millennia of darning the weft in at a snail's pace before some genius figured out the principle of the heddle—apparently in the Neolithic (about 6000 B.C.?), somewhere in northern Iraq or Turkey. From there the idea must have spread slowly to Europe, to the Orient, and eventually by boat to South America. It is such a difficult concept that it may have been invented only once. But it is what made weaving an efficient process.

What, then, is the history of this relationship between women and textiles? When did women begin to take up and develop the fiber crafts? How did women and their special work affect society, and how did the societies affect them? These interactions will form the story of this book.

2

⟨⟨⟨⟨

The String Revolution

... a threefold cord is not quickly broken.
—Ecclesiastes 4:12

Some forty thousand years ago, at the beginning of the last phase
of the Old Stone Age (called the Upper Palaeolithic), human beings
began to act very differently from the way they ever had before.
For some two million years they had fashioned simple stone tools,
and for half a million they had controlled fire and hunted coopera-
tively in groups. But forty thousand years ago, as the great ice
sheets that had covered the northern continents retreated by fits
and starts, humans started to invent and make new things at a
tremendous rate, like a slow-ascending firecracker that suddenly
explodes into a thousand sparks of varied color, shooting in a
thousand directions.

These newly creative hunter-gatherers produced novel tools—
such as awls, pins, and various chisellike burins—but they also
began to sculpt animals, people, and other information (possibly
calendrical) on pieces of ivory and bone and to make quantities
of beads for adornment. People of the Upper Palaeolithic painted
pictures of animals and drew around their own hands on cave
walls; this is the period of the famous Stone Age paintings from

Lascaux, Altamira, and other caves in France and Spain. Just as important, and more to our purpose here, these ancestors invented string and sewing and thus provided the first chapter in the story of women's long association with the fiber crafts.

As near as we can place it, the event occurred twenty to thirty thousand years ago, right in the middle of the Upper Palaeolithic. While others were painting caves or knapping fancy flints, some genius hit upon the principle of twisting handfuls of little weak fibers together into long, strong thread.

How do we know this? Nothing so perishable has survived those twenty-five to thirty-five thousand years, although by some miracle one bit of neatly spun and plied cordage has made it through from about 15,000 B.C. (see below). Our earliest evidence is indirect. We infer this humble yet crucial invention from significant changes in other objects of a sturdier nature.

The Upper Palaeolithic culture known to palaeontologists as the Gravettian (from the name of the French site where it was first recognized: La Gravette, on the Dordogne River) seems to have sprung up in central and eastern Europe, spreading gradually westward along the south edge of the great ice sheet to southern France and Spain. Radiocarbon dates suggest that the Gravettian culture lasted roughly six thousand years, from 26,000 to 20,000 B.C. During this vast time needles become common, and beads of shell, tooth, and bone turn up with increasingly small holes. The smaller beads, moreover, begin to occur arranged in neat rows across the bones (sometimes the skulls) of the deceased. Clearly these beads had been sewn onto garments, made probably of hide. In a cave near the Mediterranean border between modern France and Italy, an adolescent young man was found carefully interred wearing a cap or hairnet sewn or strung with four tidy rows of tiny shell beads. His body lay protectively around that of a smaller and much older woman—his mother?—who wore a bracelet of similar beads.

From such artifacts alone one can deduce a knowledge of sewing. But there is proof that at least some of the thread in use had

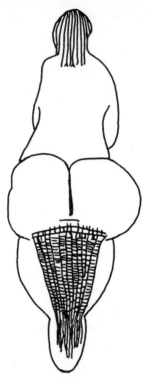

Figure 2.1. Small Palaeolithic Venus figure found at Lespugue, France, carved of bone ca. 20,000 B.C. (Gravettian culture). The woman wears a skirt made of twisted strings suspended from a hip band. Such skirts seem to have been associated with childbearing.

been twisted together from small natural fibers, rather than cut from long, stringy body parts like gut or sinew. It comes from a bone sculpture of a woman wearing a skirt made of string (fig. 2.1)

This small, plump "Venus figure" (a nickname for all the little bone, stone, and ivory figurines of women from the Palaeolithic) comes from Lespugue, in southern France, and is probably of late Gravettian manufacture. Her skirt consists of long strings hanging down the back from a hip band, and the ancient sculptor has troubled to engrave the twists in each string. Furthermore—a detail I did not notice until I began to make my own drawing from a large,

clear photograph obtained from the Musée de l'Homme in Paris—
the sculptor has shown the strings fraying out at the bottom into
a mass of untwisted fibers. These cannot be thongs of sinew or
hide; they can only be true twisted-fiber thread.

We don't know how early to date this great discovery—of making string as long and as strong as needed by twisting short filaments together. But whenever it happened, it opened the door to
an enormous array of new ways to save labor and improve the
odds of survival, much as the harnessing of steam did for the
Industrial Revolution. Soft, flexible thread of this sort is a necessary prerequisite to making woven cloth. On a far more basic
level, string can be used simply to tie things up—to catch, to hold,
to carry. From these notions come snares and fishlines, tethers and
leashes, carrying nets, handles, and packages, not to mention a
way of binding objects together to form more complex tools.
(Nets, for example, work so efficiently that nowadays they are
mostly illegal for catching fish in fresh water. Sportsmen don't
consider netting sufficiently "sporting," and furthermore, in no
time there would be no fish left to spawn more.) So powerful, in
fact, is simple string in taming the world to human will and ingenuity that I suspect it to be the unseen weapon that allowed the
human race to conquer the earth, that enabled us to move out
into every econiche on the globe during the Upper Palaeolithic. We
could call it the String Revolution.

What was it like to live in this busy new world, so different from
ages past, yet a world still without houses, stoves, and refrigerators, with nothing but rocks and wild plants and animals to supply
all one's needs? The stones and bones of archaeology yield but a
dry and lifeless picture, and a very incomplete one at that.

We can recognize an ancient campsite (if we are lucky enough
to find one) by small deposits of ashes and carbon in places where
a controlled fire burned. Stone tools of the Palaeolithic may well
have survived, too, known by their deliberately chipped edges and
regular shapes. But stone is a hard medium to work. Ancient people undoubtedly used softer materials like wood, leather, and bark
wherever these would do the job, but these softer things almost

never survive even two thousand years, let alone twenty thousand. So we must recognize that we have lost most of the tools and trappings of that time. Furthermore, material remains tell us little about the intangible parts of culture: about marriage and dinner recipes and how the world was categorized. (Anyone who has ever learned a second language knows that different cultures look at the world differently, from what colors and how many of them form the rainbow to who is counted as kin.)

Using the excavated finds as a firm pedestal, however, we can now turn a backward-looking spyglass built from the linguistic reconstruction of early languages to catch some lively glimpses of that archaic world. Words, as it happens, sometimes survive the millennia better than material objects, and they do so best in areas in which the culture changed only very slowly—as in the far north, where the intense winter cold discouraged immigrants.[1]

All across Europe to the north of the linguistically numerous Indo-Europeans[2] live speakers of the Uralic language family (fig. 2.2). Their modern tongues include Finnish, Estonian, and Lappish in the northwest, plus Mordvin and a great many others in Russia, all the way into Siberia just east of the Ural Mountains. Hungarian, too, belongs to this group, its speakers having moved into central Europe from the Urals only a thousand years ago. But as near as we can tell, the Uralic speakers of the far north are the "original" inhabitants of that area, at least since the late Ice Age. That is, they followed the retreating ice sheets—and the great herds of tundra animals—into the newly emerging land toward

---

[1] One doesn't have a term for something one doesn't know yet, so if an ancient term for something exists, what the word signified must have been a known entity. Thus a Palaeolithic hunter could not have had words for rifles and phantom jets but would have had terms for knives and nets once the objects were invented. One of the beauties of language is that it allows us to devise words for whatever we want to talk about.

[2] The Indo-European language family, which happens to include English, Spanish, French, Russian, and most of the other languages of Europe, is one of the largest in the world today, thanks in part to its expansion across the Western Hemisphere. Farther on in this chapter is a more detailed discussion of the family. See fig. 2.10.

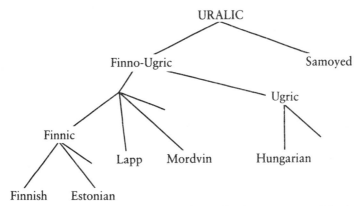

Figure 2.2. Tree chart showing the relationship among some of the languages in the Uralic family, which extends across much of northern Eurasia. Over many millennia the modern Uralic languages (at the bottom) have slowly diverged in form from a common parent (at the top).

the end of the Palaeolithic. While the inhabitants of the Near East and southeastern Europe began to settle down and develop new ideas of exploiting plants and animals through domestication and farming (the stage we call the Neolithic: see fig. 0.3 and Chapter 3), the people north of this busy center continued for thousands of years in much the old way, adopting only a few new ideas from the Neolithic south. This short transitional phase we call the Mesolithic, or Middle Stone Age. It lasted there from roughly 10,000 to 4000 B.C. or later.

The Swedish scholar Björn Collinder spent much of his life collecting and comparing the vocabulary of the various Uralic languages. Using the words that appeared in several Uralic branches, he divided his material into those terms which were clearly loans (mostly from Indo-European sources) and those which were not—terms already part of the language when the speakers of early Uralic, like those of early Indo-European, began to spread. Reading through the "native" part of Collinder's comparative dictionary is like going on a visual walk through the Mesolithic or the late Palaeolithic. With the possible exception of terms that may already refer to herding reindeer (semidomestication), and a single term referring to metal, the native expressions common to these languages suffice to account only for a Mesolithic economy, whereas words for agriculture and the specific metals are later borrowings.[3] (The italicized expressions in what follows represent the English meanings of words in the vocabulary common to Uralic speakers.)

We see, through the terms, that this land was little different from the tundra zone of the far north today. For example, their words tell us that they lived among *rivers, lakes, swamps,* and *forests.* They encountered *snowstorms* and *snowdrifts* and *trampled snow,* but they also had a verb for *keeping warm,* as well as words for *fire* and *coals.* Summer was, understandably, called *thaw-time.*

What might life have been like on a bright *morning* in thaw-time? The prime objective, of course, was to get food for the day—and more if possible, to preserve for the winter ahead. As in other preagricultural societies, with no crops to provide a regular food source, the women and children undoubtedly spent much of the day gathering wild plant food close to camp (a fairly safe task), while the men wandered farther afield hunting animal food. To deal with the youngest children while they gathered, the women had *portable cradles,* probably made from short poles and soft hides. To help in their collecting, they fashioned containers such as *baskets* and *birchbark pails,* by *peeling the bark* from *birch, willow,* and *linden* trees.

Among the tastiest things to collect were the various sorts of wild *berries* and *seeds* that ripened through the summer, as well as *eggs* from the *nests* of the many *birds* that roosted there. (As for species, we hear of *grouse, sparrows,* and *crows.*) But these people also knew of *intoxicating mushrooms,* which they almost certainly

---

[3] Even for the metal, there is no linguistic concensus on which metal was meant, and therefore, the term probably referred originally simply to metals in general. Pure, soft metal occurs here and there, and we know that such metal was picked up and used long before people learned to smelt it. (See Chapter 3.)

collected from time to time for ritual purposes. Narcotics of all sorts seem always to have been in demand for hallucinogenic rituals. By their means the participants could quickly come to see the inhabitants of the spirit world—dead ancestors and the like—of whom they could inquire about the future, cures for illness, lost objects, or other mysteries.

Collecting had its little hazards. A variety of *sticker bushes* like nettle, thistle, and wild rose grew in the area, for which the inhabitants had a single name. After all, what you needed to know about them was not their botanical classification but the practical fact that those plants were the kind that hurt! The foragers also encountered *snakes, lizards, worms, ants,* and—scourge of the tundra—hungry little *flies* and *midges.* It is with relief that we catch sight of *butterflies* among the flying swarms.

The things collected may have included more than food—for example, the soft local *mosses,* usable as stuffing for cushions and sleeping pads. For although these early people did not have permanent houses, they built seasonal shelters of *wood* and perhaps hides, to shelter themselves as comfortably as possible from the elements while they moved around at intervals to follow the changing sources of food. In fact, they had a special word for *tent poles,* which they could have fashioned from *aspen or poplar, spruce, fir,* or any of the other abundant trees.

They also built *raised wooden storage frames* for *hoards* of food to be preserved for leaner seasons. The seeds kept well just as they were, while berries, fish, and thin strips of meat could be dried for later use. But to keep these precious stores safe from the prowling *wolves* and other predators, they had to build protective *fences.*

While the women gathered plants and eggs, the men presumably searched out moving prey; interestingly, they designated *hunting and fishing* with the same word. As weapons they could use *nets, lines, traps, arrows,* and *knives.* To stalk their prey, they had regular *paths,* and they knew how *to ford* streams. The quarry must have included animals like *reindeer* and *hares,* as well as *fish* of all sorts—especially types of *salmon* and *pike.* The *snares* we hear of may have been used to catch birds as well as fish. If the kill or the catch was big enough, *sledges* made with *runners* could serve to *drag* or *carry* it home.

Back at camp, when the food was brought in, there was much to do. The meat could be cut up with knives, some to be dried and preserved for winter, some to be eaten on the spot. We don't know who did the cooking, but we can deduce that *soup or porridge* often graced the menu. To make it, they *boiled* the ingredients in *water* and *fished them out* of the *cooking pot* with a *ladle*. They also knew how to *roast* food on a *spit*. *Fat* and *oil* were so important to this cold-climate diet that they merited several terms.

There were other jobs besides preparing the food. The warm furs of hares, reindeer, and *foxes* needed to be prepared and preserved for winter wraps by carefully *scraping the hides*. The baskets and birchbark pails, as well as the hunting and fishing nets, lines, and snares, needed making and later mending. To manufacture the latter and to sew the hides, *string* was prepared from *fiber plants* (which, like the sticker bushes, got a single catchall function-based name) or from *stringy body parts*—indiscriminately gut, sinew, veins, or tendon. These people also knew how to *twist* various *fibers* into *rope* to *tie* things up and into thinner thread to *stitch* on *patches* and *fasteners* with the help of a *needle*.

In their *bags* of tools, besides knives, needles, and string, they had *picks, flints, combs, scoops,* and *glue,* along with *borers* for *boring holes*. They tell us they also knew how to *carve*. Of some of these early activities we have the physical remains, but we wouldn't have known about gluing, for instance, if they hadn't left the words behind.

During at least some *months (moon-ths)* of the *year,* the camps must have included more than just a *mother* and *father* with their *children* because terms for both the older and younger male and female *relations* of both *husband* and *wife* have come down to us. So we can imagine them sitting around the campfire of an *evening* in larger groups, making and mending tools and wraps while they swapped interesting stories of their adventures, of their *friends or comrades* and of the women's *suitors*. Sometimes people would *wrangle, admonish,* or *curse* and sometimes *get high.* But they also knew how to *give presents* and *distribute goods.* It is noteworthy that the word for *language* also sometimes meant "the news," "a report," or "a legend." Despite the friends and relatives we noticed, there just weren't very many humans around yet, and news of anything at all, even a new technique or tool, must have seemed very interesting. (To get a sense of this, imagine how hungry for news you would feel upon being released from a snowbound hut in Alaska after six months of winter.)

It would have been people living in a world much like this one, around 15,000 B.C., who produced our oldest preserved fiber artifact (fig. 2.3), a neatly made specimen found accidentally by the abbot A. Glory as he and other archaeologists were working in the famous painted caves of Lascaux, in southern France. He recounts the incident:

Figure 2.3. Earliest preserved string, reconstructed: a heavy cord twisted from three two-ply fiber strings, found fossilized in the painted caves of Lascaux, France, ca. 15,000 B.C.

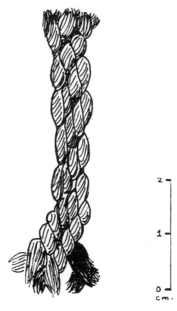

About two in the morning, exhausted with the work of copying the engravings on the ceiling of the apse, my helpers . . . and I were going to relax by hunting for new drawings and by exploring new galleries. I picked up a compact lump of clay which sealed this fissure [running between two galleries]; the clod broke into several pieces, which I took into my hands with the intention of pulverizing them to verify their makeup. As I examined the profile of the first bit, . . . I noticed a fine black line which crossed the surface from one end to the other. . . .

Mechanically with the tip of the blade of my pocket knife I tapped at the unexpected black line . . . The little lump of clay split open into two slabs like the leaves of a book. I saw immediately the carbonaceous imprint of a sort of fillet with twisted lines stretching the entire length of the lump. I interpreted this as the remains of a plaited vine, or some such thing.

The second piece opened the same way, but the positive and negative traces appeared to me to represent a more complicated interlace. The third lump broke both lengthwise and crosswise, and the fourth was not touched, to serve as witness . . .

Intrigued by these unexpected finds, we dissected square by square the rest of the clay covering, but to our great disappointment we could disclose nothing further, except for numerous particles of soot as everywhere in this layer, resulting probably from the debris of the torches . . . which had once served for light. . . . Seen [later] in the crisp light of day, there was no doubt possible: the fresh imprints, both concave and convex, in the first piece presented the very clear characteristics of a twisted cord formed of several strands on which one could distinguish even the puffiness of their twists."

Laboratory analysis showed the piece to have been made from vegetable fiber—too far disintegrated, alas, for tests to determine the plant species—and twisted from three two-ply cords (fig. 2.3). The plied cords, moreover, had each been formed by twisting their component strands in the other direction from that in which they had originally been spun. Such opposite twisting keeps the cord from coming apart once finished (see Chapter 1)—an important principle that craftworkers had discovered even at this early date. Abbot Glory concluded that the threefold cord had probably served to guide these early people down the dark and treacherous passage from one gallery of the cave to the other. Nor, as the proverb says, was it quickly broken.

We know for a fact, then, that twisted fiber string and thread were available in the Palaeolithic and that by 15,000 B.C. people possessed as much skill as anyone could wish for making cordage. After all, they had probably been practicing for five to ten thousand years already. Contrary to what one often reads in the literature, Palaeolithic peoples did not need to wait for the domestic plants and animals of the next great era, the New Stone Age, or Neolithic, to have fibers to use. For the relatively short lengths of string necessary for Palaeolithic tasks, an abundance of raw material lay for the taking in the wild.

Even today people unaccustomed to buying everything they want ready-made will manufacture bits of string and rope on the spot, using whatever is at hand. A Swedish archaeologist exploring central Asia in the 1930s described Chinese camel pullers in Mongolia who would "simply snatch a tuft from a camel shedding its hair and in a moment turn it into a piece of string for repairing a pack-saddle or the like, by twining it against the thigh. . . ." In the absence of tame animals, however, wild plants will do quite as well. Flax, hemp, nettle, ramie, jute, sisal, esparto, maguey, yucca, elm, linden, willow—the list of usable plants goes on and on, in both the New World and the Old. Indeed, all the earliest string and thread that we possess consist of plant fiber, starting with the cord from Lascaux, from 15,000 B.C. and continuing with the finds of string and cloth preserved from early Neolithic sites in the Near East, between 7000 and 5500 B.C., and the earliest-known artifacts of cord, netting, and basketry in the New World, dating to 8500 to 6500 B.C.

Nor must one go through the long and laborious process of freeing the fibers from the woody matrix within which they grow, as we do with our crops of fiber plants. The winter weather does that quite well, if not so efficiently, to lone plants, slowly rotting away the plant material around the fibers. I have only to walk out into my yard and collect off the back fence the long, dew-retted fibers of the passion fruit vine that volunteered to grow there last year. Singly the filaments will readily snap if I tug at them, but collected in a bundle and given a few twists around each other, they form a yard-long hank of string as good as any from the store.

The transient life-style of the Palaeolithic hunters and gatherers would have required such an at-need and on-the-spot approach to making string. If you have no settled home, you must carry all your possessions, so you tend not to acquire much—no more than absolutely necessary. It is thus still with the !Kung of southwestern Africa, who continue to pursue a hunter-gatherer way of life. Acquisitiveness is a Neolithic invention. String nets to catch a meal and carry it home for the family, plus wraps to keep warm and a few small tools and light containers to hold and prepare the food, for thousands of years were possessions enough. The heavier crafts like pottery awaited the advent of permanent houses to store things in.

Hence the first craft other than chipping stone blades and carving wooden implements (another perished product) and the first important craft not dangerous to the children must have been the fashioning of objects of and with string and fibers. We have no direct record of who did what chores in that distant time, but we will not be far off in surmising that the women were already involved in this innocuous task while they tended their toddlers around camp.

It is also on a carving of a woman that we found our first clear evidence for fiber string. Let's return to look at this woman again (fig. 2.1). Her skirt is fashioned of cords suspended from a twisted hip band and hanging only in the rear. Almost all the Venus figures are completely naked, but a few others wear clothing. All these come from Ukraine and European Russia, which lie as far toward the eastern end of the Gravettian culture as Lespugue lies toward

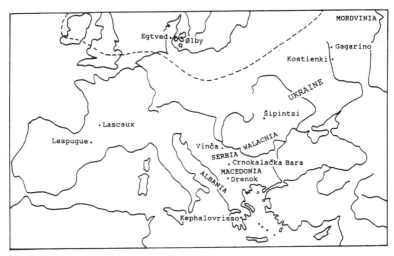

Figure 2.4. Map of the area of Europe in which Palaeolithic artifacts of the Gravettian culture are found, showing regions and some of the sites in which ancient or modern evidence occurs for string skirts (see fig. 2.1 and 2.5–2.9). The dashed line indicates the approximate southward extent of the northern ice sheet at the start of the Upper Palaeolithic.

the western (see map, fig. 2.4). A few of the Venuses from the site of Kostienki wear simple bands or sashes, but the Venus of Gagarino (fig. 2.5 a) sports a string skirt: a shorter, tidier skirt than her French sister, and this time hanging only in the front, but covering just as little, which is to say, nothing at all of what modern Western culture demands that a woman keep covered.

A skirt so skimpy, made of loose strings, can't have been very warm, and it certainly doesn't answer to *our* notions of modesty. So what was it for? Why did people who owned so little go to all the trouble of making and wearing a garment that was so nonfunctional? And what's more, why did women choose to wear such a thing for so many thousands of years? We have representations of women in little string skirts, here and there in this same broad geographical area through the next twenty thousand years, and even, around 1300 B.C., some actual string skirts preserved or partially preserved for us in the archaeological record.

Figure 2.5. Stone Age figurines of women wearing string skirts: from (a) Gagarino, Russia (ca. 20,000 B.C.); (b) Šipintsi, western Ukraine (ca. 3500 B.C.); (c) Vinča, Serbia (4500 B.C.); (d) Crnokalačka Bara, Yugoslav Macedonia (ca. 3000 B.C.). Compare figs. 2.6–2.8. The bindings on the feet of (d) look very much like the crude bast shoes with cloth leg bindings used by Russian and Ukrainian peasants into this century.

During the Neolithic, as people settled down in one place to practice the new art of farming (making it much easier for us to locate where they lived), we find an increasing array of clay figurines of women in string skirts, from sites in central and eastern Europe—the old heartland of the Gravettian culture. (In this area the Neolithic, or New Stone Age, lasts from shortly after 6000 B.C. to the introduction of metal, around 3000 B.C.) We have such statuettes from various parts of Ukraine and the Balkans (fig. 2.5 b–d).

In Denmark and northern Germany, moreover, in addition to figurines, we have the remains of string skirts on the bodies of young women buried in log coffins during the Bronze Age, late in the second millennium B.C. One of these skirts (fig. 2.6), made of woolen cords stained a rich brown by the acidic groundwater that preserved it, is complete; we can inspect its mode of manufacture. The thick plied cords that form the skirt were anchored by being woven through a narrow belt band, from which they hung down

Figure 2.6. String skirt of wool preserved on the body of a young woman found at Egtved, Denmark, and dating to the fourteenth century B.C. (Bronze Age). She wore it wrapped around twice and slung rather low on the hips so it reached to just above the knees. The skirt is now displayed in the National Museum in Copenhagen.

to a length of about fifteen inches. At the bottom they have been caught together by a twined spacing cord, which serves to keep them in order. Below that, the ends have been looped into an ornamental row of knots, making the bottom edge so heavy that the skirt must have had quite a swing to it, like the long, beaded fringe on a flapper's dance dress. The belt band on which all depends is so long that the skirt was worn wrapped around twice, rather low on the hips, and tied in the center front with the generous ends of the band. Other finds of less well-preserved string skirts show much the same design features, except that some were finished off at the bottom by encasing the ends of the cords in little metal sleeves (fig. 2.7). These, too, would have given the skirt a consider-

Figure 2.7. Remains of a young woman laid to rest in a short string skirt and other finery, from Ølby, Denmark (Bronze Age). The ends of the strings were encased in little tubes of bronze. The rows of tubes (largely fused together now by oxidation) show how short the skirt was: the original miniskirt.

able swish to it, by their weight, as well as caught the ear with the click and the eye with the gleam of the metal.

European scholars were horrified, when the complete skirt was dug up at Egtved, that their ancestresses should have worn so indecent an apparel and proclaimed that the lady must have worn a linen shift underneath it, now disintegrated without trace, to hide her nakedness. The figurines indicate otherwise. The Egtved girl at least wore a woolen blouse, but the spry young girls in the bronze images wear nothing at all but a string skirt of the same design, and a rather shorter one at that.

In no case do the string skirts—whether Palaeolithic, Neolithic, or Bronze Age—provide for either warmth or modesty. In all cases they are worn by women. To solve the mystery of why they were maintained for so long, I think we must follow our eyes. Not only do the skirts hide nothing of importance, but if anything, they attract the eye precisely to the specifically female sexual areas by framing them, presenting them, or playing peekaboo with them. In all the Venus figures the breasts, belly, and pubic area are heavily emphasized; that is how the sculptures came to be called Venuses. Hands, feet, and head are often barely carved at all. To us, with our modern city standard of slim "fitness," these women may seem unattractively fat. But many other cultures view plumpness as the essence of female beauty, as our own culture did in, say, Rubens's day. Of course, fat played a different role then. A woman who becomes too thin will become temporarily infertile (as modern female athletes discover). So a fat woman is in a far better state to survive and to support her child with her own milk during seasonal famine. In short, obesity helps ensure successful reproduction.

Our best guess, then, is that string skirts indicated something about the childbearing ability or readiness of the woman, perhaps simply that she was of childbearing age, having reached menarche but not yet menopause, or perhaps that she had reached puberty but was not yet "married" (whatever that might have meant in the particular society: still a virgin, or still without child, or still without a regular mate)—in other words, that she was in some sense "available" as a bride. The notion of marriage, as opposed to mere mating, is so important to the human race that the need to negotiate this problem has been seriously suggested as one of the most powerful drives toward the development of language.[4] Indeed,

[4] The argument is that monogamy is a more successful strategy of reproduction for women than polygamy because, by obtaining the services of a single male, a woman can better protect and feed her children. For the male, however, the best strategy for representation in the ongoing gene pool is polygamy—as long as the children survive. But if the children seriously require his help, then monogamy may be necessary. In that case he and his family may want recompense for what

clear signals as to the marriage status of women are common around the world, from the tiny gold band around the fourth finger to signs visible from far away, such as the squash blossom hairdo of the unmarried Hopi girl and the glittering coin-covered cap of the newlywed Mordvin wife. Depending upon the society, such a marker might carry with it a considerable sense of honor and specialness, certifying the wearer as possessing the mysterious ability to create new human life.

If this is the case, then we do well to look at the gently comical tale which Homer tells, in the fourteenth book of the *Iliad,* of how Hera set about to seduce Zeus.

Hoping to divert her all-powerful husband's attention from the battlefield of Troy for a while, Hera goes to her divine apartments to dress herself in a way that her spouse will not ignore. She washes, puts on perfume, braids her hair, and dons a "divine garment" and golden jewelry. Then she carefully ties around herself, for this special occasion, her "girdle fashioned with a hundred tassels." Finally she goes to Aphrodite, goddess of sexual love, and asks sweetly if she might borrow Aphrodite's girdle as well. In other words, to make very sure of her quarry, she asks to use the divine archetype of all such girdles, into which, Homer says, "have been crafted all the bewitchments—in it are Love and Lust and Flirtation—persuasion that has stolen away the mind of even the carefulest thinkers." Aphrodite obligingly takes off her special girdle (she wears it constantly, it seems, as a badge of her office) and places it in the hand of the queen of the gods, instructing her to put it on under the fold of her breast. (This is the literal wording and describes exactly how the Venus of Gagarino wears hers. But the modern translators, not understanding the garment, usually tamper with the passage.) Aphrodite tells Hera that with this girdle on, "what you wish for in your mind will not go unaccomplished!"

---

he is giving up, while the woman and her family may want assurances that he will not let down his end of the bargain. It is these intricacies of negotiation that language can make plain.

Nor does it. Zeus spots Hera coming toward him across the mountaintops, forgets everything else, and demands that she lie with him then and there.

What could this be, this "girdle of a hundred tassels," but our string skirt? The form is right, in fact unique, and the signal that Zeus picks up—that it has to do with making love to a woman—is very close to what we have surmised. That the archetypical one is owned by Aphrodite falls closer still; in her hands we might almost call it a mating girdle.

The string skirt is still alive and well, preserved in many a folk costume in the old heartland of the Gravettian culture of twenty thousand years ago: south-central and eastern Europe (see fig. 2.4). What's more, the symbolic function that we deduced from the ancient examples is preserved right along with the form.

Far to the east lie the Mordvins, just east of Moscow and west of the Volga River and Ural Mountains. They speak a Uralic language related to Finnish and the other northernmost languages on the European continent (see figs. 2.2 and 2.4). Well into this century custom had it that a Mordvin girl would don a long black string apron at the time of her betrothal (fig. 2.8 a). Hanging only in the back, like that of the Venus of Lespugue but wider, it marked her as a wife. Its function, claims a Finnish woman who has researched the local costumes thoroughly, was that of "the symbol of a married woman," and as such it "belonged to the same category as the woollen and often fringed loin drapings of the Southern Great Russians, the Bulgarians, the Serbs and the Rumanians." Women wore very simple ones for every day, but quite elaborate ones for festive occasions.

The typical peasant costume in most of the central Balkans and Ukraine consists of a white chemise of soft vegetable fiber (linen, hemp, or more recently cotton), over which the woman usually wears a pair of aprons, one in the front, the other in the back. Among the Vlachs of eastern Serbia and in the Banat area of Romania just to the east, as well as among the Walachians of southeastern Romania (fig. 2.8 b), the solid-woven part of the

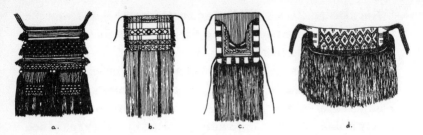

Figure 2.8. String skirts among recent folk costumes: (a) Mordvin, back apron (black); (b) Walachian (Romanian), front apron (red, worn with a back apron identical except for not having the lozenge pattern); (c) Yugoslav Macedonian, front apron (red with black; see fig. 2.9 for the accompanying sash); (d) Albanian, front apron (black with red lozenges). (See map, fig. 2.4, for locations of these areas.)

apron is remarkably short, half to seven-eighths of the length being occupied by an enormous fringe predominantly of black (Serbia) or red (Romania). Furthermore, the women decorate the front apron, at least, with a woven pattern of lozenges, generally taken as a powerful fertility symbol. These lozenges, usually with little curly hooks around the edge, rather graphically, if schematically, represent a woman's vulva. In parts of Romania the young, unmarried woman attached to her apron at the waist a chain with rings and keys hanging from it—another unsubtle image of the mechanics of sex. But if she reached the age of thirty without having borne children—woman's most important work in an expanding society—she had to move the chain to the bottom of her costume, to show symbolically (it is said) that she had trampled and wasted her childbearing capacity and duty.

All these motifs reinforce one another. In medieval Russia the iron lock plates of the storerooms and storage chests were often wrought in the form of a hook-surrounded lozenge, while as far back as the mid-first millennium B.C. keys to women's jewelry boxes were being made in phallic shapes. The image of inserting the key to unlock the bounty of the storehouse needs no further explication, and it links the ring-and-key "jewelry" directly to the lozenges on the aprons they adorn. Everything—lozenge, ring and key, and string apron—is clearly there to promote, protect, and celebrate female fertility.

Farther south, in Macedonia, there remain many vestiges of the string skirt, all done in fiery reddish orange. A friend brought me a Macedonian outfit from her costume collection to try on (see figs. 2.8 c and 2.9). The front part consisted of a short woven apron with a piece appliquéd onto it that exactly framed the pubic bone underneath. Below this hung a weighty fringe nearly double the length of the solid part. We tied it on to me and began to wrestle with the other half, a girdle perhaps twelve feet long, woven with white and black threads in opposite directions and terminating in a great fiery cascade of red fringe at either end (fig. 2.9). I couldn't help noticing that these fringes were divided and wrapped, redivided and wrapped again in an ever-widening pattern, much the way I knew some of the Bronze Age belt ends to have been worked.

"OK, we start by holding one end against one side of your rear," said my friend, "then wrapping this whole length of belt band around you about six times . . . and tucking the other end through so it hangs next to the first one. . . . What I really need now is a hook to make them stay together. . . . Oh!" she exclaimed in surprise. "There's a little hook right here where I need it; I never noticed it before." Proof that we had put it on right, the hook anchored the two ends of the girdle beside each other so they formed a solid mass of apron and fringe in the back. Because the wool of the fringe had been combed before spinning, the fibers lay maximally close together, creating a very dense, almost uncomfortably hard cord, which was so heavy that it swung with a life of its own.

That was the greatest surprise of all: the independent life of what now enveloped me. I danced around the room from one mirror to the next, fascinated by the way the heavy fringes moved, completely differently from any other garment I had ever worn. I felt exhilarated, powerful; I wanted to make them swish and jump,

Figure 2.9. Red and black woolen fringed sash, used to form back of string skirt on costume from Drenok, in Yugoslav Macedonia (see fig. 2.8 c). Surviving Bronze Age sashes from Europe show a similar method and pattern of dividing and wrapping the threads.

see what they would do next. My friend laughed and admitted that it made her feel the same way when she wore the costume and that she was always as reluctant as I to take it off. For days afterward I pondered the unexpected strength of the experience.

A sense of powerfulness? Is that a part of the symbolism of the skirt? The ability to create new life must surely have been viewed as a form of ultimate power. Exhilaration in wearing it? Was that, too, part of the reason why this garment lasted for twenty thousand years?

However that may be, I also began to realize that the other bright orangy-red Macedonian aprons, which have much larger woven parts than this one but also much heftier fringes than the typical European apron, were "changed later forms" of the string skirt, as linguists would say of words evolving through time. (The processes are remarkably similar, as we shall see.) Such aprons exist not only in the Yugoslavian area, but also in the section of Macedonia now ruled by Bulgaria to the east. To the west, Albanian women (fig. 2.8 d) still wear string aprons with long black cords (like the Vlach and Mordvin ones) and with the lozenges across their very narrow woven tops (like Slavic and Romanian ones).

Greece, too, preserves traces of the string skirt—for example, in the Argolid (see map, fig. 2.4). Most women now wear modern Western clothing there, but some of them still possess string skirts for childbearing emergencies. The women's folk costume of older times had included a special girdle known as a *zostra*, made of red wool in a kind of knotless netting called sprang.[5] It was worked to about twelve feet long, with a deep fringe. "The women of [the town of] Kephalovrisso consider the *zostra* as sacred," the researchers tell us. "They place it on the abdomen of the woman

[5] The method of manufacture plus the color make me wonder whether we perhaps possess a girdle of just this sort from the Bronze Age. Two woolen textiles were found at Roswinkel, in the northern Netherlands, one being a fragment of red knotless netting, like the Greek *zostra*, and the other a belt woven with alternating groups of threads in a way that suggests number magic (see Chapter 6). Sprang itself dates back in Europe to the Neolithic at least.

who has a difficult labour and maintain it does work wonders. . . . Very few old women still know how to make a *zostra*. Young women inherit it from their mothers and usually refuse to part with it, as they like to keep it as a charm." I have heard its aid is also sought if the girl is having trouble conceiving. One could describe it as a talisman to help out the forces of modern medicine where the crucial age-old matter of bearing children is at stake.

The very name for this special girdle is ancient: *zostra* from Classical Greek *zōstēr*. It comes from the same root as the word *zōnē,* meaning "belt," which Homer used for the hundred-tasseled girdles of Hera and Aphrodite and from which English *zone* has been borrowed with a slight shift of meaning (now a belt of land). The ancient Greek word is, in fact, a changed later form of the Indo-European word for a belt—any kind of belt—that is also pre-served in Albanian, Slavic, Baltic, and Iranian.

Languages constantly change, but only slowly and according to some fairly regular principles. As a result, linguists can reconstruct many of the details of earlier forms of language. We have already appealed to language sources and will do so again many times in this book, since the terms for the products of women's work, like food and clothing, generally survive longer than the objects them-selves. Unfortunately one of the principles by which languages change is through loss. (For example, the old terms for the trap-pings of a horse-drawn buggy are dropping out of our language because we now use cars instead.) As a result of such limitations, the farther back in time we go, the less we can reconstruct; we are doing well when we haven't lost sight of our quarry by the time we get back to the start of the Bronze Age.

And so we find it with Indo-European words for clothing. I have mentioned the Indo-European family before. This huge group of languages (fig. 2.10) already extended across most of Europe and half the Near East (all the way to the middle of India—hence the name we have given it) before Columbus sailed to the "New World." The numerous tongues had developed from a single lan-guage or closely related group of dialects apparently spoken in a

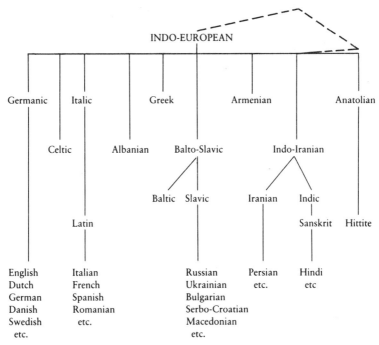

Figure 2.10. Tree chart of languages in the Indo-European family, which—before Columbus—extended from northwestern Europe to northern India. It is now the dominant family of the New World as well. Compare fig. 2.2, showing a tree of the Uralic languages. The Anatolian branch, clearly related to the others, may in fact be sister rather than daughter to the Indo-European family.

fairly small area in the Neolithic, probably in southeastern Europe near the Caucasus. Early in the Bronze Age, however, the speakers of these constantly and gradually changing dialects began to fan out across the continents, losing direct contact with each other. So what had once existed as a single Indo-European language, where people could understand one another (if only imperfectly, thanks to regional differences), slowly became a set of mutually unintelligible—but still closely related—languages (fig. 2.10). Such are Greek, Albanian, and Slavic; such also are the "Romance" languages of western Europe (French, Spanish, Italian, etc., all of them changed later forms of the "Roman" language, Latin) and the "Germanic" group farther north (including English, German, Dutch, Danish, Swedish, and Norwegian). The reconstructed language from which all these modern tongues came is known for convenience as proto-Indo-European, since we don't know what those early people called themselves.

What strikes me so about this word for "belt"—*zōnē, zostra,* and their cousins—is that it is one of only two terms that we can reconstruct for clothing in proto-Indo-European. The other term, significantly, is the generic word for clothing which Homer uses for the vague other "garment" that Hera puts on first as she dresses to visit Zeus. That word is *heanon,* from the same Indo-European word root as *vest, vestment* (which we have borrowed into English from Latin) and related also to the Greek *Hestia,* Latin *Vesta,* the name of the goddess of the hearth and home. (The semantic connection between "clothes" and "hearth and home" seems originally to have lain in things that help you keep warm.) Thus, when we reconstruct linguistically back as far as we can in Europe—admittedly, merely to about the Early Bronze Age (third millennium B.C.), when the Indo-European groups began to lose contact with one another—we see only a general word for a warming wrap and a word for a belt. Clothes don't get much simpler.

Can this picture be right? Is this all that these people wore? Yes, in essence it seems so. Slightly later some of these speakers borrowed the notion of the tunic, word and all, from their Semitic-speaking neighbors to the southeast. But three garments—white tunic, belt, and oblong or tubular overwrap—remained the basis of the European peasant woman's costume from then until the present. Even the modern business woman who wears a white blouse, woolen skirt, and belt to work dresses in a barely changed, later form of Bronze Age European clothing. After all, if it works well, why alter it? Fashionable details may come and go, but the fundamentals of how we clothe our bodies are remarkably conservative.

The "string skirt" or "tasseled girdle" appears to have been fundamental to women's clothing in that part of the world since long before the Bronze Age, and it has retained one of the old and fundamental names.

The Palaeolithic is a remote era that ended more than ten thousand years ago, yet it yields some remarkably sharp details. People were already making a diverse array of things from twisted fibers, one of which, the string skirt, was specifically associated with women and with women's ability to bear children. We can guess, therefore, that women were already heavily involved with the making of thread and such clothing as existed, as part of their work. Note, too, that this first type of clothing for which we have good evidence is symbolic rather than purely utilitarian and suggests the relative importance of women and their work.

Within the Palaeolithic, "fiber craft" would have been largely a matter of people making short lengths of string specifically for the job of the moment. Fibers from wild plants would have sufficed, stripped directly from trees or vines, or noticed and gathered after the rain and sun had retted them naturally by disintegrating the rest of the stem and leaving the fibers bare. But it probably didn't take the remaining ten to fifteen thousand years of the Palaeolithic for people to figure out how to speed nature along by helping with the retting process. (The archaic verb *to ret* means "to make [something] *rot*," just as *to fell* a tree means "to make [the tree] *fall*.")

From the beginning of the next age in the far north, the Mesolithic, we have well-made hunting and fishing nets composed of fiber stripped from the bark of elms and willows, from sites in Finland and Lithuania. This technology fits perfectly with the linguistic data from proto-Uralic and suggests that people had also learned early of the strength and pliability of these materials. Bark fibers are as useful for making baskets, mats, fences, and weirs as for making string.

We also have the evidence for the fashioning of string skirts. The Gravettian skirts show the simplest of designs; the cords merely hang from a twisted belt band. No doubt the women to whom it was so important an object put some thought and time, over the millennia, into making it sturdier, perhaps also neater and more beautiful. The design of the earliest string skirt that has survived intact (that from Egtved, Denmark) so closely resembles the peculiar way that a warp was traditionally prepared in Europe (up until the introduction of new looms in Roman and medieval times)[6] that I have often wondered whether women in Europe had already invented weaving itself during Palaeolithic times, as a way of making a stronger and better string skirt.

String seems such a simple, almost inevitable invention, yet its appearance was a momentous step down the road of technology. Invented early, it was known worldwide. Weaving, on the contrary, is much more complicated and may have been thought up only once, much too late to spread with humankind. Many cultures were still ignorant of it as this century began.

[6] Both were made by weaving a narrow ribbed band and pulling the weft of that band out a great distance to one side to form the fringe or the warp threads, as the case might be.

3

Courtyard Sisterhood

Men may work from sun to sun,
But women's work is never done.

Welsh rabbit: oddments of cheese melted with leftover
ale and served over toast for supper when the hunters
fail to come home with a rabbit.

Toward the end of the Palaeolithic era, some ten thousand years
ago, the way women in particular lived their lives began to change
dramatically, as the result of a seemingly small but new idea. Here-
tofore families had always been on the move, shifting from one
temporary abode to another as sources of ready food came and
went with the seasons. Now, as the great ice sheets and the vast
herds of tundra animals retreated northward across Europe, some
humans in the rapidly warming south stopped following the animals and began to settle down, obtaining their food locally. The
era that followed, with its multitude of cultural changes, we call
the Neolithic, or New Stone Age.

These settlers didn't know it—they would not have possessed
such a concept yet—but this life of permanent abodes started the
greatest pyramid scheme of all time. A pyramid scheme starts

small and gets bigger and bigger, leaving the last people to pay for all. (Chain letters are often of this sort.) When you settle down, you begin to acquire things to make your survival and that of your children easier; soon you need more tools and helpers—off-spring—to care for the ever-increasing number of things and surviving children. At the end of the Palaeolithic, around 8000 B.C., the entire continent of Europe contained scarcely five hundred thousand people—roughly today's population of Florence, Italy, or Denver, Colorado. Population experts estimate that Earth as a whole had five million humans then, less than half of what greater Los Angeles alone has today. It took the next fifteen hundred years for that number to double to ten million. Today, by contrast, we are doubling our billions of world inhabitants in a mere twenty-five years and have nearly reached what will be the ultimate layer of this pyramid, one way or another, as we run out of fresh water and breathable oxygen, not to mention wood and metals. We find ourselves stuck with the final bill for some five hundred generations of uncontrolled acquisition and child producing begun in the Neolithic.

In sum, settling down changed radically the relationship of people to one another and to the environment, as it altered how people now came to behave. To understand the relations between women and their new work in a sedentary world, we must therefore first understand what made settled life such a novel project.

Why did people stop being nomadic? Archaeologists used to debate the question in chicken-or-egg form: whether people first discovered how to domesticate plants and animals, then settled down to tend the fields they had planted, or whether they settled first, then began taming what they found in the vicinity. It was even argued for a while that people stopped moving around because they had invented pottery, a commodity too heavy and breakable to carry about. But we now know that true pottery was invented several thousand years after permanent settlements began.

Evidence from recent excavations in Turkey, Syria, and Israel

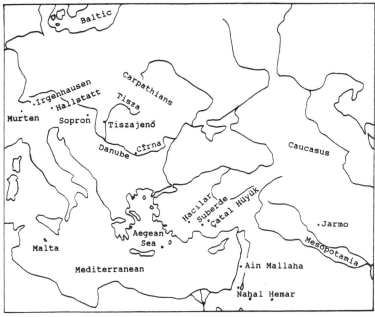

Figure 3.1. Map of Neolithic and other sites important to the early history of textiles.

shows that at least in some cases people settled first, then domesticated their food supply. Huge stands of wild grain began to flourish in that area, as a result of the warming postglacial climate, from about 10,000 B.C. on, and people apparently began to find it possible to live off this wild grain and the animals it supported. Thus early settlement sites like Ain Mallaha in Syria and Suberde in Turkey (fig. 3.1) give evidence of permanent dwellings and storage pits, but only wild food. Furthermore, the first sign of domestication that we have, present at some of the earliest settlements, is not something that was eaten: It is the dog. This creature, which willingly chooses a human as the leader of its lifelong pack, was humankind's first friend, it seems, as well as its best.

The very act of stockpiling ripe grain for winter in the new village could well have led people to the idea of helping nature out by planting seed themselves. A woman going to the family storage bin during the early spring rains might find that the last of the winter store was already sprouting into new plants. Or perhaps some grain, dropped on the way home from the harvest, had sprung up just outside the doorstep. A little water during dry spells and a little weeding during wet ones ensures the crop—in a most convenient place.

But soon an interesting symbiosis develops between the humans and their favorite plants. When it ripens, wild grain breaks off very easily from the stalk it grew on (as anyone knows who has gotten a sock full of seeds just by walking through a field of tall, dry grass). That is how the plant spreads its seeds to propagate. In the wild a seed that does not fall off the stalk easily is less likely than its more readily dehiscent neighbors to settle into a good spot to germinate, but conversely it is *more* likely to be sitting there waiting to be found when the human collector comes by. The varieties of grain thus select rapidly toward kinds that cling firmly to the stem, once people gathering and sowing seed come into the equation. In fact, the plant becomes dependent upon the humans to wrestle its seeds free and plant them. Such changes in seed form constitute some of the clues we have that purposeful planting began between 10,000 and 7000 B.C.

Animals, too, change under domestic conditions. With the old-style Palaeolithic kills (the only alternative to daily foraging), it tended to be feast or famine: Everyone got together and rounded up a herd of something tasty, slaughtered the lot, gorged, and then went hungry again. Dry-curing a stock of meat could help even things out, but then you had to haul it about, and meat, even dried, is heavy. Once you settle in one place, however, different problems and solutions arise. If you kill a big animal far from your permanent residence, you must somehow convey the meat back home. You can no longer bring home to it. (The remains of animal bones at the early village of Suberde show how the hunters there solved this problem. Instead of carrying the largest and heaviest bones all the way home, the villagers cut them out at the kill site and used the hide as a bag in which to drag home by the shanks the rest of the carcass, now considerably lightened. This causes a peculiarly skewed distribution of bones at the dwelling site that archaeologists have nicknamed the schlepp effect.)

But what if you rounded up some middle-size animals, not too big to handle and not too small for the bother, walked them home on their own four legs, and stored them *alive,* in a pen full of fodder, until you needed them one by one for food? Refrigeration on the hoof, as it were. True, the jumpy ones will probably break loose or get killed first for their trouble, but the more docile ones might last till spring and, like the grain, might then be found quietly reproducing. Thus selection in captivity tends toward docility and smaller biting equipment—shorter muzzle, less prominent incisors, weaker neck muscles—and less of a premium on invisibility to predators. (Protection from predators over more than one generation allows variations in hair growth and color that would otherwise make the animal nonviable.) These traits, too, show up in the archaeological record from the early Neolithic on.

To the hothead, being "kept" is exploitation; to the docile, symbiosis. It's partly in how you look at it. Individuals that could not have survived "in the wild" can live out their lives under protection. (Ants grow great flocks of aphids by protecting them, then "milk" them for their sugar. Exploitation or symbiosis?) Humans themselves, compared with other primates, show the typical signs of domestication in their reduced jaws, claws, neck muscles, and hair—women even more than men. We partially domesticated ourselves first. In any case, many other species thrived under human care, and the humans rearranged their lives to care for the plants and animals that now came to depend on them.

These new labor arrangements differed from one region to another as a function of just which domestic animals, if any, became critical to the local food supply. Plants in themselves are compatible with child raising, but some animals are not—especially the large draft animals used for plowing. Thus farming societies tend to divide into types depending on whether the plants are grown using a plow (*agriculture,* meaning "field culture") or by hand-tending alone (*horticulture,* "garden culture").

But it was not until some four thousand years after people had begun domesticating animals that they started to harness creatures to pull plows. So our next tale is of horticultural settlements, where the women were usually in charge of the kitchen-gardens and thus of the main food supply, along with the young children and the burgeoning fiber-crafts.

Permanent abodes changed women's lives dramatically. Not least, it allowed women to stop carrying their children around. Women today who belong to hunter-gatherer societies, such as the !Kung in southwestern Africa, space their children three to four years apart. They can't physically handle more than that, and that number of children (considering that they don't all survive) is quite sufficient to keep the population going without overloading the resources of food and water. But once the family settles down, carrying the small children constantly is no longer necessary, so the babies *may* come oftener, and there is always need for more hands on a farm, so more babies come to be *wanted*. Furthermore, the risk of disease and epidemic is far greater where larger numbers of people live in close quarters and among their own refuse. Cholera, typhoid, plague, and diphtheria all were diseases spread by such conditions, terrifying in their speed, devastating in their toll, and checked only recently by modern sanitation, immunization, and antibiotics. Babies are the most vulnerable to such attacks; thus, under those conditions, babies soon *needed* to come more often to balance out the higher death toll.

This new Neolithic ethic of bearing large numbers of children (still practiced by many today, even where modern medicine now keeps most of these children alive) is evident both in the increasingly rapid rise of population during the Neolithic and in the representations of people: almost always women, and usually— unlike the few male figures—fat. These numerous figurines seem to be continuations of the Palaeolithic Venus figures, but with some marked differences.

At Jarmo, a Neolithic village that flourished around 7000 B.C. in Iraqi Kurdistan, plump women are modeled sitting down instead of standing—perhaps a more characteristic pose in a stationary life. Jarmo is one of the earliest villages we know with firm evidence of both plants and animals being domestic. By 6000 B.C. at Çatal Hüyük, in south-central Turkey, we see a strong and overt preoccupation with fertility and childbirth. Amid a frightening array of bulls' heads (plaster over actual skulls, with enormous horns), we see a no less scary plaster wall relief of a pregnant woman with her legs spread and her arms raised, concentric circles like a bull's-eye on her stomach (fig. 3.2). In another case a sculpted man and woman lie in close frontal embrace, and still another statuette shows an enormously plump woman sitting as she begins to deliver (fig. 3.3). But this is no ordinary scene of birthing: The lady's hands rest on a pair of formidable felines, perhaps lionesses, suggesting that she is in supernatural control of life.[1] Many other figurines of plump women, mostly either sitting or lying, often with children clambering on them, come from the slightly later site of Hacılar nearby. The height of this reverence for obese women, however, comes with the reclining sculptures from early Malta (fig. 3.4). Such females—special priestesses? queens?—may remind the modern observer of nothing so much as a termite queen, whose only job is to lie quietly all her life, eating food and bearing young—plump, pampered, pale and immobile. Or they may remind one of Odysseus' description of his men arriving at the palace of the king of Laistrygonia (possibly in the vicinity of Malta):

And when they entered the famed halls, they came upon his wife, who was big as a mountain peak; and they were appalled at her.

Settling down and being able to grow as much of something as one wanted not only changed the patterns of childbearing but also

---

[1] A not unsimilar cult of the dread goddess Kybele and her wild animals persisted in western Turkey in Classical times.

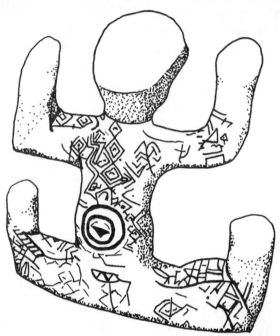

Figure 3.2. Relief sculpture of a pregnant woman, from the wall of a shrine at the early Neolithic town of Çatal Hüyük, in Turkey. The hands, feet, and face are mostly gone now, but the preserved parts of the skin are covered with tiny red-painted designs, mostly forms of lozenges but here and there resembling plants. They probably imitate body paint used magically to help a woman through the dangerous and painful ordeal of childbirth.

inevitably changed the types of tasks to be parceled out. In the fiber crafts, vast new supplies made it now possible to consider making big pieces of cloth rather than just narrow bands and belts. But to do that, the craftswoman first had to redesign her loom.

Our earliest clear proof of woven cloth comes once again from Jarmo, Iraq, in the form of two little clay balls with textile impressions on them. The cloths are fine and neatly woven in not one but two different weaves, details demonstrating clearly that people had been weaving long enough to have become highly skilled at it. Unfortunately no vestiges of weaving equipment or work spaces

Figure 3.3. Clay statuette of an obese woman giving birth while seated with her hands on a pair of wild animals; found at the early Neolithic town of Çatal Hüyük, in Turkey, ca. 6000 B.C.

Figure 3.4. Neolithic figurine of a reclining woman, from the Mediterranean island of Malta. All the early female sculptures from Malta show great obesity.

turned up at this site, so we can't say whether the Jarmo weavers had solved the problems of large looms yet. A look at all the Neolithic evidence for textiles together yields more data, however.

By plotting this evidence in both time and space, we can discern traces of at least two large Neolithic looms of quite different design, and we see, furthermore, that the loom types spread in roughly opposite directions across the landscape from the innovative area where Jarmo and Çatal Hüyük lie. One of these is the horizontal ground loom (fig. 3.5), still used today by Bedouin

Figure 3.5. Wooden model of a Middle Kingdom Egyptian weaving shop, showing two horizontal ground looms pegged out for use. Two weavers squat beside the warp to help each other with the weaving. This type of loom has been used in the Near East from sometime in the Neolithic until the present day. Other women are shown processing flax, spinning, and measuring warp thread on pegs on the wall. Eleventh Dynasty, ca. 2000 B.C.

women in the Near East. This device migrated mainly south and southeast: through Mesopotamia and the Levant, down into Egypt, and apparently eventually all the way to India. Since this loom is made entirely of wooden sticks (seldom preserved and hard to recognize), most of our evidence for it comes from representations of its use. In these depictions, incidentally, wherever one can tell the gender of the weavers, they are women (cf. fig. 7.5).

The other type is the warp-weighted loom (fig. 3.6), set nearly vertical, which was still being used twenty-five years ago by women in rural Scandinavia. This loom, by contrast, can be traced spreading largely north and west across Europe from a focal center in Hungary. It is much easier to trace than the ground loom because, although most of this loom, too, was composed of wood, the warp was kept tight by a series of weights, which were generally made of baked clay and hence are much less perishable. Although representations of this loom are far fewer and later, those we have show women once again as the weavers.

What I find most fascinating about these two early looms is that neither is logically derivable from the other, but both are easily derived from the simple band loom. With a band loom, the weaver normally ties the near end of the warp in a single bunch to a post or her own waist and the far end to something else, like a tree or another post or her big toe. If the weaving is tied to the weaver, the tension on the warp that is necessary for weaving is provided by simply leaning back. It couldn't be simpler. As one wishes to make a wider and wider fabric, it is possible to spread out the near end of the warp on a bar, rather than attach it all in a single bunch. But as the spread increases, if the far end is still tied in a single group, the warp threads develop a steep angle that makes the weaving difficult. That end needs to be spread, too. If, then, you take the bar at the weaver's end (called the cloth beam) and hang it up, tying stones on to the bottom of the warp in little bunches to provide the necessary tension, you have the makings of the warp-weighted loom. But if you stake the cloth beam to the ground, and

Figure 3.6. Women weaving together on a warp-weighted loom, as depicted on a Greek vase of about 560 B.C. (See fig. 9.4 for the entire scene.) On this loom the warp hangs down from a beam supported over the weaver's head.

stake an identical bar some yards away to which you can tie the other end of the warp, thread by thread, to keep the tension, you produce the ground loom.

Thus the two types of loom appear to have been independent ways of solving the problem of how to make wider cloth. Once invented, they spread outward, meeting and competing with each other in Turkey, it seems, but otherwise creeping slowly for thousands of miles in opposite directions. It is interesting, too, that the seminal zones for these large looms are the areas in which flax first became domesticated, the stretch from northern Iraq to southern Europe. Such deductions strengthen my hunch that the Palaeolithic women of southern Europe had already invented belt weaving (as part of their concern with symbolic belt-based clothing like the string skirt) and that knowledge of this useful craft had spread southeast by early Neolithic times to the areas where domestication was invented.

Consider, too, the geographical areas where each loom came to be used. Egypt and Mesopotamia are hot, dry regions where it seldom rains. A woman can go outdoors and stake out her loom as big as she pleases for days, weeks, or even months without fear of disaster. Not so in Europe, where snow covers the ground half the winter and rain is frequent all summer. Outdoors is no place for a loom, but neither can the family afford to have the weaving all over the floor of the living space. So hang it from the rafters, or prop it on the wall! It takes almost no floor space that way and is protected from the elements.

In the Tisza Valley in Hungary, excavators have dug up the remains of several Neolithic huts from around 5500 B.C., some equipped with sets of clay loom weights along with the cooking pots and other simple gear. In one cottage (fig. 3.7) the weights sat in a heap beside a pair of stout postholes near one wall. Since these posts have no discoverable function in holding up roof or walls, they almost certainly formed the supports for a vertical warp-weighted loom—a loom measuring 185 centimeters wide and thus accommodating a cloth 4 to 5 feet in width. Furthermore, we see

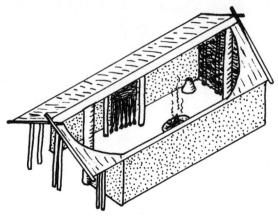

Figure 3.7. Cutaway reconstruction (from the floor plan) of a sixth-millennium-B.C. Neolithic house at Tiszajenő, Hungary. In addition to the hearth and a storage jar set into the floor, one can see the reconstruction of a warp-weighted loom, set up at a slight angle to the wall so that it could receive light from the doorway in daytime as well as from the hearth fire at night.

that the woman of the house had cleverly set up her loom so she would get the best light on it during the day, since it faces the doorway, and also set it near the hearth as well, so as to get light from the fire at night and during the long, dark winters. Apparently women already expected to work long hours.

In Europe conditions in the Neolithic and Early Bronze ages fostered a "courtyard and outrider" economy. There were no draft animals, so the women with their children underfoot could take responsibility for the entire basic food supply: cereals, legumes, and such other fruits and nuts as might be available, plus eggs and an occasional lamb or mutton stew. That freed the men to go outside the community (outriders) for other resources entirely, if needed, returning at intervals with their contributions. Since war did not yet constitute significantly more of a problem than it had in the Palaeolithic, the men did not have to stay home all the time simply for defense. (The rarity of warfare had to do with both the sparseness of the population and the lack of great difference between haves and have-nots.) We see families clustering their houses together into little villages for mutual aid and support, but fences, when present, seem to be designed more to keep sheep and children in than enemies—other than wolves—out.

In such a world the women could bring their smaller crafts out into the communal yard in good weather, to chat together and help one another as they worked and watched the children play. The children, in turn, could play at helping, pretending to do what the big folks do, as children will. Such play can function as a sort of vocational kindergarten, teaching the children the basic steps in processes that they will have to master in earnest later. For textile work alone, in addition to spinning the thread and using it to sew, make nets, and mend, these activities included the many steps of preparing the dried flax or hemp for spinning. First the women place the dried plants in a stream or in the dew long enough to rot the unwanted parts of the stem away from the tough fibers—a process called *retting*. Then they beat and twist loose the woody parts of the stem (called *breaking* or *braking*) and comb the fibers until they are free and clean (called *hackling;* a dog's hackles, when raised, look like the coarse teeth of a hackling comb). Archaeologists have found tools for breaking and hackling flax in the muddy lake beds that surrounded some of the Neolithic villages in Switzerland, along with hanks of flax in all stages of preparation. Unfortunately they were not found in such a way as to give us further clues to how the inhabitants organized their work.

In tending their garden plots, once again the women could work together while the children played or slept nearby, as we can see from the many ethnographic studies of horticultural societies. In Europe well into this century the women often sang or chanted ritual songs to set the rhythm of the endless repetitive motions of handwork in the fields. The slow, droning chant also has the interesting cognitive effect of blunting one's awareness of the pain of aching muscles and of the length of time spent. Here, too, the children could learn their future tasks bit by bit, in the process becoming participating members of the social community. I remember how proud I was as a child of four to be sent to the top of the apricot tree to pick the last of the fruit. It was wartime, food was scarce, and I was the best and lightest climber. I could contribute something no one else could.

If the summers encouraged this sort of sisterhood, European winters invited communal work even more. When the farm is covered in snow and modern electronic entertainments are millennia into the future, how do you while away the time? You carry on what small and useful crafts you can, giving you a sense of bettering your life, and you make it more fun by having a party at the same time. Just as the pioneer women in rural America got together for sewing, quilting, and husking bees, just as Hungarian farm women still have regular "work parties," so the women of prehistoric Europe gathered at one another's houses to spin, sew, weave, and have fellowship. How do we know this? From the cloth itself.

All over Denmark, preserved by the boggy groundwater, lie treasures of Bronze Age information in the form of wonderfully preserved burials. Bog water is highly acid, and acid preserves skin and leather, hair and wool, horn and fingernails almost perfectly. Many times it has happened that a peasant cutting peat for fuel out in the bogs has come upon a well-preserved dead body and called in the police to see who had recently been murdered. Fingerprinting the perfect swirls on the victim's hands yields nothing in the police files, but archaeological sleuthing soon shows that despite the perfectly preserved face, hairdo, and woolen clothing, the deceased died some two to four thousand years ago.

At the site of Trindhøj, straight west of Copenhagen on the Danish mainland of Jutland, a man went to his grave around 1300 B.C. wearing a patchwork tunic, a white fringed shawl, and a huge brown cloak woven of coarse wool. Two Danish archaeologists, Margrethe Hald and H. C. Broholm, analyzed the weave of the cloak and discovered that the weft threads in this enormous cloth often cross each other, shifting from one row to the next right in the middle of the textile. The only possible explanation is that several weft bobbins were in use at once. That is, three women had to have been weaving on this cloth simultaneously, passing the bobbins to each other as they met in the middle somewhere and then changing the shed. Other cloths show similar telltale signs.

We have more evidence of women working together. A famous Classical Greek representation of the warp-weighted loom (figs. 3.6 and 9.4) shows two women working beside each other at their loom (while others help prepare the wool and fold the finished cloth) in exactly the way that the ethnographer Marta Hoffmann found Norwegian and Finnish women still doing twenty-five years ago (see above). The loom is often so wide that this must have been fairly common practice, although it was not absolutely necessary. Homer, for example, depicts the lady Calypso working alone on her desert island:

And she, singing indoors with a beautiful voice,
wove at her loom, walking up and down with the golden bobbin.

Being alone, Calypso had to provide her own entertainment, too.

Prehistoric women in Hungary already provided entertainment for each other. In a charming scene from a Hallstatt urn (fig. 3.8), we see one woman spinning, another weaving at a great warp-weighted loom, two others with their hands above their heads as though they were dancing, and a fifth, shorter figure (male or female?) holding a stringed instrument that is either a lyre or a frame for making the kind of plaiting called *sprang*.

In this same part of Europe, well into this century, women wearing clothes remarkably similar to the Hallstatt ones (fig. 3.9) still met at one another's houses for working bees. The continuity is remarkable. Perhaps the most common activity before "modernization" was spinning, since it took so much longer to spin than to weave a given amount of fiber; estimates put it at seven to ten times as long, using a hand spindle. (How much time it took to

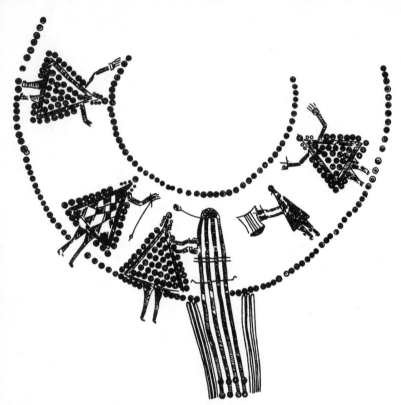

Figure 3.8. Women spinning, weaving (on a warp-weighted loom), and entertaining one another with music and dance. The scene is incised on a vase of the Hallstatt culture (mid-first millennium B.C.), from Sopron, Hungary. Compare the triangular-looking costumes with modern Hungarian folk costumes (fig. 3.9).

spin the yarn for a given area of cloth depended, of course, upon how thick the yarn was, exactly as in knitting. Fine yarn takes longer per unit of weight to work up.) Girls were taught to spin when they were ten or twelve, and they looked forward to that time, since spinning is a pleasant task. It is also an activity easily dropped and easily resumed in the excitement of courting. For the men came to these workplaces, too, whether indoors or out, bringing their small crafts of leather and wood—but they came primar-

Figure 3.9. Hungarian village girls wearing costumes similar in their peculiar shape to those depicted in the area twenty-five hundred years earlier: see fig. 3.8. (From a photograph taken ca. 1950.)

ily to entertain the women and keep them company. Tales were told, songs sung, and music and games played, especially those games we would call dances. The same word serves for both "dance" and "game" in many languages—for example, *igra* in Serbo-Croatian.

When one is having so much fun, it is hard to stop, and that may in part explain a peculiar anomaly in the Neolithic evidence from central Europe. Archaeologists would peg these Stone Age people as living in a subsistence-level economy—forced to work fairly hard just to feed themselves and to stay warm and dry. By this model, little time and energy would remain for fun and frolic. Cloth survives poorly in most of Europe, subject to the destructive effects of alternating wet and dry weather; yet our surviving textiles from the Neolithic are astonishingly ornate. Clearly these Neolithic women were investing large amounts of extra time into their textile work, far beyond pure utility, far beyond our concept of "subsistence level."

Life remains hard in these same parts of rural central Europe today, yet the tradition of making fancy cloth persists there. During the long, boring winters not much useful outdoor work is possible, so the energy overflows into indoor crafts. Furthermore, one finds the attitude that if you have to make a bedspread or a cushion anyway and will have to use it for the rest of your life, you may as well make it pretty and be able to enjoy both the making and the using.

How do we see this love of embellishment in the Neolithic? Take, for example, the linens of Switzerland, dating from 3000 B.C., from such sites as Robenhausen, Irgenhausen, Schaffis, and Murten, which lie clustered around the lakes in the center of the country. The women who made them lived in a swamp, squashed between forest and lake, far from the centers of European culture downstream on the middle reaches of the Danube. To stay above the lakeshore mud, the inhabitants drove hundreds of wooden pilings into the soft ground to stabilize it before laying their clay hearths and building their wooden houses on top. Little corduroy pathways of logs joined the houses to one another and to the higher ground where the forests began, helping the villagers stay dry-shod as they moved about. The frequency with which they added piling shows the constant urgency of keeping ahead of wet and rot. Whatever fell into the muck below was lost for good—to them, but preserved for us, since the perpetually soggy, airless, alkaline lake mud happens to preserve plant material quite well. (Note that alkali, which destroys animal remains, has exactly the opposite effect from acid bog water, which destroys plants but preserves animal skin and hair.)

Thus we find quantities of wooden tools—a rarity on most archaeological sites—from bowls, ladles, pounders, and tilling sticks to the panoply of utensils needed to prepare flax: breaks, hackling boards with little thorns set into them in neat rows, and spindles with clay whorls. We find hanks of spun thread ready for use (all that labor, only to be dropped into the mire!) and clay loom weights—sometimes in a row across the floor, showing that the loom was in use when the particular village was eventually destroyed. The trail of loom weights indicates that the warp-weighted loom and its associated weaving technology had spread here during the fourth millennium B.C., moving up the Danube from its home in central Hungary. We find baskets and bags of all sorts, and textiles—fancy ones.

Stripes, checkers, triangles; braided fringes, knotted fringes, beadwork, and fancy edges. Weaving stripes into the cloth with an extra pattern weft was the most common, but sometimes the weavers put in triangles or squares, which is not a simple task like stripes. An especially elaborate piece (fig. 3.10) from the site of Irgenhausen, near Zurich, has triangles within a complicated pattern of checkers-within-checkers-within-checkers , formed by lacing in a whole handful of pattern wefts. Emil Vogt, who painstakingly analyzed all the blackened remains of this large cloth, concluded that there would have been no point in weaving the pattern in that particular way unless the weaver had been using at least three hues so the patterns would stand out. Would that we knew what these colors were! When workers at the National Museum in Zurich wove a replica (fig. 3.10), they used conservative brown and beige on white, but we know that plants and other substances producing reds, blues, and yellows grew in the area, too, and that some of these dyes were already in use elsewhere in Europe.

The Stone Age clothmakers of the Swiss lakeshores did not stop with adding color, however. The creator of another textile, found at Murten, pierced groups of little fruit pits and sewed them carefully onto the cloth on either side of some woven stripes. Someone also attached this piece to a second cloth by means of half a dozen rows of knotted netting, thus giving elasticity to the join. For clothing?

Figure 3.10. Modern replica of a Neolithic linen cloth found in a lake bed at Irgenhausen, Switzerland, dating to 3000 B.C. or a little after. The original fragments are so blackened that we can no longer determine the original colors, but careful analysis of the weave structure (which made it possible to weave this replica) shows that at least three colors must have been employed. (Swiss National Museum, Zurich.)

Above all else, these weavers loved fancy borders. The ribbed side borders were not difficult, but the unique problems of setting up a warp-weighted loom meant that the cloth had to begin with a special edging at the top to secure the warp threads. Then, having neatly framed the cloth on three sides, these weavers threw all their ingenuity into devising a bottom border. One can imagine the women working together and egging each other on as they finished off the bottom edges of their cloths. The fanciest involved weaving a ravelproof band right across the warp ends with its own decorative pattern of ribs and triangles, while any ends left after all that were braided and knotted into a fringe for good measure.

The inhabitants of Neolithic Switzerland were not the only Europeans making fancy fabrics. We catch more glimpses in central Germany, where the dead were laid to rest in great ossuaries, their oak rafters apparently draped with patterned textiles. (We see from this that cloth already served other purposes than just clothing people.) Periodic firing of the ossuaries from the outside, probably to keep down the odor and contagion, preserved bits of the fabric where insufficient oxygen made the cloth char rather than burn. Although most of the actual scraps of cloth were lost again during recent wars, we can see stripes, checkers, and lots of little chevron patterns as we peruse the sketches made at the time of discovery in the late nineteenth century.

Neither Germany nor Switzerland stood at the center of this European weaving culture, however, but in its backwaters. Its "frontwaters" lay in Hungary and along the lower Danube, where the warp-weighted loom first developed. With the textiles in the backwaters so ornate, what then must they have been like at the center of the tradition? Back in 5000 B.C., along the Tisza River, nearly every house had the weights for a loom already, while later on, the figurines from Hungary sport fancy patterns on their persons, sometimes apparently as body paint (still found in remote parts of the Balkans today) but sometimes also on clothing.

All over central Europe women were inventing more and more elaborate textiles, regardless of modern economists' models. One of the key issues to understanding this "extravagance" is time. Not only were there infinitely fewer entertainments tugging at one's attention in a preindustrial rural setting, but expenditure of time was viewed very differently from the way it is within an industrial economy. To us, time is money—to be "saved," "spent," "bud-geted," "invested," or (horrors!) "squandered." For them, money was irrelevant because it hadn't been invented yet, nor would it be for another twenty-five hundred years. So there was nothing to weigh time *against;* it simply was what it was. Furthermore, it was an *automatic* resource, unlike food or material goods (including money). Time was thus constantly available for use to promote survival, whether directly (e.g., by preparing food and building shelter) or indirectly—that is, by trying to elicit symbolically what was wanted. The latter is a use that many of us have forgotten. Ethnographic parallels worldwide show that enormous time is often put into "simply" decorating people and things with effica-cious symbols believed to promote life, prosperity, and safety (cf. fig. 3.2). For example, many a Slavic folk costume is decorated with red embroidery at neck, sleeve, and hem. Both the designs and the bloodred color carry symbolic life powers, while the potent signs are carefully located to ward off sickness demons that are looking for openings through which to attack. Thus "art" is at once pleasing and thoroughly functional—a double winner.

Weaving was not the only craft into which artistic time and energy were being poured in the Neolithic. From Hungary on south through the eastern Balkans, all the way to Thessaly in Greece, we find a profusion of astonishingly elegant pottery cov-ered with sophisticated swirling designs. The idea of baking a con-tainer molded of clay in order to make it hard and waterproof had developed in the Near East around 6000 B.C. and soon spread to southeastern Europe. There is no direct evidence of whether men or women were making the pottery, even when we see the baking of the clay moving soon from low-temperature firing in the family hearth to much hotter firing in courtyard ovens. But a case has been made that the elaborate painted designs that soon developed in southeastern Europe represented a variety of fertility symbols, core among which are eggs. The painting of the eggs themselves at Easter, the time of renewed growth, is still an important annual ritual in the Balkans and Ukraine, and the designs painted on them are replete with ancient symbolism. In the United States, on the contrary, the meaning is so far weakened that painting Easter eggs is now viewed as a children's pastime while the highly fertile rabbits associated with them have devolved into commercialized cuteness. Once again, female fertility was a dominant theme among the cultures of the Neolithic, and the women may have been in charge of this new craft, too, with its cargo of fertility symbols. To these arguments we can add that vase making was certainly another courtyard art and would combine well with child rearing. The resulting pottery, moreover, was used chiefly for the women's daily chores of storing, cooking, and serving the food.

Strong parallels to many of these archaeological details can be found in another culture overflowing with women's courtyard arts, the Hopi of the American Southwest. There the potting, vase painting, basket making, and weaving all are women's work, and although the weaving of patterned rugs is recent, the elaborate no-two-pieces-alike painting of pots is not. (I have often been struck, in fact, by the similarities between the Hopi-Papago designs and those of Neolithic Anatolia and southeastern Europe.) Certain aspects of the Hopi designs are traditional to the culture, but other features have typically been handed down from mother to daughter within the family, for the women worked together constantly and learned principally from one another. Indeed, a woman lived her whole life in the dwellings owned by her mother and her mother's clan, whereas the man divided his time and allegiance between his wife's household (to which he contributed the food he produced) and that of his own mother, where he had many ritual duties. As for property, the matrilineal clan owned the plots of land in which the main food supplies of corn and squash were grown. The men did some of the crop tending but also spent much of their time out pasturing the flocks, which they passed down from father to son. Thus the women remained permanently settled in a single place while the men spent a great deal of their time moving around. In short, Hopi society was horticultural in much the same way as the Neolithic and Early Bronze Age societies of

Europe seem to have been. For that reason the Pueblo Indians have sometimes been used as a model for trying to understand the archaeological record in Neolithic Europe.

Thus textiles flourished in the early horticultural economies of southeastern Europe between 6000 and 2000 B.C., when the women could handle the subsistence farming and the crafts while the men could go out of the community to hunt, fish, tend flocks, and barter for luxuries such as shell beads and obsidian blades. Obsidian, or volcanic glass, is much sharper than flint but is found in only a very few places. Settlers wanted it particularly for scything grain, and men had to establish huge trade networks to obtain it, as the planting of domestic grain spread.

In the Near East, although we have little information on textiles during this period, we have data on food. They suggest that the style of life may have paralleled that in Europe, since at first the fields of grain that provided the central food were hand-tended. If anything, however, life in parts of the Near East must have been harder, for the women spent so many hours of their lives at hard labor over heavy stone grain grinders that the work permanently deformed their bones. Archaeologists have found the toe, knee, and shoulder bones of the women in the early farming villages of northern Mesopotamia to be squashed and deformed in ways caused by pressure from kneeling and pushing heavy objects with the arm and shoulder—clearly the metate-like stone grinders that we find on the sites (cf. fig. 8.7). Nor were the men always out hunting, for their bones often reveal the same deformities.

The picture conjured up by these and other excavation details is not such a pleasant one. Southern Europe provided a fair number of "orchard crops," such as nuts, olives, and edible fruits (fig. 4.1), which require relatively little work for a fair return of food. The forests, moreover, although making the clearing of fields for grain difficult, abounded in game. In Syria and Iraq, on the other hand, we find an abundance of sickles and stone grinders for cutting and grinding cereals but much less evidence for most other types of food, although people herded sheep and goats where suitable graz-ing existed. Wheat and barley grew copiously in wet years and stored well, but converting them into the major food supply was punishingly hard work. The second most common food came from the legume family, including peas, lentils, and chickpeas, which we associate with Near Eastern cuisine even today. Eaten regularly together, the cereals and legumes provide the body with complete proteins and thus with a viable diet, even without the addition of meat.

Developing a diet not dependent upon meat was fortunate, because around 4000 B.C. came a meat-related discovery that soon brought the Neolithic to a close. People in Mesopotamia began to realize that their primary domestic animals—sheep, goats, and cattle—could be exploited in a far more efficient way than by kill-ing them for their meat and hides (the sole use for which they had been domesticated). Kept alive and used efficiently, they could provide a constant supply of "secondary" products: of milk foods, wool, and muscle power. The old strategy allowed only one chance at food and clothing from each animal—one feast, one hide—and you got the maximum of meat for the minimum of care by slaughtering when the creature had barely reached adulthood. But now people saw that if you kept at least the females alive, you could milk them for years and could eat the meat in the end any-way, although it wouldn't be so tender.

If cattle were central to this change, so were sheep. The inbreed-ing of domestic sheep over thousands of years had led to some varieties that had a fair amount of wool, which molted every year in the spring. Wild sheep, and thus the early domestic sheep, had coats that were predominantly hairy—technically, kempy—with some underwool. The coarse kemps are rather stiff and simply shatter like dry crackers if you try to twist them, whereas the underwool is so short and downy fine that it wads up and doesn't spin either. So sheep had to change a lot before they had usable wool. It seems to have been about 4000 B.C. that people realized they could get a steady supply of clothing from the live sheep.

Around that time we see a shift to killing the animals at a ripe old age. Older ewes alone might mean purely a milk flock, but old males, and castrated at that, can only be exploited for wool. These *wethers*, in fact, produce the best fleeces of all. Wool, for its part, is a wonderful fiber: warmer and more resilient than linen (although scratchier), and far easier to dye. A new phase in textiles and the work associated with them was about to begin.

The third benefit of keeping the animals alive was to exploit them for their strength, in particular to help with the heavy jobs of plowing the fields, threshing the grain, and transporting seed, harvest, and equipment. (The wheel, too, was invented about this time.) By using a team of oxen to pull the weight, the farmer could use a heavier plow to dig a much deeper furrow and produce a better crop.

This above all—the use of huge draft animals in large fields to grow the basic food—permanently removed the food-producing portion of the economy from the women's domain. Why? Because such activity was no longer compatible with child raising. Thus the allotment of tasks shifted once again, first in Mesopotamia and gradually in a widening circle beyond.

Another radical change in the organization of human life began soon after, marking the start of the Bronze Age. People living in metal-rich regions had long known the usefulness of metals, starting with the soft ones that happen to occur in pure form, like copper and gold.[2] But such soft metals are more suitable for ornaments than for tools. It took the discovery that metals can be alloyed into new and harder materials by mixing them while molten to open a way finally to vastly improved tools: metal axes, cauldrons, chisels, knives, and—a metal-dependent invention—the sword. The problem for most people at that time was that,

---

[2] At Çayönü Tepesi, in eastern Turkey, not far from a rare source of pure copper, excavators found little copper tools, such as hooks, made by hammering and abrading. The site is an early farming village of about 7000 B.C. It was in just such ore-rich areas as eastern Turkey and the Caucasus that metalworking gradually developed during the course of the Neolithic.

although copper is rather commonly found in Europe and the Near East, the hardening metals aren't.

The most widely useful alloy of soft metals is copper mixed with tin, giving the alloy we know as bronze. Tin, however, occurs mostly only in a few places far away from the early centers of civilization, like eastern Iran, Spain, and Cornwall (in Britain). Another effective hardener is arsenic, and it was used briefly in the steppes north of the Caucasus at the beginning of the Bronze Age, but arsenic bronze soon died out—perhaps because people noticed that families using cookware of arsenic bronze soon died out. Unfortunately the arsenic will dissolve out of the bronze into the acid of the food. Probably the smiths working with the arsenic died, too. Obtaining tin, even if it required great trouble, was worth the effort.

This need for tin steadily increased trade in goods and ideas, for people all over the Near East and soon Europe began to want these newfangled tools. But bronze won't grow in gardens. That was a new problem. Somebody had to go out and find the ores from which it could be made—or find someone else who had ore and was willing to trade. So the great metal search began, and it became men's work, if only because the distances were far too great for the toddlers to travel. Mines, too, once you find them, are no place to have little children under foot, nor is the smithy—too many hammers and hot sparks flying about. Thus metalworking became men's work as well.

So much trade and exploration, so much movement of people and new ideas began to alter society dramatically. At the same time, the ever more efficient production of food supported ever larger congregations of people, until the once-tiny villages and towns had become immense cities. For it was about this same time, toward the end of the fourth millennium B.C., that truly urban civilization sprang up in Mesopotamia, a civilization that included writing, laws, contracts, tax records, and much else that literacy enables. It took almost a millennium for the principal changes to reach southeastern Europe, but by 2500 B.C. the sedentary vase painters and weavers were gone, abruptly swept away by warlike swarms of new people hunting for ores from the Caucasus to the Carpathians to the Alps. The old days of simple Neolithic courtyards were gone. Ahead lay the heady chemistry of new and far-ranging human contacts, catalysts for yet other developments in women's contribution to society through their textile arts.

4

Island Fever

By how much the men are expert above all other men in
propelling a swift ship on the sea, by thus much the women
are skilled at the loom, for Athena has given to them beyond
  all others
a knowledge of beautiful craftwork, and noble minds.
                    —Homer, *Odyssey,* 7.108–11

In at least one area of the Mediterranean world, a basically horticultural system survived more or less intact until late in the Bronze
Age—namely, on Crete. Heir to millennia of textile innovations in
cloth-crazy Europe and fed by a new and richer source of colored
fiber—namely, wool—the art of weaving flourished in Minoan
Crete as never before. The era, which ran from about 3000 to
1400 B.C. is recent enough that a much fuller set of artifacts has
survived, allowing us a considerably more detailed view of the life-
style. As usual, wherever we catch glimpses of the clothmakers
themselves, they are invariably women.

Crete is an island, and the immigrants who reached Crete obviously arrived by sea—at first a few stragglers but already carrying
early stocks of domestic grain and animals, and then, at the very
end of the Neolithic, around 3000 B.C., a great influx of settlers.

Many sailed from southwestern Turkey, but some perhaps from the facing shore of Africa: from Libya and the Nile Delta. Technology was accruing rapidly, and soon after the start of the Bronze Age we begin to see pictures of increasingly sophisticated boats in the Aegean, with banks of oars to propel them through the sea and presently with muscle-saving sails as well. Other people could stay land lovers, but it behooved the populace of a seagirt land to perfect the use of wind power.

Island Fever: That's what some archaeologists call the enormous amount of effort that isolated cultures invest in unusual activities. Products of this effect include Stonehenge in England, the Easter Island avenues of stone faces, the multiroomed halls made of enormous boulders on tiny Malta, and the pyramids of Egypt (an "island" in a nearly impenetrable sea of desert sand). The mechanism seems to be that such cultures, living in the first flush of new technology but before travel to their land was easy, could afford to expend on communal works all the energy that other cultures needed just to defend themselves from the people around them. Sudden expansion and proliferation in a new and protected environment are well known in the biological world as well—for example, in the Hawaiian Islands, where the small number of species that reached the islands alive (such as honeycreepers and caterpillars) evolved with explosive rapidity into the many new ecological niches.

The great unfortified palaces of Crete—so huge and rambling that they gave us (through the Greek language) the word *labyrinth*—and, indeed, the whole amazing Minoan civilization, including its textiles, must to some extent have been powered by Island Fever. There are no walled towns or garrisons on Crete, villas sprawl unprotected about the countryside, and the lines of watchtowers seem set for signaling information with flares rather than for defense. Secure in their island stronghold, the women could continue to tend their gardens and their looms while the men launched forth on the dangerous sea, to catch fish, to trade in faraway places, and to explore for resources not found on the island.

This does not mean that men never helped with the food at home. Indeed, oxen existed on Crete (along with fearsome wild bulls), as did some sort of plow eventually, but for all the thousands of pictures of their life that they left us on wall paintings and carved gems, the Minoans never portrayed scenes of plowing or of draft animals in action. Apparently these were not a pivotal part of that life. Farmable land both fertile and flat is scarce on Crete, while the steep, sunbaked slopes more readily support orchard crops of olives and grapes, nuts and pomegranates—crops that provide more food for less labor than cereals do (fig. 4.1). The steepest slopes of all offer pasture to sheep and goats, which in turn yield milk for cheeses, wool and hair for weaving, and finally meat for the stewpot. All these foods, together with flavor-intense wild honey and local herbs like thyme and coriander, have been part of Aegean cuisine from then until now. Men might assist, but land and crops could be managed by the women alone for long periods.

In this comfortable setting it is no wonder that the women had leisure to pour unprecedented energy into making beautiful cloth. They had, in addition, a new plaything: wool.

Flax had been in use around the Mediterranean since the Palaeolithic, whereas wool, on the backs of woolly sheep (as opposed to hairy or kempy ones; see Chapter 3), had been introduced into the Balkans from the Near East only around 3500 B.C., late in the Neolithic. White wool, unlike flax, is easy to dye, and wool, in addition, grows naturally in different shades—from black, gray, and brown through ruddy and tawny to cream and white—according to the pigmentation of the individual sheep.[1] Patterned textiles depend largely on the use of color. White-on-

---

[1] A closely parallel effect can be observed in the third millennium B.C. in China, where the discovery of how to unwind silk from the cocoon of a particular species of silkworm revolutionized the technology of clothmaking. Silk, like wool, is

white designs are handsome but extremely subtle; contrastive colors are more vividly satisfying. Thus the arrival of wool marked a new era in textile development.

By 2300 B.C., the people of Crete had turned the herding of these new, woolly sheep into a major part of their economy. The Minoan culture itself, fertilized by ever-increasing trade, stood ready to burst into full bloom, and so, we can deduce, did textiles. Our first evidence comes from a prehistoric village near Myrtos, almost the only thoroughly excavated Minoan site dating to this early period. Lying on the south coast of Crete atop a steep, windy little hill looking out across the deep blue Mediterranean toward Egypt (well beyond the horizon), Myrtos is a convenient place for watching for the return of the fishermen and sea traders, if not for lugging the daily water up the hill. The houses are party-walled together in a tight clump. An occasional narrow alley winds through for access, with steep little steps here and there to accommodate the sharp rise in ground.

The Myrtos dwellings proved chock-full of evidence for textile manufacture. Simple clay spindle whorls turned up in many of the rooms, as though women did their spinning anywhere and everywhere (just as in rural Greece today). In one room the diggers unearthed a shallow clay dish with a "handle" on the inside, and fragments of another: special bowls for wetting linen thread as it is being worked. New linen is so stiff and full of slivers that it is much easier to handle damp. The bowls were designed to receive a ball of thread straight into a puddle of water in the bottom (fig. 4.2). The end of the yarn ran under the loop of the interior "han-

---

easily dyed, producing a wide range of bright and attractive colors. Furthermore, its particular properties, so different from the plant-stem fibers used previously, led to major innovations in weave structures. For example, to bring out the wonderful shininess of silk, the weavers began to develop satin weaves, in which one set of threads (usually the warp) almost totally hides the set at right angles. They also developed new types of pattern weaving based on how the warp is treated. The same sort of thing happened with wool. The Europeans developed twill weave and patterns based upon it, and the Near Easterners invented weft-faced tapestry weave—in each case to exploit the peculiar properties of wool.

Figure 4.1. The steep Aegean hillsides, like this one in eastern Crete, are best suited to raising orchard crops. Here, in a photo taken by the author in 1962, the upper slope is planted with olive trees, and the lower (bottom right) with grapevines. At the top of the vineyard is a well for irrigation (grapes need more water than olives). The water was traditionally raised by means of a bucket hung from one end of a long pole balanced on a forked tree trunk (visible in the center of the picture). A huge stone lashed to the pole counterweighted the bucket, to ease the work of raising the water.

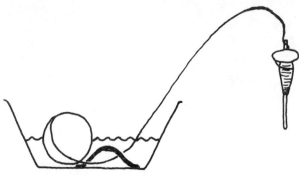

Figure 4.2. Fiber-wetting bowl and its use. To spin plant stem fibers like flax and hemp, which are more easily worked when damp, several cultures have independently invented wetting bowls to speed the process. The bowls are formed with a loop inside on the bottom. Water is put in the bowl, and the partly formed thread is passed under the loop to force it through the water on its way to the spindle. The ancient Egyptians and Minoans made such bowls, and similar ones are still employed in Japan.

dle," an arrangement that not only forced the thirsty linen through the water but kept the ball from jumping out as the spinner pulled on the thread while she plied it or added twist to make it stronger. This peculiar technology, better known from wall paintings and looped bowls that survived in Egypt and also from a similar archaic tradition of thread making in modern Japan, is appropriate only for working with bast, the stem fibers of plants. Since flax (linen) is the indigenous bast fiber of the Mediterranean countries, the presence of such a bowl, locally made and with a characteristic worn spot under the loop from the thread's constantly running past, demonstrates beyond doubt that the women of Myrtos were working flax.

They also processed wool. Numerous sheep bones turned up in the Myrtos excavations, but most of them came from adults of both genders, a distribution indicating that the people expected to harvest the sheep flocks for wool. In two or three of the houses, large spouted tubs overhung runoff areas arranged beneath, and in one case a channel cut into the soft bedrock directed a substantial flow off down the hill. (Note that if you are pressing grapes and olives for wine and oil, you do *not* want the liquid to run away, so this installation was designed for other purposes.) The material from one of the tubs was analyzed and found to contain remains of animal fats—most likely from washing wool. Sheep were undoubtedly eaten, too, but this was not where they were cooked, since there was no hearth or fire pit, no way to heat these tubs. Smaller cooking bowls and a large stone grinder lay nearby. Were these for preparing food, or perhaps for grinding and extracting dyestuffs?

Clay loom weights occurred, but not scattered like the spindle whorls. Instead they were concentrated largely in two areas at the site—the same two areas as the main tub installations. The weights in at least one case, however, lay in the upper fill, having fallen from above. Peter Warren, the British excavator, suggests reasonably that the loom had been set up on the flat roof and, further, that its beams had been made of oak, since he found charred oak in the fill as well. One of the sets of loom weights is of the small, disk-shaped variety associated with the pattern weaving of wool. Some of these weights have grooves across the top, possibly for a bar to stabilize them and stop them from clanking so loudly with each change of the shed during the weaving process (see Chapter 1).

Greek island villages are not so different even today from what we see at Myrtos (fig. 4.3). Steep and narrow streets wind between the little party-walled houses, everything whitewashed to reflect the heat. Upstairs, shaded from the sun and raised into the breeze above the worst of the dust, the women work together at preparing the food and the clothing, chatting while they wait for the men to return from fishing and sponge diving at sea.

All in all, at Myrtos, two or three areas at the site seem well equipped to take the production of cloth from start to finish. If we pull the evidence together, we can see that both linen and wool were being processed, that spinning and weaving took place in considerable quantity, and that the wool was probably also being

Figure 4.3. Steep village street with whitewashed houses and rough stone-slab paving, on the Aegean island of Mykonos. Although the scene is 1962, it could well be 1500 or 2200 B.C., to judge by the remains of excavated Bronze Age towns.

dyed. Several dye-producing plants and animals were available in the vicinity of the village, while small pierced stone weights—found in abundance at much later dyeing installations—occurred all over the site. The windiness of the hill could have played a part as well, since dyers always seek a steady wind to help the fabrics dry and to remove the sometimes dreadful stench of the dyestuffs. It all adds up to label Myrtos as a perfect place to make colored cloth. But the excavator Peter Warren stopped shy of suggesting anything so radical as *patterned* textiles.

Warren published his admirably thorough description of the excavated site in 1972. What he could not know then, since the research had not yet been done, is that the Europeans had already been making ornate patterned cloth for millennia and that, not long after the little coastal village of Myrtos burned down, the Minoans were already exporting their versions of it to the Nile Valley. The exported textiles had patterns so complicated that one has to assume a long running start on learning to make them—back at least to the time of Myrtos.

What were the pretty patterns the Minoans liked so much to weave?

The first favorite on exports to Egypt, to judge from copies painted there from around 2000 B.C. onward, consisted of blue heart-spirals set point to point (much like the design typical today on a wrought-iron fence) with a red diamond between each pair of double hearts, all on a white ground (fig. 4.4). It must have been stunning. At any rate, the women of Crete wove that design for at least another thousand years, for we catch glimpses of it here and there both in Egypt and in Crete, all the way down into the Iron Age long after the fall of the Minoans. Patterns favored in the Egyptian market a little later included rows of yellow or white spirals, often running on the diagonal with red and blue rosettes alternating in the spaces between.

The Minoan men who carried these beautiful textiles to Egypt did not go home empty-handed, let alone empty-headed, from their long trading voyages. (The journey from Crete to Egypt was

Figure 4.4. Two renditions of a favorite Minoan textile design, the double heart-spiral, as recorded by Egyptian artists. Left: on the tomb ceiling of a Middle Kingdom nobleman, Wahka II (at Qau, ca. 1900 B.C.). Right: on the (heavily damaged) kilt of an Aegean visitor to the Egyptian court at Thebes ca. 1450 B.C. (tomb of Menkheperraseneb). The color schemes are very similar on all known renditions: blue spirals with red palmettes and partly red lozenge figures.

about five hundred miles, and often more than a thousand miles to return because of the prevailing wind directions.) One thing they brought back from Egypt was the idea that one could paint scenes on walls. From then on we see their own depictions of themselves, including what they wore. For centuries Cretan men wore simple loincloths, sometimes with fancy borders and always fastened with cinch belts. But the women clothed themselves in ever more gorgeous attire—another tip off that they were the ones in control of producing the stuff.

Even the simplest costumes are fancy. The earliest representations, some clay figurines around 1900 B.C. (two or three centuries before the frescoes begin), already show women in large bell-shaped skirts with open-fronted bodices. Not only are these flaring skirts and open bodices features we associate with the Minoans, but they are clearly old within the culture and basic to a Minoan woman's concept of normal clothing. One of the little statuettes (fig. 4.5) is both complete and painted, in an outfit reminiscent of

Figure 4.5. Clay figurine of a Minoan woman of the early second millennium B.C., from Petsofá, Crete.

the flamboyant ladies of 1780 at the court of George III. On the woman's head sits a large, eye-catching chapeau, boldly decorated with black and white stripes; her bodice sweeps up to a high peaked collar behind her neck, while her dress has an equally bold light-on-dark design, just like the elegant new style of pottery of that period, the so-called Kamares ware.

Two to three centuries later we see that flounces had become the rage among ladies of fashion. The frescoes show them, thus colorfully attired, dancing in gardens and courtyards (fig. 4.6), while lively crowds of fellow citizens look on from surrounding bleachers. (We have found just such bleacherlike arrangements of stone steps at every Minoan palace yet excavated.) The men in the

Figure 4.6. Wall painting of a beautifully dressed woman dancing (?) in a garden, from the villa at Hagia Triada, an important Minoan port town in southern Crete, mid-second millennium B.C.

paintings sit together in one area, gesticulating with their arms, and the women sit in another section, largely in front of the men, in animated conversation—perhaps over the performance, their own splendid jewelry and gracefully piled hairdos, and their elegant dresses.

The plainest dresses are merely striped; the fanciest ones display a mind-boggling array of all-over patterns: grids of tiny diamonds filled with various little squiggles, complex figures of three- and four-pronged interlocking shapes (petals, stars, lobes, or crosses), as well as spirals, "yo-yos," and rosettes. Bright tassels and patterned edgings replete with zigzags, spirals, rosettes, wavy lines, and simple bars trimmed the outfits, along with thick sashes, sculpted aprons, and colorful hair bands.

We also have a fairly good idea of how the Minoans must have obtained the brightly contrastive colors—red, blue, yellow, and white—that made pattern weaving so much fun.

Natural dyes come in two fundamental types. With the simpler kind, called direct dyes, what you see is pretty much what you get. Thus, if you chop and simmer the root of the madder plant, which still grows wild on Crete, you get a dark red soup which will dye wool an orangy red; if you simmer the stamens of the saffron lily, found on many Aegean islands, you will get an orange broth and a bright yellow dye color. Minoan reds and yellows probably came mostly from madder and saffron, although red may also have been obtained from kermes, a type of insect the female of which contains a gorgeous red dye (our word *crimson* comes from *kermes*). Warren notes the presence of the kermes-bearing species of oak near Myrtos.

Dyes of the other type are called vat dyes and are much more complicated to process. One of the most popular vat dyes even today is indigo blue, the natural chemical used to color blue jeans. The Minoans probably obtained the dye from a European plant called woad; the word is so old that we know the proto-Indo-Europeans already knew of it. The indigo plant itself was not imported into Europe from India (whence it got its name) for another two thousand years. The people of Crete also extracted royal purple (so called because the Roman emperors later decreed that only they could wear it), deriving it from several varieties of sea snails, such as murex. We have their shell heaps from the early second millennium on to prove it. Each little mollusk produces only a single drop of the splendid dye, so purple-dyers had to catch and slaughter hundreds to tint a single piece of cloth. Depending on the water in which the sea snail grew, its dye could vary from purplish blue through deep purple to cherry red.

The advantage of vat dyes is that they don't wash out. To make madder and most other plant dyes colorfast, one needs a mordant, a chemical which fixes the dye. Soon after the height of the Minoan culture we have evidence of the mineral alum, the best natural mordant, being imported into the Aegean from Cyprus, so perhaps the Minoans knew of its use already. But all the way up until the invention of synthetic dyes in 1856, reds and blues were the easiest colors to keep from either washing out in water or fading from long exposure to light. (Hence the flags of most countries that became political entities before 1856 are colored red, white, and/or blue.) It is probably no accident that these were the colors that the Egyptians depicted their Aegean visitors wearing.

Since dyestuffs other than sea purple don't leave durable evidence like shells behind, and dye sources can seldom be determined unambiguously from the chemistry of their residues (even when we are lucky enough to have dyed objects preserved), we often can't prove that an available dyestuff was actually in use. But occasionally we are lucky, and in one case we also get a charming glimpse of women at their work.

A recently discovered set of frescoes, still under restoration, from a Minoan-style house on the volcanic isle of Thera shows women out on a saffron hunt (fig. 4.7). A young girl has decked herself out in a handsome yellow bodice with blue edging and red tassels, a divided skirt with blue, yellow, and white flounces, gold hoop earrings, and gold and silver bracelets. Most of her head is lightly shaved (boys' heads were treated similarly, and still are, in modern Greece, to cure or prevent ringworm). Only a forelock and a single ponytail have been spared. As she plucks the stamens from the lilies on the craggy lava rocks before her, she looks up toward an older girl, whose locks have just grown out but are not yet very long. The latter, in turn, keeps picking saffron with one

Figure 4.7. Young women in fancy Minoan-style dress, picking saffron—the stamen of a lily used as a yellow dye, as a spice, and as medicine for menstrual cramps. Wall painting from a mid-second millennium house on the Aegean island of Thera.

hand while she carefully holds her collection pail with the other and glances back over her shoulder at her young companion. A third woman, a young matron with long coils of black hair, fancy necklaces, and a garland of flowers over her elaborately patterned dress, holds out a string of beads in her hand, while a fourth girl, with sprigs of flowers and greenery stuck into her hair, has sat down to rub a bare foot she stubbed on the jagged rocks. Her mouth forms an "ooh" of mild pain. Yet another girl empties her basket at the main collection point, while a sixth girl looks back, wearing a polka-dot veil over her head and shoulders. Her head is still partly shaved, but she has several long locks. It has been suggested that she is the cause of this scene, that the saffron hunt is part of her rite of passage to the state of womanhood, since saffron is not only a dye but is considered in the Greek islands even today a specific for women's menstrual pain. The use as a dye for clothing is closely connected. In Classical Greek times, yellow apparel was considered appropriate for women only, including goddesses like Athena. The comic poet Aristophanes got a lot of mileage out of this by jokingly portraying the more effeminate Athenian politicians as dressed in yellow.

Thus the archaeological finds on Crete and the Aegean islands repeatedly give us solid evidence of a textile industry strong in technology and tradition and closely tied to the women's cultural as well as economic and medical concerns. Those, however, who enjoy reclothing the dry bones of archaeology and reanimating a long dead way of life can go a few steps farther, with Homer.

High Minoan civilization fell, sometime between 1500 and 1400 B.C., weakened in part by devastating volcanic eruptions and quakes in the Aegean. The Bronze Age in turn ended around 1200 B.C., two generations after the Trojan War. Thus Homer, around 800 B.C., lived in an entirely different age as he composed his oral epics of the battles at Troy and of the difficult homeward journey of the Greeks after they had won the war. Without a doubt Homer worked from orally transmitted material; some of the objects he describes, like a helmet made of boar's tusk, had not been seen in the Aegean for centuries, although they are now known from archaeology. Classicists argue incessantly over how much he made up. Some have even suggested that all of it is fiction. But ethnographers working with oral histories learn that remarkably little of this sort of material is freely invented. The point of passing history along orally is that it contains information viewed by the tellers to be important. Making it up defeats the purpose, although embroidering it a bit from other known information can make it more fun and memorable.

Consider, then, the famous tale which Homer tells of Odysseus shipwrecked on the island of the Phaiakians. It is an idyll, a sort of fairyland, but also a perfect picture of the kind of horticultural society we have just been visiting. Minoan Crete, last of its kind in Europe, was long gone, so Homer knew of this life-style—with considerable accuracy—either from some long-standing oral tradition or from a small enclave of emigrants still keeping to the old horticultural ways nearby. Either way we can profit from Homer's tale, by taking a brief walk through the sort of life that the luckier of Bronze Age Aegean women lived.[2]

THE LAND OF THE PHAIAKIANS

Half dead from swimming, the shipwrecked Odysseus struggles ashore at night onto an unknown island at a sandy rivermouth and burrows into the warm, dry leaves of a nearby thicket to sleep. He is awakened the next afternoon by the cries of young women who have been washing clothes in the river.

> *Girls can be seen even today at work and play on the riverbanks in rural parts of the Balkans, much the way Homer describes.*[3]

They took the garments in their arms from the wagon and carried
   them into the dark water,
and stomped them in the pools, making a lively contest of it.

[2] Because the interest and importance of the details are not always immediately obvious to one not thoroughly acquainted with the archaeological and ethnographic literature, I have chosen to present the story with a running commentary at the side. My readers may thus choose to read the two strands in any order they wish without losing track of what relates to what.
   Homer knew of Crete, of course, but mostly of a Crete full of Dorian Greeks with a few "true Cretans" and other minor ethnic groups scattered about. Nowhere does he specifically equate the Phaiakians with either the Minoans (whom he also has heard of; see below, on dancing) or Crete, although when Odysseus gets home he tells everyone the "lie" that he has just come from Crete.
[3] Many a Serbo-Croatian courting song mentions that the young man saw the girl of his desires when she was at the river doing this chore. One, for example, begins: "I saw Jovana washing her white linen in the stream. . . ." Nausikaa, in fact, was prompted to go to the river by a dream that she should begin to prepare for marriage. Textiles not only made up much of the trousseau but were among the main gifts to the wedding guests in rural European weddings up into this century.

Then after they had washed and cleaned away all the grime,
they spread everything out in rows on the shore of the brine,
    wherever
the sea had scrubbed the pebbles on the beach especially clean.
Having bathed and anointed themselves with olive oil,
they had their lunch on the banks of the river
and waited for the clothes drying in the rays of the sun.
Then after both Nausikaa and her maids were satisfied with food,
tossing aside their headgear, they played ball,
and white-armed Nausikaa led the song for them. [6.90–101]

It is their shout, when someone misses and the ball
goes into the river, that wakes up Odysseus. Hid-
ing his nakedness behind a convenient branch, he
delicately approaches their leader, the young princess Nausikaa, who gives him food, a tunic, and oil
for bathing and then directs him to the nearby
town, which lies between two harbors. She
explains to him that

There the men busy themselves with the tackle of their black
    ships—
the ropes and the sails—and they sharpen their oars.
For bows and quivers are of no concern to Phaiakian men,
but rather masts and oars of ships and the balanced ships
    themselves,
in which, rejoicing, they cross the gray sea. [6.268–72]

> *The Greeks, by contrast, loved to hunt, so Odysseus
> learns right here that he has arrived in a society rather
> different from his own.*

Nausikaa tells Odysseus to ask in the town for the
house of her parents, and then gives him the following careful instructions:

Go quickly straight through the hall until you reach
my mother—she is sitting by the hearth in the light of the
    fire,

spinning sea-purple roves of wool, a marvel to see,
leaning against the pillar, and her maids sit behind her.
And there the seat of my father is leaned, opposite her,
where he sits and drinks wine like the immortals.
Passing him by, on the knees of my mother
place your suppliant hands, in order to see your day of
   homecoming
with great rejoicing, even if you have come from very far.
For if *she* takes friendly thoughts in her heart,
then there is hope for you to see your friends and reach
your well-built house and your native land. [6.303–15]

> *Different again. No married woman ran the Classical Greek household or made its principal decisions.*[4] *These peculiarly un-Greek instructions, however, are perfectly in line with what we know of matrilineal societies in which the men spend much of their time away. Since the woman owns and controls the house, she has control of which guests may stay in the house.*

At the city gate who should meet him to give him
directions but his old friend Athena, goddess of
useful knowledge, disguised as a young woman.

[4] Women were virtually household prisoners in fifth-century Athenian society in particular, as the legal orations of Lysias show (see Chapter 11), and this seems to have been the typical state of affairs from shortly before the time of Homer onward. There are many exceptions, however, in the Mycenaean world, most notably with Helen of Troy. Not only does her husband, Menelaos, carry on a ten-year war to retrieve her, but then, far from punishing her (as later Greek husbands of wayward wives were known to do—usually by death), he sits around placidly while she tells stories of her escapades to their guests! The reason that he had to fetch her back can only be a matter of succession: that the right to the throne of Sparta passed through her female bloodline, not his. Without Helen, Menelaos could not be king. This analysis is borne out by every detail known of the family: Helen is the queen even though she has two brothers, the famous twins Kastor and Polydeukes (Pollux in Latin), and her daughter Hermione—not one of Menelaos' sons—becomes the next ruler of Sparta after her death. (See Atchity and Barber, "Greek Princes and Aegean Princesses," for a full discussion.)

> *Everywhere else in the Homeric epics Athena disguises herself as a man. So far everyone important on this island has been a woman, and Homer seems to be going out of his way to show that.*

Athena warns him first that the islanders are very suspicious of strangers on their own shores, since they rely on their ships for defense of their land. Then, as they walk along, she tells him the genealogy of Nausikaa's parents, Arete and Alkinoos. The Earth-shaker Poseidon had a son Nausithoos by the daughter of one of the Giants, and Nausithoos in turn had two sons, Rhexenor and Alkinoos. Rhexenor died young,

> leaving only a single daughter,
> Arete; her Alkinoos made into his wife
> and honored her as no other woman on earth is honored.
> [7.65–7]

> *Let's translate that. Poseidon, the god first of earthquakes and next of tidal waves and the sea, mates with the daughter of a Giant—a euphemism for a volcano. Odysseus is now among people for whom seismic activity is the most important of all "supernatural" forces, as several other points in the story show. Arete, an orphaned heiress, is married by her paternal uncle—incest in many cultures, but precisely what the law requires for lone heiresses in the early law code from Gortyna, in Crete. Although written in Greek about 450 B.C., this huge inscription contains many laws that are very unlike Greek laws elsewhere, especially those relating to marriage, heiresses, and the often considerable property of the women. The differences, which include easy divorce initiated by either partner and what anthropologists call tribal cross-cousin marriage (typical of matrilineage), have been attributed to strong local holdovers from Minoan society. Homer may have made up all the*

names—*Arete simply means "virtue"—but not the*
rules of cross-cousin marriage so foreign to the
Greeks.

Athena continues:

> Thus most heartily she was honored, and still is—
> by her children and by Alkinoos himself
> and by the people, who, viewing her as a deity,
> greet her with words when she walks through the city.
> For she herself lacks in no way of noble intellect;
> and she resolves the quarrels of the women to whom she has
>   good will, and their menfolk. [7.69–74]

> *The women of similarly structured societies among*
> *the Pueblo Indians also had the right to arbitrate*
> *quarrels and to say whether a stranger would or*
> *would not be allowed to stay within the home. They*
> *also had the system of cross-cousin marriage. Thus*
> *Homer's details are entirely consistent with modern*
> *ethnology.*

Odysseus is astonished at the opulence of the
house. First to meet his gaze is the gilt and faience-
tiled courtyard with its statuary. Next come the
house itself and its gardens:

> Inside, seats were placed at intervals along the wall, straight
> through to the inmost room from the threshold, and
>   on them
> delicate, well-spun draperies were thrown, the work of the
>   women.
> There the great-hearted Phaiakians would sit,
> drinking and eating; for they held the [seats] in perpetuity.
> And indeed, young men of gold stood on well-built
>   pedestals
> holding flaming torches with their hands,
> lighting up the nights for the feasters throughout the halls.

A common feature of Minoan palaces (but not Greek ones) is a huge room near the kitchens, apparently for massive communal dining. We are also just beginning to find evidence of life-size, fully realistic Minoan statuary of ivory and gold.

And fifty serving women belonged to the house,
some of whom grind on the millstone the ruddy grain,
while others weave at the looms and twirl their spindles
as they sit, restless as the leaves of the lofty poplar,
and the liquid olive oil runs down from the linen warps.
By how much the Phaiakian men are expert above all other
    men in
propelling a swift ship on the sea, by thus much their
    women
are skilled at the loom, for Athena has given to them
    beyond all others
a knowledge of beautiful craftwork, and noble intellects.

Here is the central expression of women's work in this kind of society, exactly as we have come to expect it. We also see that the men's arena of activity is far from home and the soil—down at the harbor and out to sea.

But outside the courtyard near the doors is a great orchard
of four acres, and around it on either side runs a hedge.
And there tall trees have grown luxuriant—
pears and pomegranates and shining-fruited apples,
and also sweet figs and plump olives. [7.95–116]

Truly, a horticultural economy raised to fairy-tale perfection. Yet every fruit mentioned was important to the Aegean economy.

And beside the last row of vineyard, tidy garden beds
of all sorts grow, ever shining;

and in it are two fountains, one of which sprinkles
the whole garden, while from the other side the second
　　flows under the courtyard's edge
toward the lofty house, whence the citizens draw water.
[7.127–31]

*Minoan sites are known for their highly advanced
technology in waterworks. Those who built the palace at Knossos piped supplies of fresh water through
the buildings in stone channels running under the
floors, accessible at intervals, and built extensive
drains for the sewage as well. Elsewhere in the palace
the water runs in clay pipes, subtly tapered to keep
the water moving. Open pools surrounded by a
broad stone lip were constructed in a frescoed portico
at the end of the road to the palace, where dusty trav-
elers could sit comfortably, wash their feet, and cool
off before entering the royal domain. Down the steep
east side, just beyond the royal living quarters, the
Minoans constructed what seems to have been a pleasure garden with little pools and channels of running
water fed by a gurgling cascade.[5] Truly they loved
their gardens.*

Entering the house, Odysseus does as he has been
instructed, casting himself at the feet of the queen,
and is accepted as a guest, to be fed, housed, and
entertained before being given safe convoy home.
The entertainments include athletic contests, the

[5] The staircase leading down the east retaining wall to the garden is unique in
having beside it an open channel that carried whatever fresh water had not been
used up in passing through the palace. The channel curves to match each step of
the stair, enhancing the pleasant sound of the rushing water. At the bottom,
shaded during the hot afternoons by the steep wall retaining the hill, it runs along
two flagstone terraces through a series of tiny square pools, much too small for
washing laundry, as the excavators suggested. The entire arrangement is much
more likely to have been a pure pleasure garden. One of the Knossos frescoes
depicts a splashing fountain rather like the one described by Homer.

singing of a bard, and dancing. Watching the dancers, Odysseus exclaims to Alkinoos,

> You boasted that your dancers were the best,
> and indeed it has been shown to be so. Awe seizes me as I
>   look on them! [8.383–4]

> *We have a remarkable number of Minoan representa-*
> *tions of dancing: not only the frescoes from Knossos,*
> *mentioned above, showing women dancing in a great*
> *courtyard, surrounded by bleachers full of lively spec-*
> *tators, and others from both Knossos and Hagia Tri-*
> *ada (fig. 4.6), but also, for example, a small set of*
> *clay figurines of women joined in a round dance.*[6]

Finally the Phaiakians heap Odysseus with gifts,
listen to the long tale of his adventures, and take
him home across the sea to Ithaca as he sleeps. But
as the sailors return, Poseidon vents his wrath on
them for saving his enemy, Odysseus, by destroying the ship within sight of the harbor. The citizens
are terrified by the memory of an oracle to the
effect that Poseidon would one day destroy a convoy ship and pile a mountain on top of their city, in
anger because they gave safe passage to everyone.
Seeing the one part fulfilled, they rush off to make
sacrifices in hopes of averting the second apocalyptic disaster. And that is the last we hear of them.

> *Just such a disaster had actually happened in the*
> *Aegean around 1600 B.C., when the island volcano of*
> *Thera, sixty miles north of Crete, erupted with great*

---

[6] One is reminded of yet another Homeric passage, the description in the *Iliad* of
the many scenes depicted on the shield of Achilles. Among them (18.591–4) is a
dance floor
> like the one which once, in broad Knossos,
> Daedalus built for Ariadne with the beautiful plaits of hair.
> And there, youths and maidens worthy of a large bride-price
> were dancing, holding each other's hands by the wrist.

violence, burying the Minoan towns on its flanks under a hundred feet of volcanic ash before partially collapsing into the sea.

Centuries later the people at Tanagra (four miles from the Aegean coast and twenty-five miles north of Athens) were still burying their dead in Cretan-style clay coffins painted with running spirals and with mourning scenes of women in Minoan-looking flounced skirts (fig. 4.8)—at a time when all others in Greece were burying their dead coffinless and wearing baggy chemises and tunics. So at least a few people long maintained some of the old customs, perhaps even down into Homer's time. Whether or not, like the Amish of Pennsylvania today with their horse-drawn plows and carts, they still used archaic ways of producing their food, they clearly kept their habits of dress from a bygone age, as

Figure 4.8. One of many painted clay sarcophagi from the town of Tanagra, in eastern Greece, showing mourning women wearing strikingly Minoan-looking dress. Such clay coffins are known elsewhere only from Minoan Crete, rather earlier. The Tanagra examples date mostly to the thirteenth century B.C.

the Amish in bonnets and long dresses do also.

It is by their clothes that we recognize them instantly as a breed apart, an isolated remnant of a life-style that had grown and flourished for millennia but now languished far from the stream of change. And it is to the central importance of clothes as social indicators that we will now turn our attention.

5

⋙

More than Hearts
on Our Sleeves

"Clothes make the man"—but
women made the clothes

The advent in the fourth millennium B.C. of colored thread, in the form of various natural and dyed hues of wool, triggered a major revolution in the clothes that women wove for their families to wear. Already in the Early Bronze Age, soon after 3000 B.C., we see the forms of dress proliferating from a small number of rather simple types into much more complex regional costumes. The Bronze Age, in fact, witnessed the development of many of the basic modes of dressing that we find characteristic of the cultures of the world today. Since the production of these new garments affected the lives of women in both what they wore and what they spent their labor on, we will find considerable interest in a closer look at the structure, meaning, and ramifications of the changes that occurred at this time.

Why do people wear the clothes they do? Why do people wear clothes at all?

Most people will reply that clothes are for warmth, yet this argument does not hold up against the evidence. On the one hand, the inhabitants of very hot climates such as the Arabian Desert may wear lots of clothes—for protection against the sun and sand. On the other, the human body can adapt to much lower temperatures than pampered Americans usually think it can. I recall my astonishment, upon coming to New England from a lifetime in a hot climate, at seeing a fellow graduate student wheeling his tiny children through the snow in light shirts and cotton pants. Then I learned that the family was from Finland and that to them this constituted warm weather: thirty degrees above, not thirty below. In fact, most clothing is worn for social reasons—to mark sex, age, marital status, wealth, rank, modesty (whatever that may be within a particular culture), place of origin, occupation, or occasion.[1] A few candid souls may, as the saying goes, wear their hearts on their sleeves, but we all wear a great deal of our pedigree and social aspirations written all over our apparel. The economic developments of the Bronze Age caused major cultural differentiation in most of these categories, and clothing types could now proliferate to mark the new variety.

Relatively few Neolithic figurines wear clothes, and those that do are predominantly female. The simplest of straight skirts, often ankle-length, characterizes the common garb for women in central Europe, Egypt, and probably Mesopotamia. One imagines these skirts as wraparound, so that the person would have enough room to walk, but the depictions are too sketchy for certainty. Some European women wear a string skirt, the old Palaeolithic carrier of social information (see Chapter 2), while a few in both Europe

---

[1] To discover the nature of this practice, look around you. Does a party guest wear expensive silk? Cheap polyester? Motorcycle boots? Lace gloves? We deduce much from such clothing about the owner. If the veiled woman is all in white, she's the bride; if in black, she's the widow, or at least in mourning. If the man's bow tie is white, he is host or guest, but if it's black, he's probably the waiter. And if he has no ribbon at all around his neck, some clubs and restaurants won't serve him any dinner.

Note, too, how specific these codes are to a particular culture. In China, for example, white is for mourning whereas the color for weddings is red. In nineteenth-century Russia leather boots were a sign of wealth. Modesty, likewise, is culture-specific. In China a woman's feet were traditionally considered her most private part, and if caught undressed, she would cover them first.

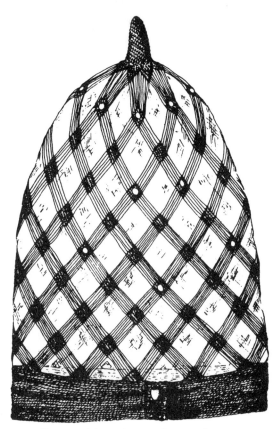

Figure 5.1. Needle-netted linen bag with stone button, thought to be a ceremonial hat and thus the oldest preserved clothing. From Naḥal Ḥemar Cave, Israel, ca. 6500 B.C.

and the Near East wear only a belt or sash. Such raiment is simple in the extreme.

Ritual, however, already occasioned the use of unusual attire. One of our earliest finds of actual textiles, from a cave in Israel known as Naḥal Ḥemar (ca. 6500 B.C.; see map, fig. 3.1), includes an elaborate net bag with a small stone button on it (fig. 5.1). The use of this linen net gradually became clear as the excavators sifted through the contents of the cavern in the mid-1980s.

The little cave in question burrows into a sheer cliff just above the floor of a canyon in the Judean Desert, near the southwestern tip of the Dead Sea. From the cave mouth one can see across arid heaps of stones to small tar seeps welling up from below the earth—tar that the early Neolithic people traveled out to this distant and desolate spot to fetch. Between trips they stashed some of their gear in the little cave, using it as a convenient natural storeroom. Among its abandoned contents archaeologists discovered stone and bone tools, raw materials, and half-finished objects. One concludes that while here, the cave visitors spent time manufacturing things.

The half-finished containers in particular demonstrate that the natural tar or asphalt in the gully formed the main attraction. Pottery had not been invented yet, and these people exploited the tar to make waterproof vessels by thoroughly caulking their baskets and other fibrous containers with it. The sticky stuff invited other uses as well. The ancient artisans left a curved sickle with sharp flint bladelets set in with tar, as well as a human skull onto which someone had begun to model in tar a hairnet something like the one found in the cave. From contemporary sites, such as Jericho (only fifty miles away and already a thriving town five thousand years before Joshua), we know that members of this culture saved the skulls of important ancestors. After the flesh was gone, they remodeled the facial features with plaster, placing shiny oval cowrie shells where the eyes had been. People must have been carrying out such grisly work at this site, for cowrie shells, too, figure among the many remains in the cave, along with beads, cloth, figurines, and fright masks painted with violent red and green stripes. So much elaborate work went into the preserved linen hairnet (and into the shell-ornamented remains of a second such net) that the headpiece must have served for more than everyday wear—perhaps for the same ritual or magical ceremonies in which the modeled skulls and gaping masks found use.

Far away, in Hungary and the Balkans, people marked ritual by other means. Clay statuettes of both sexes (often sitting formally enthroned) were covered with geometric or swirling designs, some of which appear to be decorations on clothing (woven? painted?). But in other cases these patterns run straight across obvious anatomical details such as the navel or pubic triangle, as though they were right on the person's skin—body paint or tattooing rather than patterned clothes.

Archaeologists seldom see the skins of the people they dig up, but a tomb frozen solid by permafrost in the Altai Mountains of central Asia proves that decorating human skin is an antique art. It contained a man's body embellished from shoulder to ankle with tattoos of rams, a giant fish, and all manner of toothsome griffins. This find, which had to be excavated with buckets of hot water rather than trowels, probably dates to the fourth century B.C., Iron Age rather than Neolithic, but the sure-handedness of the designs shows that tattooing was no new art. The practice of painting designs on one's skin persists in parts of the Balkans and Turkey right up to this day. At Neolithic sites in the Balkans, small seal-like blobs of clay often come to light, with incised geometrical patterns on them quite suitable for stamping paint onto textiles, skin, or walls—a way of producing multiple copies of the same design quickly and easily. (Once again, I have seen rooms of modern peasant houses in northern Yugoslavia and Hungary—as well as local textiles—handsomely decorated with just such tiny stamped designs.)

What we know of Neolithic pigments and dyes suggests that most of them would not have survived a washing. So the sort of swirling body art and textile paint seen on the figurines would have been quite temporary, as in parts of Africa today. We children of industry view such wash-off art as a scandalous waste of time and effort, but if we had to put in the hundreds of hours needed to make a *garment* by hand from scratch, we might see the practice of repainting one's dress appropriately for each festival during the year as a tremendous savings, a necessary frugality.

In general, then, our picture suggests that Neolithic clothing was rather spare, with occasional elaborations in the sphere of ritual. Our first insight into what caused matters to change so radically in the Bronze Age comes from a pair of widely separated but parallel events late in the Neolithic. One occurred in China, the other in Europe, and both cases involve the advent of a new and more versatile textile fiber.

All through the Neolithic, weavers in Europe and the Near East employed flax, and in China they worked with hemp. Both are bast fibers—that is, derived from plant stalks. About the time metalworking began, or a little before (late fourth millennium in Europe, late third or early second in China), animal fibers became available: wool in the west and domestic silk in the east. Both of these animal fibers insulate the wearer better than the plant basts, and both of them also accept dyes much more readily than bast. It was this second feature, color, which suddenly made it possible to send a vast new variety of social signals by means of cloth and clothing. Overnight, dress became far more than a wrap for cold nights or a shield from the sun. Only in Egypt, where wool never came to be used much, did the clothing itself remain fairly plain— white linen garments of simple design—while social signals came to be marked almost exclusively by jewelry.

In Europe we have the evidence to trace some of the changes in dress occasioned by colored thread. We have already seen in Chapter 2 that the proto-Indo-Europeans of the Early Bronze Age handed down words for only the simplest of attire—belts and a general word meaning merely "what you wear" (or perhaps "what keeps you warm"). We also saw that many of them soon borrowed a word and the garment it represented—the tunic—from their Semitic neighbors to the south.[2] This tunic itself was a plain

---

[2] The word *tunic* comes into English from the Latin *tunica,* which itself was borrowed from some West Semitic language. In Hebrew, for example, the garment is called *kutton-eth.* (The Romans took the word in as *ktuni-ka* and simplified the beginning. The Greeks took the same word and made *khitōn* out of it.) The Semites, for their part, had borrowed from the Sumerians some names for the linen that this garment was made of. Thus cuneiform records show that the East Semitic Akkadians had *kitinnu,* meaning "linen; linen cloth," and *kitû,* "flax, linen," which latter was ultimately borrowed from Sumerian *gada,* "linen."

linen garment of simple cut, a tubular body wrapper with places for head and arms.

Why should this linen garment have been borrowed into Europe just *after* the advent of wool? Wool may be colorful, but it is also scratchy against the skin. The soft white tunic, made of smooth plant fiber (linen, hemp, nettle, and later cotton), served as a convenient buffer between the skin and the otherwise wonderful new wool—all the more convenient because linen is so easily washed, bleached, and dried to clean it of body sweat. Thus the sartorial strategy became one of wearing a soft white tunic as a foundation garment, with the colored woolen clothes over the top for warmth and for show. We still dress by much this principle today in Western society—largely white shirts, blouses, slips, and T-shirts as foundation beneath our colorful woolen sweaters and jackets, skirts and trousers.

Tunics developed in two major directions. The simpler variety consisted merely of a big rectangle of cloth, just as it came off the loom. The wearer draped it suitably over the body and pinned, tied, or belted it into place (fig. 5.2 a and b), while the manufacturer had it easy since no cutting or sewing was required to shape the dress. But that was also its drawback: One had to redesign the garment each time one dressed, and it wasn't always easy to keep it in place. (Many a quip has been made over the years about the poor Venus de Milo losing her drape altogether because she has no hands—fig. 10.1.) The more complicated type of tunic dealt with this problem by taking several rectangles of cloth and sewing them up into tubes: one tube for the torso and two smaller ones sewn on for the arms (fig. 5.2 c).

In Mesopotamia, where linen had been important for thousands of years, Sumerian women wore simple shoulder-to-ankle tunics wrapped so that the right arm and shoulder were bare (figs. 5.2 b and 8.6). The representations of this fashion date from the late fourth millennium B.C. onward. The men, when they wore anything at all, evidently preferred a longish skirt made either of a sheepskin with the shaggy fleece on the outside, or of a shaggy-

Figure 5.2. Types of simple tunics found in the ancient world: (a) Greek type, made by folding cloth and suspending it from two points at the shoulders (usually belted as well); (b) Mesopotamian type, made by wrapping the cloth around the body (see fig. 8.6); (c) Mycenaean and Slavic type, made from three tubes of cloth.

weave textile. (Women sometimes wore tufted skirts and cloaks, too.) It is only in the mid to late third millennium that we see the habit of wearing linen tunics spreading to the menfolk, a date which accords with the apparent time of the linguistic borrowing farther north and with the time at which the eastern Semites began to get the upper hand in Mesopotamia. Probably the tunic had already become characteristic of these Semites, without our having the evidence to demonstrate it.

Meanwhile, just to the south of the western Semites, the Egyptians were working on sleeved tunics, after perfecting short and knee-length kilts for the men and a simple shoulder-strap jumper for the women, all in plain linen. The earliest complete garment yet found by archaeologists anywhere in the world is a highly sophisticated Egyptian linen shirt from the First Dynasty, ca. 3000 B.C. (fig. 5.3).

Sir William Matthew Flinders Petrie had dug up this shirt during his 1912–1913 seasons at the site of Tarkhan. Even as far back as the First Dynasty, dead men and women embarked for the next

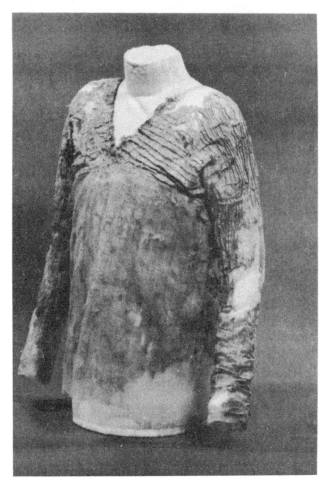

Figure 5.3. World's oldest preserved body garment: linen shirt from a First Dynasty Egyptian tomb at Tarkhan, ca. 3000 B.C. The shoulders and sleeves have been finely pleated to give form-fitting trimness while allowing the wearer room to move. The small fringe formed during weaving along one edge of the cloth has been placed by the designer to decorate the neck opening and side seam. Creases inside the elbow (making the lower half of the sleeves angle forward) prove that the shirt had actually been worn. It was found inside out, as though stripped off over the head. (UC 28614B': photograph courtesy of the Petrie Museum, University College London, where the piece is on display.)

world with linens and other useful goods piled high around their coffins. In the case of tomb 2050, robbers had already ransacked the burial in ancient times, chucking a good deal of linen out into the hot, dry sand, which soon blew over the cloth and protected it rather well until uncovered by Petrie's spade. A meticulous British archaeologist, Petrie concentrated on recording the minutest details of Egyptian daily life at a time when most museums and scholars prospected only for splendid works of ancient art and discarded the rest of what they uncovered (see Chapter 12). As with so much else of a homely nature that he found, and that no one else wanted, he tucked the ragged prize into his study collection and took it back to University College London. There it hibernated until 1977, when two women curators interested in textiles found it as they began to sort through the heaps of dirty "funerary rags" in storage. It proved a fine piece, with seams, fringes, and elaborate pleating largely intact after five thousand years. Moreover, creases at the elbow still make the long, slim sleeves bend forward at a comfortable angle, showing clearly that the shirt was actually worn. In fact, it was found inside out, just as the wearer had left it after stripping it off over the head. The linen rectangles from which the tunic was stitched together had been woven with a fringe of weft running along one edge, and these edges had been placed so as to adorn the neck opening and the side seam. What's more, the linen had been carefully pleated in row upon row of tiny tucks, not sewn but simply pressed in, to give it both elasticity and a trim fit. All this before 3000 B.C.!

It may well have been a simple version of the Egyptian shirt that the western Semites adopted in the next centuries and passed on up the coast to Syria and then Anatolia (roughly modern Turkey). There we find a long sort in use when we begin to get depictions of clothing in that area in the second millennium B.C., and from there it passed westward with Mycenaean Greeks along with the Semitic-based word *khitōn* to refer to it (see fig. 5.2 and note 2 above). Short-sleeved tunics appear in Mycenaean palace murals of 1400–1200 B.C. If we keep our eyes open, however, we can also detect long-sleeved ones in some of the shaft burials of 1650–1500 B.C. at Mycenae. In several of these royal graves, very thin gold foil surrounded the wrists of the deceased—foil so thin that it could not have held shape alone but had to have been supported by a cloth sleeve.

This sleeved and rather long garment, which I will refer to as a *chemise,* became the basis of clothing in much of the Balkans, central Europe, the steppelands, and the Caucasus.[3] In Classical Greece and Rome, however, the simpler, sleeveless, draped tunic prevailed, probably brought in at the end of the Bronze Age by less sophisticated Indo-European tribes that invaded and infiltrated from the north during the period after 1200 B.C. Breezy in the extreme, it suits the warm Mediterranean climates. Our earliest Greek find of complete clothing conforms to this kind: a white linen tunic with a bright pattern-woven sash, dating to about 1000 B.C. Notice that the Classical tunic does not hang at all the way the Sumerian one does; instead of being spirally wrapped, the cloth is folded in half and suspended equally from both shoulders (fig. 5.2).

With the foundation garment—soft white tunic or chemise—in place, people began to elaborate and embellish woolen overwraps. That meant that the average housewife needed to learn to work both wool and flax, which require very different handling. But for her effort, she got much fancier and more diverse clothes to wear. The earliest-preserved example of this new mode of dress comes from the burial of a chieftain in the Kuban area, just north of the

---

[3] The English word *chemise* comes, via French, from Latin *camisia,* itself probably a borrowing from Celtic. Note that words for types of clothing frequently bounce about from one language to another, the way *tunic* and *chemise* have done. For one thing, many people enjoy borrowing novel forms of clothing from other cultures. (The Romans, for example, avidly imported cloth and clothes from the Celts to the north of them.) The second big reason is that textiles and garments were favorite forms of booty during raids and other warfare. This fact is fossilized in our language with the term *robe,* which came from the verb *to rob.*

Caucasus, around 2500 B.C. He was laid in his grave wearing a white undergarment embellished with red tassels; over it was a black and yellow plaid wrap apparently of wool, and over that a fur wrap. Such an outfit is also just about what one would expect from comparative reconstruction based on more recent folk costumes of Eurasia and is heavily (though not exclusively) associated with the groups of Indo-Europeans expanding through Europe and the steppes. But to understand that remark and to decipher the interesting history of the European woolen overgarment, we need a new tool.

We can learn a lot about the development of ancient dress from applying the methods of comparative analysis (developed by linguists for language study) to the costumes themselves, not just to the words for them. To the extent that habits of speech and habits of dress occur largely below the level of conscious thought, they behave the same way. That is, we just *use* these tools as a means to some end without contemplating the basic tools themselves. (Most people, for example, don't sit around asking themselves why the word *spoon* contains those sounds. They just ask for a spoon to eat their breakfast with and get on with life.) Constant subtle changes and adjustments in these unconscious habits go on everywhere all the time, causing the forms of speech—and dress—in one area to end up different from those in another. The changes also happen much more slowly in a peasant culture than in a crowded urban environment. Since the changes occur at different rates in different places, they are reflected gradually across space, and a folk-costume map can end up looking rather like a dialect map.[4]

Approaching matters thus, we can coax into view the historical

[4] In applying this principle to the archaeological world, we must beware of eighteenth- and nineteenth-century nationalism, which artificially heightened and overcodified local differences. Thus the beloved tartans of the Scottish clans did not exist as such before the rise of Scottish nationalism in the 1800s. People wore woolen twill cloth, and plaid was a favorite type of pattern; but that was about all. On the other hand, even though details were added, the basic local notions of what constituted the proper approach to clothing men and women were not

evolution of the woolen outer garments that Europeans now placed over the soft white tunic or chemise. Like the tunic, its simplest form is a plain rectangle of cloth straight off the loom. The men of Homer's epics, for instance, each wore a big woolen rectangle over the tunic, using it as a cloak by day and as a blanket by night. Later Scotsmen did likewise: Their pieces of plaid wool (often worn with a shirt) used to be some sixteen feet long, half being belted around the waist like a skirt, with enough pleats tucked in each time to allow free movement, and the other half being thrown over the shoulder as a cape. Stories have it that the Scots were able to outlast the English soldiers in running warfare because the Highlanders would take off their kilt-cloths after dark, roll up in them three or four times, and remain warm enough to sleep out the night under any bush. Unfitted clothing has great versatility.

Women had cloaks, too, but a tradition arose among them of tying smaller squares on in addition, to use as aprons. (I have often thought, while puttering around my kitchen garden, that aprons must have been invented by prehistoric farm wives. The apron shields the undergarment and is always available as an impromptu basket of variable size to carry miscellaneous produce and wayward tools or toys, with the sacrifice of only a single hand to hold up the corners.) In parts of the Balkans (especially Romania) and Ukraine, this simplest, most archaic type of European folk costume could still be found into the middle of this century: a white chemise and a pair of narrow aprons, one in the front and one in the back (fig. 5.4 a). Nearby, dialectlike, one finds a slight but important variant, in which the back apron has become so wide that it wraps most of the way around, the small gap that it leaves in the front being overlaid by a small front apron (fig. 5.4 b). Sur-

---

changed. (Some modern debunkers have gone so far as to claim that even the idea of plaid was new to the Celts at that time, but archaeological finds such as those discussed in the Introduction show that to be untrue. Celts had been making simple two-color plaid twills for a good twenty-five hundred years when nationalism took hold.)

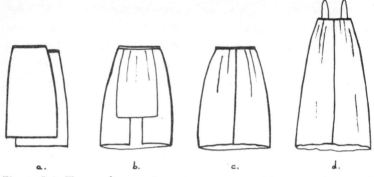

Figure 5.4. Types of women's uncut overwraps: (a) narrow front and back aprons; (b) wraparound back apron with a small front apron to cover the gap; (c) wide apron sewn up into a skirt; (d) skirt raised and lengthened to form a simple jumper.

vivals of this style can be found also in the Banat and Serbia, just to the west, and northward at least into Orël, Tula, and Penza provinces in central Russia, just south of Moscow. Like the string skirt (see Chapter 2), which it partially replaced, the woolen back apron came to signal women's marital status.

The next variant in time and space comes with the idea that the wide back apron does not have to be rewrapped every day, nor does it have to let in the cold in front. One can sew up the square of cloth into a tube—a skirt—and belt it on somehow, either with a sash to bind it on or with a drawstring (fig. 5.4 c). In fact, we possess a plaid woolen skirt with a drawstring from the Danish bogs, dating to the Iron Age. (Because an outfit required a huge expenditure of time, effort, and materials, older folk costumes are usually constructed so that the person could grow in the usual directions—taller or fatter—without making the garment useless. A fixed belt band is less accommodating than a drawstring.) The skirt, of course, has become a particularly common element in Western clothing, still worn over the chemise, which itself has only recently been split at the waist to form a blouse or shirt above and a slip or petticoat below.

In the clothing "dialect" to the north of skirt territory, we find a similar woolen tube over the chemise, except that the top edge has been hauled up under the armpits, with the effect of keeping more of the torso warm (fig. 5.4 d). Since the skirt doesn't get much purchase up there, it requires shoulder straps to stay up. This, in effect, is the design of the Russian *sarafan* and the jumperlike overdress found in parts of Scandinavia.

Thus an apparently wide array of traditional garments, scattered across thousands of miles, turns out to reflect an underlying unity of concept, a basic way of approaching the notion of clothing. The tradition we have just traced lies behind *our* way of dressing, but of course, it is not everybody's. Traditional notions of what constitutes basic clothing differ radically from one part of the world to the next. Most of us do not recognize that fact now, because so much of the world has recently adopted traditional Western dress. Consider, however, how differently conceived the Indian woman's sari is from our tailored dresses or how different the Scotsman's kilt is from a Western business suit. And each of these differs widely from the Hawaiian girl's grass skirt, the Japanese woman's elaborate kimono, the African man's dignity robe, or the Australian aborigine's loincloth.

Returning to our European playground, we can discern that another ancient tradition by which women fashioned their attire lurks in the Balkans, in addition to the blanketlike wraps of uncut woolen cloth. Minoan women, approaching the problems differently, based their clothing on cutting and tailoring, traits especially visible in the tightly fitted sleeved bodices and rounded aprons (figs. 4.5–7 and 6.3). A not unsimilar costume (considering the variety of clothing in the world), with big skirts and a sculpted bodice, appears on figurines from the Danube in the Bronze Age—e.g., at Cîrna (fig. 5.5 left). Since Minoan weaving techniques tie in closely with those developed along the Danube, I suspect that this tradition of cutting and tailoring is linked, too, and is ultimately responsible for the woolen jumper with deeply cut neckhole so prevalent in parts of Bulgaria and Serbia (fig. 5.5 right). Even some of the details of ornamentation on recent folk costumes

Figure 5.5. Left: Bronze Age clay figurine of a woman, found in a cremation urn at Cîrna, southern Romania (mid to late second millennium B.C.). Right: Typical Bulgarian folk costume of the nineteenth and early twentieth centuries A.D. Note the similarities of cut and decor to the Cîrna figurine of thirty-five hundred years earlier.

of the Balkans resemble with astonishing closeness the Bronze Age representations of women's wear (see Chapter 6). But then, when the string skirt has lasted twenty thousand years, other traditions can make it through four thousand.

Women's dress was not the only kind to evolve. We left the Indo-European man wearing a white chemise or tunic, a belt (preferably red), and a woolen cloak. To judge from their first distribution, trousers were invented about 1000 B.C. in response to the chafing of tender parts incurred in the new art of horseback riding. The man's chemise was then shortened (*shirt* means "cut short") to allow the straddling position. Horses had been domesticated long before on the steppes, where they served to pull carts and chariots for a couple of thousand years before riding on the horse's back became common. Riding revolutionized life on the steppes, however, just as it did for the Plains Indians on the American prairies, because it meant that the humans were now faster and more mobile than the animals they chased. They could manage such large flocks, in fact, that the herds alone provided a good living for relatively little work. On both continents we see formerly sedentary people pulling up stakes and riding off after the herds. The great grassy steppeland, much of it far better suited to grazing than to agriculture, became a giant pastureland controlled by trousered nomadic riders. They inhabit it still today.

At the east end of the Eurasian steppes the Chinese watched the same transformation of herding early in the first millennium B.C. and recorded it with dismay. To them it spelled attack: swift, repeated raids on the rich Chinese farmlands by mounted barbarian nomads in search of food, women, and, above all, silk cloth. In vain the Chinese rulers tried to bribe the raiders with silk and grain to stay away. Finally, in self-defense, one of the Chinese kings, Wu-ling of Chao, ordered his people (in the words of an ancient Chinese historian) "to adopt barbarian dress and to practice riding and shooting." Trousers and riding, as we saw, went together at the west end of the Eurasian continent, too, and the Chinese adopted both, around 400 B.C., from the same source as the West had. Thus prepared to fight fire with fire, Wu-ling led his men in a successful foray against the nomads and then began building sections of defensive wall to keep them out in the future. Affairs were more manageable after that, but hardly solved. A couple of centuries and many pieces of wall later, another emperor joined the sections into what we now know as the Great Wall of China, and in 174 B.C the emperor Wen wrote to the leader of the nomadic barbarians as follows, suing for peace: "We .. send you from our own wardrobe an embroidered robe lined with patterned damask, an embroidered and lined underrobe, and a brocaded coat . . . ; one sash with gold ornaments; one gold-ornamented leather belt; ten rolls of embroidery; thirty rolls of brocade; and forty rolls each of heavy red silk and light green silk." Bright-hued silk and silken cloth, manufactured by countless Chinese women, finally induced the roving horsemen to leave the land in peace for a little while.

Figure 5.6. Left: Cypriot bronze stand from Episkopi-Kourion, showing man wearing long kilt and turned-up-toed shoes. Right: Mycenaean vase from Attica, in form of a leather shoe (compare fig. 5.7). Fourteenth century B.C.

It was these same irrepressible nomads yet a millennium or two later who contributed the last major feature of many eastern European folk costumes, the fitted jacket. Undoubtedly they had invented their jackets, too, in the struggle to stay warm and dry while dashing about on horseback.

Besides the line of development leading to the shirt and trousers, and besides the Minoan loincloth, the Bronze Age gives evidence of a third men's tradition in the northern Mediterranean: that of the short wrapped kilt. Of uncertain origin, perhaps starting as an animal skin wrapped around the hips (as the Egyptians saw at least a couple of Mycenaeans doing), it is so simple that, like the apron, it might well have been thought up independently in several places. Yet for all that, it is not particularly common in the world.

In Cyprus and in Egyptian paintings of visitors from the North Mediterranean, the kilt is associated with another article of apparel: plaited leather shoes, often with turned-up toes and worn with highly decorated socks or leggings. This distinctive footwear is also depicted in great detail on a Mycenaean pot modeled in the form of such a shoe, with all the minutiae painted on (fig. 5.6). There is no doubt that the slipper is constructed just like the *opanci* still made today all over the central Balkans and Turkey (fig. 5.7)—another incontestable survivor of several thousand years. The shoes are very comfortable, and the turned-up leather

Figure 5.7. Traditional leather shoes with turned-up toes *(opanci)* from various parts of the central Balkans. Compare fig. 5.6. The turned-up tips help keep one from stubbing one's toes in the rocky terrain.

at the tip is particularly suited to protecting the toes from getting stubbed on rocky ground. They do not fare well slogging through mud or sand, however, so one concludes that they evolved to cope with just the sort of dry, mountainous areas where they persist today.

In such ways have the underlying clothing traditions of the world grown up, from a combination of available materials and felicitous inventions to meet the needs of climate, terrain, and life-style. We have followed these traditions in only one large region, but along the way we have seen how old such customs can be. Once a viable form had evolved for a given econiche, what need was there to replace it? Having established the fundamentals, people of a particular culture just kept adding new ideas and modifications on top of the old.

The frosting on these increasingly diverse and distinctive "layer cakes"—these accumulations of types of attire used in different regions of the world—comes in the surface decoration of the individual garments. As with the forms of the clothes, the observer can gather large amounts of social and geographical information from looking carefully at patterns, colors, and placement. The cultural codes of surface decor are so arbitrary, however, compared with the forms of the garments themselves, that we will have to treat them within a different framework.

6

≷≷≷

Elements of the Code

Know first who you are, then
deck yourself out accordingly.
—Epictetus, *Discourses,* 3.1

Human beings, the quintessential social animals, constantly send
and receive complex social information. Our most acute sense is
vision, yet eons ago the human race selected sound, not vision, as
its primary channel for linguistic communication.[1] That kept our
newly evolved hands free for using tools and allowed us to send
and receive messages even when we weren't looking or couldn't
see, for instance, in the dark of night or in a thick forest. But how
to deal with the need to send certain social messages *continuously,*
like "I'm married" or "I'm in charge here"? Sound waves die away
the moment they leave your mouth, yet saying something over and
over is a bore, and tiring, too.

---

[1] Oral speech, as we know it, is on the order of 150,000 to 100,000 years old, to
judge by the fossil evidence for the evolution of a mouth and vocal tract adapted
to oral speech. For comparison, writing was first invented a mere 5,500 years
ago, and a widespread, standardized sign language for the deaf was developed
only in the last century. (Upright stance, together with "modern" hands and feet,
developed about 4 million years ago.)

Visual symbols, so easily made permanent or semipermanent, provide the answer. For instance, one can carry a scepter to mark one's continued authority or set up a stone circle and stand inside it to mark a religious event in progress. A scepter, of course, engages your hands—a disadvantage—and a stone circle, being too heavy to lug about, keeps you in one place. Painting the body itself with symbols avoids both these problems, and we know that people did this in prehistoric times (see Chapter 5) and still do, especially in the tropics. In colder climates, however, where putting on a warming wrap will cover up these emblems, the easiest and most adaptable solution is to hang a suitable cloth outermost on the person, place, or thing to be marked and remove it when it is no longer appropriate. Thus an embroidered towel slung over the shoulder, a gift from the bride, marks the groom's kin at a Croatian wedding, and a handsome cloth wrapped around an object in Japan marks it as an honored present. The bride, too, is "wrapped" in a ceremonial white gown in Western society, as she is "given away." Clothing, right from our first direct evidence twenty thousand years ago, has been the handiest solution to conveying social messages visually, silently, continuously.

It also became the normal solution, as we see from some notable counterexamples. European societies in the Middle Ages developed heraldic devices adorning shields and banners (another type of cloth) to announce in some detail who was who. Why? Because knights had gotten completely covered up in armor. Thus no one could see much of them or their clothes anymore. Similarly today, where commuters are swallowed up in the armor of their cars for hours on the freeways, they have resorted to bumper stickers and vanity plates to display their individuality. That is, when you can't *see* the clothes, people invent new visual devices to carry the social signals.

Note, however, a critical difference between modern bumper stickers and message T-shirts on the one hand and medieval heraldry on the other. Today in America we assume that everyone can read. We have only to locate a place to *write* the message. But writing wasn't even invented until roughly fifty-five hundred years ago, not long after the wheel and woolly sheep came along, and even then the script was so complicated that only a very few—and highly privileged—individuals could read and write. It wasn't until a script as simple as the Greek alphabet had both been invented and become widespread, a good three thousand years later, during the "golden age" of Athens in the late fifth century B.C., that message senders could assume some literacy in the general population. The Classical Greek and Roman urban citizens could read and write, even (!) women and slaves in many cases. But all of that was lost in the barbarian wars that followed. So during medieval times messages like family lineage had to be signaled by symbolic coats of arms, and shop signs needed to be pictorial: a loaf of bread for a bakery, a sheaf of wheat for a miller, a steer's head for a butcher shop. Widening literacy, born with the printing press and the Renaissance, is but a few centuries old.

Cloth, like clothing, provided a fine place for social messages. Patterned cloth in particular is infinitely variable and, like language, can encode arbitrarily any message whatever. Unlike language, however, it is not organized around sweeping syntactic patterns that can compress large amounts of information into simple rules. Hence one has to learn the textile and clothing code one element at a time. Within this riot of information, we will seek the chief goals of such systems and ferret out the basic principles.

What did ancient people try to accomplish when they deliberately made cloth bear meaning? A good look at folk customs and costumes recently in use reveals three main purposes. For one thing, it can be used to mark or announce information. It can also be used as a mnemonic device to record events and other data. Third, it can be used to invoke "magic"—to protect, to secure fertility and riches, to divine the future, perhaps even to curse. Today clothing is also used as an indicator of fashion, but the subtleties of that expression, which change so very rapidly, are largely beyond our ability to reconstruct in the ancient world.

The string skirt announcing the readiness of a woman for childbearing, discussed in Chapter 2, is an excellent example of the first category, the announcement of information. In the mountains of south-central Asia Kafir women wear distinctive headgear but remove it for a few days each month to indicate a temporary nonreadiness, menstruation.[2] Examples abound in Western society, too: for instance, the indication of mourning by wearing black.

Social rank, too, has probably always been encoded through symbols in the material, design, color, and embellishment of the clothing. In Rome, for instance, the emperor and no other enjoyed the privilege of wearing a robe entirely of "royal purple." Lower nobility, freeborn boys, and certain priests could sport at most a purple stripe, and others no purple at all. Both the Egyptians and the Sumerians were already marking their kings with crowns in the late fourth millennium. Because the top rulers were virtually always male, the royal headdress in Egypt also came to symbolize virility and included a false beard. When Hatshepsut, the step-mother and regent of Thutmose III, chose to take the throne herself around 1500 B.C, she faced the incongruity of needing to assume clearly male regalia as "pharaoh." Her statues—what was left of them after Thutmose III got through destroying them following her death twenty years later—are quite recognizable for the feminine delicacy of her face and the ever so slight modeling of her breasts, despite the traditional male kilt, false beard, and pharaonic wig that mark her as "king."

Cloth is also used to mark someone as a participant in a ceremony. In the Minoan scene of picking saffron discussed in Chapter 4, one of the young women wore a special veil with red polka dots, apparently to mark her as the center of the ritual. Minoan women

[2] They also wear small string skirts over their clothes, but I have not been able to determine what significance is attached to them. The Kafir people are Indo-European; Kafiristan is former Nuristan. These particular women lived in the Birir Valley of the Karakoram Mountains, at the northeastern tip of Afghanistan and Pakistan, according to information gleaned at the Ethnographic Museum, Florence, where photos of them were on display.

Figure 6.1. Minoan woman wearing a "sacred knot" at the back of her neck, signaling that she is in the service of the deity. Fresco from palace at Knossos, fifteenth century B.C.

also signaled some kind of special function by donning a scarf looped in a large knot at the back of the neck (fig. 6.1). This scarf is clearly not directly functional as clothing, and as a symbol it came to operate by itself. Thus we see the "sacred knot" repeatedly represented alone—carved in ivory, modeled in faience, or painted as a fresco motif. In the same way, Athena's sacred garment, the aegis, came to represent her in Classical times. Such symbols could be used alone to mark the location or existence of a ritual, much as the cross associated with Jesus is used in Christianity.

Hanging up a distinctive textile is a common way of making ordinary space special, even sacred. The folk of southern Sumatra place a special ritual cloth, made by the women of the family, as a backdrop to the key participants in the most important rites of passage, such as marriage, birth, or death. Mary Kahlenberg, an expert on Indonesian textiles, tells us that these special figured cloths "identified the nexus of ritual concern and by their very

Figure 6.2. Egyptian linen chest painted to represent the lord and lady enjoying refreshments in a shady pavilion formed from bright mats (end, with window) and textiles (roof). From the Eighteenth Dynasty tomb of Kha at Thebes, ca. 1450–1400 B.C.

presence delineated a ritual sphere." For example, "the bride sits on one or more . . . during specific times in the wedding cere-mony" and "the head of a deceased person rested on one . . . while the body was washed." Similarly, in Greek representations of funerals from the Geometric period (around 800 B.C) special back-drops, almost certainly cloths, hung over or behind the deceased.

Textiles can be chosen to mark off and provide information about secular space, too. In Egypt we see gaily colored mats and textiles hung to form sun-shading pavilions, where the lord and lady are sometimes depicted taking cooling refreshment from a servant girl (fig. 6.2). As time went on, the materials for these can-opies grew ostentatious, including brightly patterned rugs imported all the way from the Aegean. The rank, wealth, and "connections" of the family could thus be seen in how fancy the tent was and in the sorts of fabrics available to the family.

In Classical Greek times, too, important banquets were sometimes laid out in tents made of fancy textiles. For instance, Ion, the young hero of Euripides' play *Ion*, sets up such a pavilion for a feast to celebrate his reunion with his father. Since his mother had orphaned him as a baby on the steps of Apollo's temple at Delphi, he grew up as a temple servant. He thus has both the right and the duty to select from the rich temple storehouses a series of ornate cloths with which to make tent walls to shelter the sacred feast.

In all these ways, textiles mark special people, places, and times and announce specific information about them. But cloth can also be used as a vehicle for recording information, such as history or mythology.

In the third book of the *Iliad* (lines 125–27), Helen of Troy is described as weaving into her purple cloth "the many struggles of the horse-taming Trojans and the bronze-tunicked Achaians." In fact, as she does so, the messenger-goddess Iris comes to her in human disguise to say that the Greeks and Trojans are no longer fighting. Helen should come up onto the city wall to see for herself that now her first husband, Menelaos of Sparta, and her new husband, Paris of Troy, have engaged in single combat for her sake while the two armies ring around to watch. The passage implies that Helen should stop weaving old events and move on to recording the new ones.

Whether or not Helen herself actually wove episodes of the Trojan War, we know that Greek women sometimes did produce large storytelling cloths and that some of these "tapestries" were kept in the treasuries of Greek temples, where they could be seen upon occasion. (Greek temples, like medieval cathedrals, served as storehouses for cultural treasures, much like our modern museums.) It is just such textiles, covered with stories of Orion (the hunter who still chases the seven Pleiades sisters across the starry sky each night), Cecrops (the snake-bodied progenitor of Athens), and various barbarian battles, that Euripides has Ion use for his temporary banquet hall. Penelope's famous cloth, which she wove by day and unwove at night to fool her suitors, was almost certainly a story cloth. Because we are told that it was for her father-in-law's funeral, most people interpret the phrase *funerary cloth* (used by Homer when he tells the story in Book 2 of the *Odyssey*) as a shroud or winding sheet. But she could have woven that in a couple of weeks and wouldn't have come close to fooling her suitors for three years. Homer's audience would have known that only the weaving of a nonrepetitious pattern such as a story is so very time-consuming, but we who no longer weave or regularly watch others weave are more easily misled. We even possess pieces of two story cloths from Greek tombs in the Black Sea colonies, where textiles are preserved more often than in Greece (fig. 9.6).

We also know from Athenian records that young women periodically wove a new woolen garment to dress the ancient cult statue of Athena on the Acropolis and that this robe had scenes on it. Two priestesses called the "workers" *(ergastinai),* helped by two young girls chosen for the privilege from among the noble families of Athens, wove the saffron-colored robe over a period of nine months. This weaving took so long, even though the statue was only life-size, because it had woven into it in purple the important story of the battle between the gods and the giants. During this horrendous uproar (a "mythical" account of a major volcanic eruption, probably the explosion of Thera between 1600 and 1500 B.C.) Athena was credited with saving her city, Athens, from destruction. The entire festival, occasion of the new dress's presentation, was apparently a giant thank-you for salvation, and the story on the dress was of focal importance.

Records of history and mythohistory on textiles are not uncommon elsewhere in the world. The Hmong women who recently escaped to Los Angeles from Cambodia are busy making picture cloths in a traditional style, depicting the incidents of recent wars in their homeland, since they do not know how to write. Pile rugs knotted recently in Afghanistan sometimes show Stinger missiles downing flaming Soviet helicopters, and the conflict between Harold of England and William of Normandy (later William the Conqueror) was immortalized in the Bayeux Tapestry. (Ironically it is not, in fact, a tapestry, which is woven, but an embroidery, which is sewn.) This 231-foot wool-on-linen strip also shows a remarkable natural event, the passing of Halley's Comet, datable to April 1066.

Third and last, cloth and clothing often invoke magic in their encoding. Within this magical world, fertility, prosperity, and protection are three of the most common objectives.

We have seen that at least one modern descendant of the string skirt, the Greek *zostra,* has moved from being a signal that the woman could bear children to being a magical talisman to help her do so safely. The hooked lozenges woven on the modern string aprons from Serbia, Macedonia, Albania, and Romania (and embroidered on other parts of the women's costumes from these areas) are also to promote fertility (fig. 2.8).[3] Another motif on these same costumes that seems to be very old is the rose, a symbol of protection. George Bolling furnishes an interesting argument that Homer portrays the Trojan princess Andromache weaving specifically protective roses onto a cloak for her husband, Hector, at the moment at which she hears that he has been killed. Her work in vain, she drops her bobbin and rushes to the city wall to see for herself, wrenching from her head, as she collapses in grief, the elaborate headdress that marked her as a married woman. She is married no more. The pathos of her patient attempt to weave a frail web of magic for her beloved in the midst of this tumultuous war heightens the power of the scene enormously.[4]

Marija Gimbutas has drawn together extensive evidence of the

[3] The lozenge is intended to represent (rather graphically) the female vulva. Europe is not the only place where this symbol is used. In Hawaii, for example, the hula dancers traditionally make a lozenge shape with their hands to signify the same thing, and novices have to be careful not to make this sign accidentally when trying to make the partly similar sign for a house!

[4] The translation of the key word *thronoi* has long been a puzzle, and Bolling's set of arguments that it means roses is not accepted by all classicists. But he has considerable evidence, and the interpretation makes good literary sense out of an otherwise random set of details in the scene. Homer is not usually so uneconomical. The passage occurs in Book 22 (lines 438–72) of the *Iliad.*

use of bird and egg motifs, from far back in the Neolithic. These two—the bird and the egg, so closely related to each other—are still common today in Greek and Slavic territory, as well as in other parts of Europe, as potent fertility symbols. Eggs encapsulate the miraculous power of new life, and birds produce eggs, a life-giving process remote (to the naïve viewer) from our own live birth, and much more abstract. It is no accident, either, that eggs are part of Easter, the celebration of renewed life in the spring. Among the early Slavs (and residually down into this century), birds—especially white ones like swans—were thought to be rein-carnations of girls who had died before having children. Called *rusalki* or *vily* (willies), they were thought to possess the powers of fertility that they hadn't used during their lifetimes and to be able to bestow that fertility on the crops, animals, and households of those who pleased them. It is noteworthy that the farther north and west you go, the more crotchety and ill willed the willies become. In Ukraine, although they are touchy and you have to be nice to them, they are extremely beautiful and are likely to favor your crops and might even do your spinning for you. By the time you get up into southern Poland and eastern Germany, they are terrifying and often ugly creatures that will harm pregnant women and will dance or run to death any men unlucky enough to see them out in the forest at night. Someone who "has the willies" is being hounded by these wraiths. Images of birds and bird-maidens were carved on the houses, barns, and gates and embroidered on the folk costumes, a tradition which undoubtedly goes back much further than we are able to document in that area. Ladles for food, in a long tradition going back at least to the mid-second millen-nium B.C. on Russian soil, were formed in the shapes of water birds. Many a classical ballet has used variations on these themes to advantage, the most famous being *Swan Lake,* in which an evil sorcerer has turned a whole flock of maidens into white swans, and *Giselle,* in which the heroine dies of a broken heart in the first act and in the second saves her now-penitent lover from being danced to death at night in the forest by her companion willies.

Snakes, frogs, and fish (egg layers all) are also thought to bring wealth and fertility to the household, in various parts of Europe. Rusalki are sometimes shown as girl-headed fish, at least one Greek vase shows a woman overlaid with a fish figure, and snakes were an integral part of ancient Greek and Minoan lore. Phidias' great statue of Athena in the Parthenon, a temple built in part to give thanks for the end of the Persian Wars in 480 B.C., shows a snake emerging from under Athena's shield, which she has just set down, Victory standing in her hand. The message is clear: It is safe to come out now and go back to running happy, prosperous households. It would be interesting to know whether the famous Minoan statuettes of young women holding up snakes, found in religious contexts, had a similar meaning (fig. 6.3). Quite likely they did. An important Slavic pagan deity named Berehinia (Protectress[5]), whose cult survived up into this century and who still appears on ceremonial towels, shows up as a figure with a full skirt and raised arms, in exactly the same stance (fig. 6.4). In her hands she holds bunches of vegetation (flowers or grain), or birds, or occasionally snakes. Or sometimes (and this is the form we see often in Greek art) she controls with her upraised hands a pair of large animals. In Greek this form is known as the *Potnia Theron* (Mistress of Animals). In Ukrainian villages in the spring the women carried an image of the Protectress around the perimeter of all the village fields, in a solemn procession in the dead of night, to ensure fertility and protection throughout the coming year. Woe befell any male so foolish as to go out that night.

Europe had no monopoly on protective images on clothing, although we know much less about their history elsewhere. In Tutankhamon's tomb, among the wealth of royal clothing preserved there, lay a richly decorated tunic. Its neckhole forms an *ankh,* or long-life sign, with the king's name embroidered at the center of the cross and surrounded by the traditional *cartouche,* a protective oval made by a magic rope—the Egyptian equivalent of

---

[5] Perhaps also to be translated "riverbank spirit" since the Slavic word roots for "protect" and "riverbank" are homonymous.

Figure 6.3. Minoan statuette of a young woman—either priestess or goddess—displaying snakes in her hands, while a creature perches on her hat. This clay figurine, another similar one, and clay models of ornate dresses were found in the temple repositories at the great Cretan palace of Knossos (mid-second millennium B.C.).

the European magic circle. Around the bottom of the tunic are panels embroidered with an array of real and mythical beasts and plants, clearly of Syrian workmanship. What messages, if any, these were intended to convey to or for the pharaoh is unknown.

So far, all our examples of encoded magic have been in the form of decorative motifs. But people have devised more structural approaches to working magic. European folktales are full of refer-

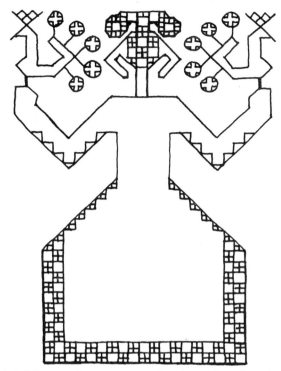

Figure 6.4. Nineteenth-century A.D. Russian embroidery design of the pagan Slavic goddess Berehinia, the protectress of women and their fertility, displaying birds in her hands. Such archaic survivals are frequent in Slavic folk art; the motif of the protecting goddess with her arms raised, hands full of birds or plants, is still in active use in Ukraine and other Slavic areas.

ences to the making of magical garments, especially girdles, in which the magic seems to be inherent in the weaving, not merely in special decoration.

One possibility is to weave the spell in as number magic. In Chapter 2 we mentioned a Middle Bronze Age belt from Roswinkel, in the Netherlands, that smacked of number magic. The weaver chose warp threads of red wool for her work, 24 spun one direction, and 24 spun the other way. (Opposite spins catch the light differently and, when placed next to each other, give a striped effect.) She divided the bunch spun one way into 3 sets of 8, and the other bunch into 4 sets of 6, and alternated them. All this is perhaps perfectly innocent, but in this same area of northern Germany, Holland, and Denmark at a somewhat later date these numbers were considered particularly sacred. The scheme is best known from the runic alphabet, which at first consisted of 24 let-ters in 3 sets of 8, and later of 32 letters in 4 sets of 8. Also important were 3 and 6. Thus the handsome red sash from Ros-winkel looks suspiciously like a "magic girdle."[6]

The Batak tribes of Sumatra generate woven magic another way. In one area, the ethnographers tell us, the women wove spe-cial magical cloths on circular warps, which were never cut because

> the continuity of the warp across the gap where the woof had not been woven in was said to be magic to insure the continuity of life from the mother to the child. . . . The birth of the child was represented by the beginning of the woof at one side of the uncut fringe. As one drew the cloth through the hands it represented the growing up of the child, and when the other side of the uncut fringe was reached, it represented the beginning of a new generation whose life would repeat that of the mother, and so indefinitely.

Thus the circular form of the cloth itself is seen as magical.

Among the Batak the act of creation itself is viewed as women's special work, not only in producing babies, who grow where noth-ing has existed before, but also in creating cloth, which comes into being where nothing has existed before. Cloth and its making are

---

[6] Scholars have assumed that number magic began with the introduction of Mith-raism into the area, via the Romans. The Mithraic religion, from the Near East, is full of number magic. But I keep wondering why Mithraism took hold just exactly here. Could it be because the local people were already into number magic and viewed the new cult as enlarging their "information" on a subject already important to them?

thus taken as analogs for life and birth, in every sense. Mattiebelle Gittinger tells us, further:

> [W]omen were traditionally responsible for the cultivation of the cotton, its harvesting, cleaning, spinning and, as today, dyeing, starching and weaving the yarns. However, the woven textile carries connotations beyond those of merely women's labor. The *ulos* [ritual cloth] is a symbol of creation and fertility. In the very process of weaving the woman creates a new object—a united whole—from seemingly disparate elements. This magical quality can escape none who see the woven cloth emerge behind the moving shuttle. Further, just as music is an experience monitored through time, so too does the total cloth emerge as the finished expression of the metrical time invested in each throw of the weft. The cloth thus becomes a metaphor for both time and fruition.

When a girl is pregnant for the first time, her parents give her a cloth made specially for her. Called her soul cloth, it is covered with tiny designs that are used to foretell her future (yet another use of magic). She will rely on this cloth throughout her life "as a guardian of her well being." In particular, "its inherent revitalizing and protective powers are sought in the time of child birth . . . and in cases of her or her child's illness." The motifs on these particular cloths, and their arrangements into zones, are thought to be very old, for they are characteristic of the sorts of designs found on prehistoric cast bronzes in Southeast Asia.

We have looked at the various purposes for which cloth was deliberately encoded: giving or recording information and invoking the powers of magic. But how did people come upon the codes they adopted?

Perhaps the most frequent means of arriving at a sign is through imitation on some level, some sort of analogy of form or color. The Batak, for example, use a circular warp in analogy with cycles of life. In Europe the hooked lozenge imitated the vulva, to assure fertility, and roses were invoked for protection, apparently because of their thorns. (As the thorn protects the rose, so the rose protects me.) The Slavs (and many other peoples) use the color red to signify vitality, in imitation of red blood; until recently men wore red sashes and women embroidered the shirts and chemises of both sexes with red motifs (roses and lozenges in abundance). Our earliest European example of a person clad in a white tunic or chemise with woolen overwrap, from the Kuban in the third millennium, already had red tassels of thread and purplish red embroidery on that tunic (Chapter 5).

As another example of analogy, note that Slavic red embroideries are generally located at the openings of the clothing—neckhole, wrists, and shirttail. This decoration was meant to discourage demons from crawling in at the openings since demons were thought to cause illnesses, bodily and mental. The notion of the demons entering is an analogic construct, based on such events as vermin creeping into food and contaminating it. The placement of the demon repellent (life-bolstering colors and designs) follows logically from such images.

The northern Mediterranean use of the color yellow, on the other hand, appears to derive from association. If the theory is correct that prehistoric women in the Aegean Islands, like their modern descendants, saw saffron as a specific medicine for menstrual ills, then their use of this bright yellow dye and medicine came to link the color with women. The women may even have come to dye their clothes with saffron expressly to avoid—to turn away—the sickness ahead of time.

Much of the time, however, as with language, the relation between the code and the meaning is purely arbitrary, as, for instance, with number magic or the Roman stripe denoting rank. But even within this group one can spot an occasional symbol that started out as something more practical. Thus veils for the bride, while a mere token now, once served to cover the sexually "unknown" woman until the proper moment.

In all these ways, then—through imitation, analogy, and arbitrary symbols often viewed as magical—human cultures have over time built a sort of language through clothing, allowing us to communicate even with our mouths shut.

7

Cloth for the Caravans

One heavy cloth
to Ashur-Malik
previously
for his caravan-trip I gave;
but the silver from it
he has not yet brought
me . . .
When the purse
you send,
include some wool:
wool
in the city
is costly.
　　—Cuneiform letter from
　　Assyrian businesswoman,
　　to her merchant husband,
　　　　　ca. 1900 B.C.

The realization that domestic animals could be exploited for wool, milk, and muscle power while alive, not just for meat when killed, revolutionized human society as profoundly as domestication itself. By 4000 B.C. in the Near East we see major changes

occurring as a result. The advent of plowing with large draft animals, as we have seen, permanently removed women, especially
those with children, from the mainstream of food production.
Draft animals were big and dangerous, but the sowing of large
fields of grain provided such an efficient source of food that there
could be no going back to the old ways. Full-scale agriculture was
a largely male occupation.

On the other hand, women had new things to occupy them. For
some, this probably included small-scale dairy farming, since the
making of yogurt and cheese from the milk of domestic animals
increased the variety of storable foods and got around the problem
that most adult humans can't digest fresh milk. The ability to produce the enzymes that break down milk sugar (lactose) in the
stomach, before it gets to the intestines and causes major trouble,
is controlled by a dominant gene but has to be selected for. Longtime pastoral populations, like the Masai of Africa and the people
of northern Europe, have developed that trait. The Masai consume
much milk, while northern European cooking relies heavily on
fresh cream and milk. Mediterranean and steppe peoples, however, developed their cuisines around yogurt, cheese, and koumiss
(fermented milk). In these products, nontoxic strains of bacteria
(which are carefully preserved and transmitted from one batch to
the next) have been introduced to break down or "predigest" the
sugar, thereby functioning also as a short-term preservative. Thus
the French consume the largest amount of milk per capita of any
nation in the world today—almost entirely in the form of cheese.
Most Chinese adults, on the other hand, cannot tolerate milk,
yogurt, or cheese in any form. Their civilization did not use milk,
and genetic selection moved in other directions.

In areas where milk did become important, the work became so
great that men and women divided it. Thus in Mesopotamia in the
third millennium B.C., where the milk herds were large, sculptures
show that men tended the flocks and milked them, but cylinder
seals depict women doing a task that resembles churning.

As the reliance on grain increased, another related task grew up that fit well with child rearing: grinding the grain for use, once it came in from the fields. Thus the equipment for spinning and weaving lies side by side with the grinders in archaeological excavations throughout the Near East—for example, at the little Minoan village of Myrtos (see Chapter 4) or the Iron Age palace of Gordion, in central Anatolia. At Gordion the servingwomen lived in special quarters. Each of these houses yielded scores of spindle whorls, hundreds of loom weights—approximately six hundred in one case—and long rows of grindstones. Our earliest European author, Homer, repeatedly yokes the two occupations to each other and to females, as we have seen in the *Odyssey* (7.103–05):

> Fifty serving women belonged to the house,
> some of whom grind on the millstone the ruddy grain, while
> others weave at the looms and twirl their spindles. . . .

Ordinary housewives daily ground the flour and worked on cloth for the household, while the rich bought slaves to do these tiresome jobs for them. Slavery now flourished—and indeed lasted until self-powered machines became available to do the tasks instead.

Using animals for muscle power solved yet another problem: It made it far easier to move goods about, especially after the invention of the axled wheel, which made a load-bearing cart possible. In a sense, the "wheel" had already been in use for some time, in the form of a spindle whorl, and log rollers had probably been in use since the Palaeolithic. The trick was to figure out how to *attach* the rolling part to a nonrotating load bed. Of course, carts needed roads—a new concept in the Neolithic—not just narrow footpaths. People had to construct such roads, or at least beat them flat, little by little. (Many a road in use today in Europe and the Near East was first laid down in the Bronze or Iron Age.) Furthermore, the earliest type of wheel (the solid slice-of-a-log kind we see so clearly in Sumerian representations of 2500 B.C.) was cumbersomely heavy. As a result of both these factors—cumbersome vehicles and few roads—pack animals were far more effective than wheeled transportation for a long time, for both great distances and difficult terrain. They still are, in remote regions.

The ability to transport large quantities of goods with animal power (however harnessed) meant that trade could blossom, and women's textiles with it. Trade in small luxury goods like shells from the seacoasts, amber from the Baltic, lapis lazuli from eastern Iran, and obsidian from scattered volcanic sites (such as parts of Armenia, central Turkey, and the island of Melos) had been trickling across the continents for a long time. Early in the Neolithic, people had discovered that obsidian (volcanic glass) made particularly sharp stone knives, and explorers hunted ever farther for sources of these precious nodules. In fact, one of the first large towns, Çatal Hüyük in south-central Turkey (see Chapter 3), grew up shortly before 6000 B.C. near the foot of a great volcano that in eons past had spewed quantities of obsidian onto the flatland around. The local inhabitants grew rich, it seems, from trading this volcanic glass. Among the crafts that flourished in the leisure provided by this relative wealth was weaving. Fine textiles of several types (both wide and narrow plain-weave fabrics, weft twining of two sorts, fringed edges, rolled and whipped hems, and reinforced selvedges) have survived where they lay buried under the house floors, wrapped around the excarnated bones of ancestors. Unfortunately the portion of the town in which people carried out their crafts has not yet been excavated, so we know nothing of that aspect of this society's organization.

The size, wealth, and complexity of this very early town, however, show the powerful effects of trading an important raw material, in a way strongly parallel to towns later involved in metal trade. As with obsidian, the advent of metal triggered a search that took people far and wide. They sought most especially for the tin with which to harden copper into bronze, as well as for gold and silver for jewelry and tableware. Luxury goods such as fancy textiles and ornate metal vessels, manufactured in the growing cities,

Figure 7.1. Map of Near Eastern trade routes, third to second millennium B.C., including important sites mentioned in this chapter.

often paid for the new raw materials with which to make more, in a never-ending cycle. All these goods traveled along the ever-extending trade routes by means of another invention, the pack-animal caravan.

An archaeologist excavating in central Turkey in 1925 located the end point of one of the most important of the ancient Near Eastern caravan routes, at a city known in early times as Kanesh (fig. 7.1). Its modern name, Kültepe, simply means "ash mound"—a frequent place-name in Turkey, where people have lived, warred, and burned one another's cities down for thousands of years. Kanesh was no exception. Enemies burned it to the ground around 1750 B.C., about two hundred years after the Assyrians, trekking westward across six hundred miles in pursuit of metals, had established a trade colony, or *karum,* there. We know from the cuneiform records that nine such karums eventually grew up, of which Karum Kanesh was the largest. It also functioned as the center of the network. (A second of the nine was recently discovered and excavated at Acemhöyük, a little farther west.) The city of Kanesh, inhabited by the native people, sat atop a high mound composed of the accumulated debris of many centuries of living there. Near Eastern houses were commonly built of mud brick, which lasts at best a few decades, and each time a house needed rebuilding, the remains of the previous dwelling were simply leveled and the new house was constructed on top. As a result, such city mounds grew rather quickly, and they can still be seen all over the landscape in the Near East today. Being high up was an advantage to defense, moreover, especially when the man-made cliff was enhanced by a city wall.

At Kanesh the Assyrian karum lies just outside the parapets of the native town. There the foreign merchants lived, did their business, and kept their records—written, fortunately for us, in cuneiform on clay tablets, which survive the millennia very well. We have accounts of their transactions with the local king and his deputies, who inspected the goods from each incoming caravan and took a hefty portion as import tax before allowing the merchants to start selling the rest on the open market. (Even so, the 100 percent profits available clearly made such taxation bearable.)

We also have many of the letters that the traders' wives wrote to them from far away in Ashur, the capital of Assyria—letters not just about how the family was getting along but also about business matters. For at least some of the wives, daughters, and sisters were in business for themselves, acting as textile suppliers to their menfolk six hundred miles away in Anatolia and taking considerable profit therefrom to use for their own purposes.

The men's trade efforts revolved principally around metals. Anatolia was rich in silver and gold, as well as in copper. But to alloy copper into a bronze tough enough for tools and weapons, the local people needed tin as a hardener. The Assyrians had access to sources of tin far to the east of Assyria, and this they transported westward across the continent, first to Assyria and then in part on to Syria and Anatolia.

Tin is heavy, however—too heavy to load much of it onto a donkey's back. But mixed with textiles, which are bulky (too bulky to put enough of them on an animal for a profitable trip), the load is well balanced. Tin and textiles: That's what the Old Assyrian traders carried for nearly two hundred years from Ashur in northern Mesopotamia to their trade colonies in central Anatolia. The tin belonged to the merchants, but many of the textiles were the produce and property of the womenfolk, as we learn in circumstantial detail from the little clay tablets.

Assyrian textiles found a ready market in Anatolia, and the women scrambled to get a few more woven before each packtrain departed, negotiating directly with the caravan drivers to carry the merchandise. Lamassi, the wife of the merchant Pushu-ken, is the woman about whom we know the most. She writes to her husband such business information as: "Kuluma is bringing you 9 textiles, Idi-Suen 3 textiles; Ela refused to accept textiles (for transport); Idi-Suen refused to accept (another) 5 textiles."

These drivers had to load their donkeys carefully for the long trip over the mountains; one letter writer warns the recipient not to pile too much on his donkeys. The cloths were put into protective bags or wrappers, roughly five to a bag but sometimes more. The cloths might be sorted by quality (ordinary or expensive), and the package might be sealed by the woman sending it. Most of the tin, too, was sealed, after being wrapped in special cloths that were also sold at the other end. Then there was usually some loose tin, purposely left unsealed so the driver could trade it as needed along the way for his travel expenses. It was so much in demand that it could function as ready cash. (Coins, the first true money, were not invented for another fifteen hundred years.) The records tell us that one particular donkey heading for Kanesh carried twenty-six cloths of two sorts, sixty-five units of sealed tin, and nine units of loose tin. Usually the goods were grouped into two side packs, carrying ten or twelve textiles each and/or some tin, plus a smaller pack across the top carrying half a dozen cloths or some "loose" tin and the driver's personal belongings.

At the other end the merchants sold the textiles and the tin for the best prices they could get, after paying the import taxes in kind to the local rulers. Then they sent the profits on the textiles back well and what poorly. A letter from Puzur-Ashur to Waqartum (apparently Lamassi's daughter) says that he is sending her one mina of silver (about a pound), and please to make more fine textiles like the one he had just received from her, preferably sending them back with the same driver bringing her the payment. But, he says, put more wool into it, and "let them comb one side of the textile; they should not shear it; its weave should be close." And don't send any more "Abarnian" textiles, he instructs her; it must be that he can't sell them readily because Anatolian tastes differed from Assyrian ones. That does not mean, however, not to keep weaving. In fact, he concludes, "if you don't manage to make fine textiles [in time for the caravan], as I hear [it] there are plenty for sale over there. Buy (them) for me and send (them) to me."

From such little remarks we glean that, unlike the women of later times who were strictly confined to the harems, these women were free to go out to the marketplaces and buy textiles from other women or buy the wool to make more cloths. They also dealt directly with the donkey drivers and sometimes were asked to attend to legal matters for their absent men.

The women's rights were still far from equal to those of their husbands. Contemporary dowry contracts from farther south in Babylonia show that if a woman refused to stay married to her husband, she could be drowned, whereas if he refused *her,* he merely paid her a fine. But women owned their own property and could engage in business for themselves. One woman's dowry tablet lists a set of weights and a cylinder seal in its own box among her possessions; she was all set up for some sort of commerce. Another Old Babylonian dowry included four slaves or servants, gold and silver earrings and bracelets, "one shekel of gold as a ring for the front of her nose," as well as "ten dresses, twenty headdresses [fig. 7.2], one blanket, two coats, one leather bag." Other gear included a huge cauldron, two grindstones for flour, four chests, a bed, five chairs, a basket, two trays, and two jars of oil, one of them scented.

Figure 7.2. Sumerian women were fond of large headdresses, like this one on a mid-third millennium B.C. statue found at Mari on the middle Euphrates. See figs. 7.5 and 7.6 for other fancy headdresses.

Not every girl was so well equipped. Of the ten dowry tablets collected and published by Stephanie Dalley, only two mention looms. The poorest girl received "two beds, two chairs, one table, two chests," plus two grindstones and two empty jars. The ten shekels of silver earnest money put down by the groom's family, we are told, had been duly tied to the hem of the girl's dress. Thus, according to the custom, when the girl was delivered and accepted, the earnest money was automatically returned and the marriage deal complete. The dowry list, however, ensured that if the man divorced her or left her a widow, she would get back everything that belonged to her personally, without his relatives being able to cheat her of it.

The particularly rich lady with the nose ring, a priestess, was supplied not only with the homemaking equipment listed above but also with "one ox, two three-year-old cows, thirty sheep, twenty minas (10 kg) of wool" plus "two combs for wool, three hair combs, three wooden spoons, two wooden *asu*-looms(?), one wooden container full of spindles, one small wooden pot-rack."

What with two looms, spindles, and all those sheep, she was set up to carry on the kind of home-based business that Lamassi was engaged in. Indeed, among the cloths regularly transported to Anatolia from Assyria are specifically "Akkadian ones"—that is, cloths from central Babylonia.

If, however, like Lamassi and Waqartum, one had no sheep of one's own, getting the wool to make the next textiles was sometimes a problem. In three different letters Lamassi asks her husband to send her wool all the way from Anatolia, complaining that in Ashur it is very expensive at the moment. (In one of these she even asks him to hide her silver in the middle of the wool, to avoid the attention of a tax collector who is after her.) Sending wool from Anatolia was unusual but not difficult. In general, the men expected to buy up gold and silver in Anatolia to send home, but when silver was scarce, or when something else profitable offered itself, such as particularly nice Anatolian cloths (some of them are mentioned as "red"), that would do, too. Since the silver and gold were rather smaller than the tin and textiles of equivalent value, many fewer donkeys went home to Assyria than caravaned out to Anatolia (some were sold off at the karum), and even those might be more lightly laden. So there was plenty of room for the wool. Sometimes the men even included presents such as jewelry for their wives. The women, for their part, occasionally sent other "good buys" to their husbands. A letter to Pushu-ken from someone else mentions that Lamassi had just arranged to send her husband ten textiles with one caravan, and with another driver a bundle of minerals.

The money these women earned was not for playing around with, however. They used it chiefly to run their households, to pay taxes, and as capital to buy raw materials for the next textiles to be woven. As a result, they complained bitterly when the men delayed payment. Waqartum writes to her brother that he told her not to go to a solicitor and that she trusted him and did as he said. "But to-day I mean even less to you than a pawned (?) slave-girl, for to a slave-girl you at least measure out regularly food rations; but here I have to live from my debt(s)." She complains that he has swiped the mina of gold that her husband dispatched to her as her profit from various cloths, which she enumerates at length, totaling "in all fifteen textiles of good quality. All this is my production, my goods entrusted for (sale with) profit. . . . My gold you have taken! I beg you . . . , send it to me with the first caravan and give me courage!"

We get tantalizing glimpses of the households they ran. Lamassi had several children; the older sons went off to join their father at Karum Kanesh, while the daughters stayed in Ashur and undoubtedly learned to weave by helping their mother. Waqartum seems to have been the oldest daughter, doing weaving for her own profit, as we have just seen, apparently in her own household. She was also a priestess, and one gathers that her husband, like her brothers, joined her father's firm in Anatolia. But there were others in Lamassi's house, as we see from the following letter she composed to her husband, Pushu-ken: "About the fact that I did not send you the textiles about which you wrote, your heart should not be angry. As the girl has become grown-up, I had to make a pair of heavy textiles for (placing/wearing) on the wagon. Moreover I made (some) for the members of the household and the children. Consequently I did not manage to send you textiles. Whatever textiles I (lit.: "my hand") can manage I will send you with later caravans." Klaas R. Veenhof, the scholar who has translated and analyzed many of these letters, remarks that "Lamassi is occupied by some important event in the family—mentioned in several of her letters . . . , apparently a religious ceremony involving [a] daughter. . . . In view of these ceremonies the family had to be provided with garments and 'textiles for the wagon.' . . . Unfortunately we do not know who the *nisi bitim* [members of the household] were, but it is possible that these people co-operated in the production of textiles in Lamassi's house." It is also conceivable that part of the profit at one time or another went to purchase slave girls who could help with the weaving and thus expand the business. Capital, then as now, can beget capital.

I shall take many garments with my tribute to Babylon; I
have collected together all the garments that are available
here, but they are not sufficient.
> —Letter to a Mesopotamian queen from her
> husband, after the neighboring city was sacked
> by Hammurabi of Babylon; ca. 1820 B.C.

Women of the merchant class were not the only ones running textile establishments. Queens did it, too, but for the "state" rather
than directly for themselves. The caravans for which these textiles
were destined carried royal "gifts" from one court to another, an
important part of ancient diplomacy which the kings arranged and
the queens, to some extent, provided for. Again we learn about
it from cuneiform letters, in this case letters to rather than from
the women.

Iltani was the daughter of King Samu-Addu of Karana, a small
city-state on the caravan route between Assyria to the east and
Anatolia to the west. She lived a couple of generations after
Lamassi and Waqartum and became queen of Karana when her
husband, Aqba-hammu, usurped the throne from her brother.
Times were tough. Samu-Addu had lost his throne to an earlier
usurper, and his son had gotten it back only to lose it to Iltani's
husband when political alliances shifted again. Assyria was losing
its grip on the trade routes, while Hammurabi of Babylon—he of
the famous law code—was on the rise, and Aqba-hammu seems to
have seen what was coming. History proved him right: Iltani's
brother fled to the great city of Mari, on the Euphrates River to
the south, and when its ruler Zimri-Lim, the strongest man in
northern Mesopotamia, refused to become Hammurabi's vassal,
Hammurabi sacked the city ruthlessly. Aqba-hammu took heed
and lost no time in paying tribute to the great Babylonian prince—
better safe than sorry.

Compared with the great palace operations at Mari, the royal workshops at Karana were small-time stuff (although officials from Mari reported the Karana palace to be especially beautiful). Iltani had at her disposal only about twenty-five textile workers, in comparison with eighty-seven in one of five textile-related workshops at Mari. Because Karana was a fairly small state, the king could not afford the luxury of a man paid to manage the palace and its business, as Zimri-Lim could at Mari, and his queen took over much more of this work than her Mari counterpart, Queen Shibtu. According to Stephanie Dalley, who has compiled the information from the tablets, Iltani had

> "some 15 women who spun and wove (2 of them brought a child) and 10 male textile workers. In addition she employed 2 millers, and a brewer named Samkanum; and 6 girls who worked . . . in an unknown capacity. 13 more women, 3 of them [each] with a child, worked for Iltani, again with an uncertain task; she had a doorman named Kibsi-etar, and a man called Anda in charge of pack-asses, also 4 other men."

A man named Kissurum supplied her with wool and did her textile accounts (cf. fig. 7.3), "which had to be checked and sealed by Iltani." The men involved with textiles—to judge from nearly contemporary archives at other Mesopotamian sites—were most likely employed in such ancillary crafts as dyeing the wool or "finishing" the woven cloth in some way (cleaning it, putting in sizing, fluffing or shearing the nap, etc.). Men elsewhere were also assigned the arduous job of making felt for pads, covers, and linings out of sheep's wool or goat hair.

Palace workers seem to have come largely from the spoils of war, from inheritance, or occasionally from gifts. While on campaign Zimri-Lim wrote to his queen: "To Šibtu say, thus (says) your lord: I have just sent you some female-weavers. In among them are (some) *ugbabātum* priestesses. Pick out the *ugbabātum* priestesses and assign them (i.e. the rest) to the house of the female-weavers." He then instructed her to select the most attractive ones from both this group and the previous batch of captives,

Figure 7.3. Hittite lady spinning, attended by a scribe holding clay tablet and stylus. Stone relief from Maraş, in eastern Turkey, ca. 800 B.C.

to send them to a particular overseer (apparently to become religious singers), and to be sure that all of them got enough rations "so that their appearance does not worsen." Slaves were valued for their work, so it behooved one to feed them. They might even be blind, but if they could still work, they merited their keep. A blind woman who ground grain is listed among the recipients of rations in another city, and her rations were as big as anyone else's. The children of slaves could grow up to become valuable slaves, too, adding to the estate. We know that women who spun and wove in the palace and had children were issued extra rations to feed them.

Iltani, on the other hand, had to live with the fact that her husband was too small a vassal to do very much plundering, and far from being supplied with lots of extra slaves, the queen was constantly being importuned for slaves she felt she could not spare. For example, one of her sisters, a priestess, writes: "The slaves whom my father gave me have grown old; now, I have sent half a mina of silver to the king; allow me my claim and get him to send me slaves who have been captured recently, and who are trustworthy. In recollection of you, I have sent to you five minas of first-rate wool and one container of shrimps." A little bribery there. Presents of slaves were not uncommon among the rich, but Dalley mentions several letters showing that giving away slaves who had served faithfully for a lifetime "was regarded as an insensitive thing to do." She cites a plea to Zimri-Lim from a woman who "begs him not to give away her ageing mother as a present." On the other hand, one wonders whether very old and very young slaves were sometimes given away as a means of satisfying a request for a slave while getting rid of a liability. Apparently Iltani once sent as a present a serving boy who was so young that the recipient complains that he has to take care of the boy rather than the other way around!

Other glimpses into daily life, through these archives, show us that most of the women working in the palaces were either making cloth—spinning and weaving (fig. 7.4)—or helping with the food. The latter involved grinding grain, drawing water, cooking, baking, and making beverages (iced fruit juices and wines were among the summer favorites). In Iltani's palace, however, Dalley points out that "the millers were men, probably for heavier work on a much larger scale." Women singers and musicians of both sexes entertained, a woman doctor was available at Mari, and no fewer than nine of the Mari scribes were women. The women who were most comfortably fixed, after the queen, seem to have been the priestesses. One of Iltani's sisters was a priestess in a nearby city, while another oversaw some type of weaving in Ashur.

The raw wool from which Iltani's workers made the palace textiles came mostly from a regular supplier, the accountant named Kissurum—presumably from palace-owned flocks out in the countryside. Occasionally, as in the case just quoted, wool came in as a personal gift and may then have been used by the queen for her own dresses. In one case she herself sent wool to a less fortunate friend living in a city that had just been plundered. Sometimes, too, her husband sent her wool directly, especially when he was in a hurry for gifts to distribute. One letter from him says: "Now, I have sent you 25 kg of wool for 50 garments. Make those gar-

Figure 7.4. Mosaic fragments showing two women working with a spindle. From Mari, on the middle Euphrates, early second millennium B.C.

ments quickly. I need those garments." Large though it may seem, the size of Aqba-hammu's requisition differs radically from those made by Zimri-Lim in Mari—in one case, six hundred garments at once, in five different colors!

Most often the king needed the cloth and garments for gifts, not only for the formidable Hammurabi himself but also for minor vassals. One letter to Iltani reads: "The king of Shirwun has arrived; he asked the caravan that was going out of Karana, but it had no garments fit for presents available. Now send me quickly any garments that you have available, whether of first-rate or second-rate quality, for presents." Some of the textiles were used, however, simply to clothe the palace personnel. Zimri-Lim received an almost comical letter from his trusted overseer of palace business, who finally turned to the king to resolve a dispute between two obstinate heads of departments. It seems that the four hundred palace workers were due new sets of clothes, but only one hundred had actually received them. When the manager looked into the matter, each of the two functionaries insisted that

Figure 7.5. Figures of women spinning (right), warping (center), and weaving (left), from four Mesopotamian cylinder seals of the late fourth millennium B.C. The women typically sat on low stools or the floor to spin. The warping frame consisted of two upright poles set in heavy blocks—seen here twice in side view and once in an awkward top view. The loom was pegged out on the ground, and two weavers squatted on either side, as in Egypt (fig. 3.5).

it was the other one's job to provide the remaining clothes, and neither would budge from his position.

The types of cloth provided were quite varied, and those intended for presents were often quite expensive. One request to Iltani reads, "Send me quickly the garments, both with appliqué and without appliqué, which you have made." Zimri-Lim, on the other hand, says he will take to Babylon, as a royal gift, a Syrian-style carpet—most likely, from what we now know of the history of pattern weaving, a tapestry-woven rug like the kilims still made in Anatolia today. Near Eastern kings right up into this century traditionally gave such carpets as royal favors.

This palace system of manufacturing and distributing cloth and clothing was not entirely new in the nineteenth century B.C. Two kings of the Sumerian city-state of Lagash, who lived just after 2400 B.C., were already setting up for big business. Lugalanda, the earlier of the two, employed twelve spinners and weavers. Year by year the number increased, until a dozen years later his successor, Urukagina, had 114, divided into several workshops or weaving houses, each with an overseer.

The people making the textiles at this earlier date are all women, mostly designated as weavers with a few extra women called spinners (figs. 7.5 and 7.4). But four spinners cannot supply thirty-seven weavers (these are the figures we have for Year 6). Spinning by hand takes much longer than weaving, so one has to assume that the weavers in these shops normally spun what they then wove. On the other hand, the craft of spinning is quicker to learn and requires far less equipment than weaving, so perhaps women with less skill were assigned to help out with the spinning, perhaps even while learning weaving as apprentices. They are recorded as receiving the lowest amount of adult rations (one-eighth of a unit), along with a few of the weavers. At the beginning a man known to be involved in other palace departments functioned as overseer of the textile women, and by the beginning of Year 6 of Lugal-anda's reign, two more men had been added as group overseers. But the rapid expansion in the next few years apparently made it necessary to promote some of the women weavers to the rank of overseer. Unfortunately, for them the title carried no known tangible benefits, only the extra responsibilities, because they still got one-sixth of a measure of rations, like the other "senior" weavers, instead of half a measure, like the male overseers.

Among the ration lists for these workshops (our chief source of information here), we see a few children listed, both boys and girls—clearly the children of the women. They are assigned a twelfth of a unit of grain each. In addition, however, there are a small number of "orphans," also both male and female and also given a twelfth of grain. It would be interesting to know whether they were assigned for apprenticeship (but then, why boys?) or for the women in the shop to act as their wet nurses or foster mothers—a second job in addition to weaving.

Although we do not know what products these particular women were making, we know from excavation that royalty was already splendidly arrayed. The sumptuous burial of a lady known in the archaeological literature as Queen Shub-ad (or Puabi)[1] astonished the world when Sir Leonard Woolley published the Ur excavation reports in 1934. Some seventy-four retainers, male and

---

[1] The exact readings of these early cuneiform signs are uncertain but need not concern us here. Many of the splendid artifacts described below are on display in the University Museum in Philadelphia and the British Museum in London.

Figure 7.6. Headdress of the queen of Ur, fashioned of gold and precious stones and worn over a huge wig. The Sumerian queen was buried with seventy-four servants, many of whom also wore elaborate headdresses. Mesopotamia, mid-third millennium B.C.

female, had been drugged and killed in the great "Death Pit" surrounding her tomb. Guards fell beside their weapons, cart attendants by their animals, musicians next to their great inlaid harps. Each lady-in-waiting departed this world wearing an ornate headdress of gold and silver, huge gold earrings, and necklaces of precious stones. The queen herself wore an even larger headdress over what must have been a huge bouffant wig (fig. 7.6). The garments of all the ladies radiated splendor. Woolley says of them:

> In the case of two or three bodies . . . a stray fragment of cloth was preserved . . . , a thick but closely woven fabric the dust of which still retained a bright ochrous red colour. Very many of

these same bodies had round their wrists beads of gold, carne-
lian, and lapis-lazuli which had not been strung together as loose
bracelets but had been sewn on to the edges of the sleeves of a
garment. . . . [Around her waist] Queen Shub-ad had a row of
gold rings pendant from a heavy band of beads which were sewn
to a cloth background.

After citing much more evidence for the positions of durable
things like beads, he concludes:

[I]t would seem, therefore, that the costume of ladies of the
court, at least, included a coat reaching only to the waist and
having long . . . sleeves; the cuffs and bottom hem of the coat
might be enriched with beads, or along the hem there might be
a row of pendant rings in shell or metal; it is likely that the coat
was fastened in front and the border with its ring pendants did
not hang loose but formed a belt in one piece with the garment.
. . . Of skirts and under-garments no traces were discovered.

Such are the problems of trying to learn about something as perishable as cloth. In another spot, however, Woolley had better
luck.

[T]here lay round the legs and feet of the skeleton a great quantity of cloth; it was all reduced to fine powder but did, so long
as it was undisturbed, preserve the texture of the original sufficiently for three varieties of material to be distinguished. One
stuff was rather coarse with a plain over-and-under right-angle
weave; the second was a finely woven cloth with a diagonal rib;
the third was a loosely woven right-angle weave fabric on one
side of which were long threads forming either a very deep pile
or else "tassels" like those on the skirts of the figures represented
on the monuments.

Clearly the palace weavers and seamstresses of Mesopotamia
were far down the road to producing sumptuous clothing by 2500

B.C., the approximate time of these burials. The labor may have been increasingly that of slave women—hapless captives of the incessant wars that had sprung up over water rights, territorial disputes, and the fun of owning sheer material wealth. But in some places, at least, an independent-minded middle class of free women continued for centuries to create handsome, salable textiles for the busy commercial caravans run by their equally business-oriented menfolk.

Even a millennium after the Old Assyrian caravans ceased to ply their routes to Anatolia, in another corner of the Near East we get a glowing picture in the last chapter of Proverbs (31.10–25) of the Hebrew woman who still worked industriously at home for the household good:

> Who can find a virtuous woman? for her price is far above rubies. The heart of her husband doth safely trust in her. . . . She seeketh wool, and flax, and worketh willingly with her hands. She is like the merchants' ships; she bringeth her food from afar. She riseth also while it is yet night, and giveth meat to her household, and a portion to her maidens. She considereth a field, and buyeth it: with the fruit of her hands she planteth a vineyard. . . . She perceiveth that her merchandise is good: her candle goeth not out by night. She layeth her hands to the spindle, and her hands hold the distaff. She stretcheth out her hand to the poor; yea, she reacheth forth her hands to the needy. She is not afraid of the snow for her household: for all her household are clothed with scarlet. She maketh herself coverings of tapestry; her clothing is [fine linen] and purple. . . . She maketh fine linen, and selleth it; and delivereth girdles unto the merchant. Strength and honour are her clothing; and she shall rejoice in time to come.

8

Land of Linen

The Egyptians do practically everything backwards from other people, in their customs and laws—among which the women go to market and make deals, whereas the men stay at home and weave; and other folk weave by pushing the weft upwards, but the Egyptians push it down. Men carry burdens on their heads, whereas women do so on their shoulders. The women piss standing up, and the men sitting down.

—Herodotus, *Histories,* 2.35–36

Herodotus, who lived in Greece in the fifth century B.C., invented the notion of history as an independent form of study, using the word *historia*—literally "research, a seeking out"—at the start of his book on the Greco-Persian Wars of 490–480 B.C.: "This is the laying out of the *historia* [research] of Herodotus of Halicarnassus. . . ." Other Greek authors soon copied the new genre. Thus began "history" as we know it. Of course, to reconstruct the details of ancient life for periods after people began to write "history" is much easier than to mine the earlier periods we deal with here. And Herodotus' book provides an especially rich mine of information, for he was curious about everything. Throughout his extensive travels to research the Persian Wars he inquired about anything that caught his attention—and threw it all into his book. Thus his visit to the land of the Nile (fig. 8.1) yielded a lengthy description of Egypt and its people.

Archaeology amply supports the view of Herodotus that the Egyptians did things their own way. Isolated for millennia from other cultures by a sea of sand, they received occasional basic ideas from others (such as the notions that one could spin, weave, and write) and then developed them locally to suit their peculiar environment. In this same way, to take a trivial example, the European settlers in New England learned of pumpkins from the local Indians and then developed pumpkin pie according to their own tastes.

By the time Herodotus visited Egypt in the fifth century, he was describing a culture in which customs had changed little in more than three thousand years. New tools were occasionally taken up. The male-operated vertical loom, for example, was introduced into Egypt around 1500 B.C. By that time, however, Egyptian women—and women only—had already been weaving linen on horizontal looms for fully three thousand years. The Middle Kingdom, which lasted from roughly 2150 to 1800 B.C., is particularly interesting from the point of view of women and their work. Egypt's isolation had not yet been penetrated by the invasions that ended the Middle Kingdom, but still the records of daily affairs are much fuller than in earlier periods.

In the magnificent Old Kingdom, which began about 2750 B.C., pictorial representations and the newly-invented writing system were largely reserved for important religious uses, ones that promoted the immortality of the pharaoh and the nobility. So we know little of daily life. But when the kings of the Sixth Dynasty fell, around 2250 B.C., the myth that pharaohs were gods incarnate and therefore invincible fell with them. Chaos, famine, and political scrambling ensued. Some commoners even had the temerity to begin wearing their kilts folded in the royal manner, with the left edge wrapped over the right, instead of vice versa. When

Figure 8.1. Map of Egypt and Palestine, showing important Bronze Age sites mentioned.

the pharaohs of the Eleventh Dynasty emerged triumphant a century later, the struggle had left its mark. Earlier rulers were portrayed with unshakable looks of eternal peacefulness, as though they expected their small, orderly world to march on unchanged forever, whereas Middle Kingdom pharaohs look uniformly worried, even harassed, with furrowed brows and sad eyes peering out at unending disruption and insecurity.

With all its uncertainties, however, life in Middle Kingdom Egypt comes across as particularly, vibrantly human. The struggles for power had taught that petty chiefs could become magnificent pharaohs—in other words, that what one *chose* to do could determine what one's life became and that heredity wasn't everything. So people piled in and did things, and they recorded their lives with great gusto and not a little pomposity in their tombs. The theory—a basic corollary of the Egyptian belief in an afterlife—was that if you recorded your wealth and achievements and comforts attained in this life, you would have them for eternity in the next life. So the tomb walls of wealthy Egyptians abound with pictures of daily work and play, and if the deceased wasn't wealthy enough to have a huge painted tomb, cheap little wooden models depicting the daily activities would do the trick (figs. 3.5 and 8.7).

From the models and paintings we learn that once again the chief occupations of women were spinning and weaving, grinding grain and preparing food. We know little about the steps of food preparation, but we can follow the process of making cloth and trace its subsequent use with some accuracy from start to finish, at least in a generic way. In Mesopotamia the accidents of excavation gave us detailed data about a few women (see Chapter 6). In Middle Kingdom Egypt, on the contrary, we know little about individual women but a lot about what people in general were doing and especially about how they did it. Our knowledge of women's work in Egypt thus falls largely within the framework of how they manufactured cloth for the society. It reveals to us something of how Egyptian women interacted both with their work and with the male half of their society.

Although the Mesopotamians of 2000 B.C. wove mostly wool and a rather smaller amount of linen, the Egyptians produced almost exclusively linen for their cloth and clothing needs. There were reasons for this. Egyptian sheep were hairy rather than woolly, and Herodotus tells us that wool in general was considered ritually unclean—not kosher, as it were. Moreover, linen was admirably suited to the hot, dusty climate of the Nile Valley, since it is cool and absorbent of moisture but sheds dirt readily from its smooth fibers.

Linen is made from the stem fibers of flax, a tall, skinny plant about four feet high with thin dark leaves and bright blue flowers. The men began the production chain by raising, harvesting, and drying the flax, as we see in the pictures. We also catch a glimpse of the process in an *Arabian Nights*-style Egyptian tale of magic. In this story a young servant girl, whose angered mistress had beaten her, threatened in revenge to inform the king. But instead, perhaps thinking better of that strategy, "she went and found her older half-brother binding bundles of flax on the threshing floor" and told him her woe. Thus we learn that the men bundled the flax after drying it and knocking the seeds loose for the next crop. Eventually, in the story, the brother scolded the little girl, so she went down to the river, where a crocodile ate her. Next her mistress repented—and the manuscript breaks off leaving us hanging. (Such are the frustrations of working with ancient sources.)

Some of the harvested flax went to the men for making rope and string; that was their special province, as it is today in the Near East. One can see teams of them, each paying out through a guide ring a strand of thick twine that he has prepared, while one strong man forces the several strands to twist around each other into a single rope as he backs slowly down the village street. It is heavy work. Some flax, on the other hand, presumably the finest grade, went to the women for making cloth.

To obtain the fibers from the dried flax, one has to keep it wet or damp just long enough to rot the fleshy part of the stem away from the tough, usable fibers. Although we have no depictions in Egypt of this necessary process, called retting, women in nearby Palestine spread their flax out in great quantity on the fields or flat rooftops and retted it from the dampness of the nightly dew, as we learn from a cloak-and-dagger scene in the Old Testament: "But she [Rahab] had brought [the fugitives] up to the roof of the house, and hid them with the stalks of flax, which she had laid in order upon the roof."

Most of the flax grown in Egypt was raised on the large estates of nobles and of the ever more powerful temples. Servant women on these estates made the flax into the linens needed. They seem to have been grouped into crews, and worked together in special weaving rooms, almost like a modern production line in a factory. Sometimes life in these weaving rooms sounds as wretched as that in the nineteenth-century sweatshops. A lament on the misery of conditions during a period of political chaos says:

> Lo, citizens are put to the grindstones,
> Wearers of fine linen are beaten with [sticks] . . .
> Ladies suffer like maidservants,
> Singers are at the looms in the weaving rooms,
> What they sing to the goddess are dirges.

Temple singers would have been too high-class, ordinarily, to weave cloth. In less stressful times, however, the women are shown attacking their work with spunk.

Paintings often include an older woman acting as an immediate overseer in the workshop (figs. 8.2 and 8.4). She has double chins or rolls of fat on her tummy. "Get to work!" she calls to the girls before her. Like a prowling watchdog, the man who manages all the shops often lurks behind her, labeled "overseer of the weavers." Several tombs known from the New Kingdom belong to men who styled themselves "overseer of the weavers of Amon"—that

Figure 8.2. Women in an Egyptian weaving shop. The woman kneeling at the center is splicing flax fibers end to end for the young girl at the right to spin into tighter thread. The pair squatting at the left are weaving on a horizontal ground loom (see fig. 3.5 for a more realistic perspective), while the older woman standing behind oversees the factory. The hieroglyphs name the activities. From the Middle Kingdom tomb of Khnemhotep at Beni Hasan, early second millennium B.C.

is, the overseer of the slave workers belonging to the great temple of the sun-god Amon at Thebes. Servitude in the temples was a typical fate of women captured in war.

Inside the workshop three or four women crouch on the floor, cleaning and separating the flax fibers and splicing them end to end into crude thread, which they roll into balls or coil into a pile on the floor. Egyptian estate managers expected to store up enormous quantities of linens; we typically find hundreds of large sheets in a single unplundered tomb. The job must have seemed endless, like filling a bottomless hole. The women probably induced the splices, which are merely twisted, not knotted, to stick together by wetting them with saliva, since saliva contains enzymes that decompose the cellulose of the flax slightly into a gluey substance. The Hebrews practiced the same method, learning it while living in Egypt; the special Hebrew word in Exodus for making thread out of flax, *shazar,* means both "to twist" and "to glue." The women in the Egyptian depictions work on little dome-shaped mounds set on the floor, much as we might use a table. The names for what they are doing are written above them in the drawings: *s-sh-n* for the women loosening the fibers from the stalks of flax, and *ms-n* over the women splicing them end to end.[1]

After the splicers finish, they pass their product to the next team of two or three girls, who have to add twist to the loosely formed yarn to strengthen it. Two problems confront these women. Linen is more manageable when wet, so the Egyptians learned to keep the balls of crude thread in a bowl of water. But any knitter who has tried to yank on a ball of thread in an open container knows that the ball immediately and invariably hops out and rolls away. So the ingenious Egyptians fashioned wetting bowls with handlelike loops inside on the bottom (fig. 4.2). If the end of each thread is passed under the loop before it is attached to the spindle, the thread is forced through the water and the ball is kept from jumping out, all at the same time.

The spinner now adroitly rolls the spindle down her thigh and drops it so it keeps turning—hanging from the attached thread— as she pulls from the bowl the crude yarn to be twisted. Eventually her spindle reaches the floor, and the spinning stops momentarily while she winds up the finished thread onto the spindle. Expert spinners, in fact, don't even have to reach down to get the spindle. They can give a sharp tug on the new thread that makes the spindle roll straight up it like a yo-yo. During all this the whorl, a small round weight stuck on the spindle shaft (fig. 8.3), acts as a

[1] The Egyptian writing system specified only the consonants, not the vowels, of the words. To reduce the resulting ambiguity, a sign that indicated the general semantic category of the intended word was often added. As a result, the system was extremely large, complicated, unwieldy, and hard to learn; that is why so few people were literate.

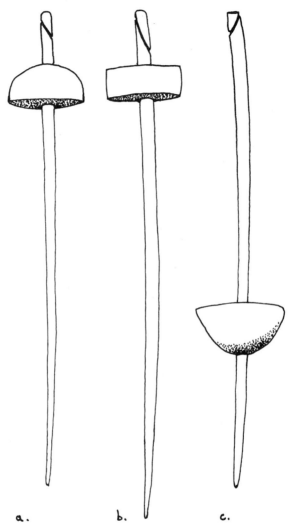

Figure 8.3. Spindles from Egypt (a) typical New Kingdom spindle, (b) typical Middle Kingdom spindle, (c) unusual spindle from Gurob (New Kingdom) made of Egyptian materials but in the European style—whorl at the bottom instead of the top and thread groove (near the top of the shaft) going the opposite direction. (Linen twists naturally in the direction of the grooves on the normal Egyptian spindles, so linen spun on the Gurob spindle would tend to be weak and come apart—it was probably used for wool.)

flywheel to keep the spindle turning as long as possible. Grace Crowfoot, a historian of spinning, has remarked that "Herodotus might have added to those manners and customs of the Ancient Egyptians which exactly contradicted the common practice of mankind the fact that they dropped their spindles whorl uppermost instead of whorl downwards."

Adding twist to a single thread gave a very fine product; we have Egyptian linens with up to two hundred threads per inch, finer than the finest handkerchief you can buy nowadays. It looks translucent, almost like silk. (A fine percale sheet today is usually one hundred threads per inch.) Twisting two or even three threads together gave a much stronger and thicker yarn, which was used for most of the cloth woven. Some of the spinners were so expert that they could keep two spindles going at once. In one mural, one of these prodigies glances over her shoulder at the women sitting on the floor behind her, who supply her with the hand-spliced yarn, and cries, "Come! Hurry!"

Among the spinners in another painting is a young boy, probably the son of one of the women (fig. 8.4). She has brought him with her to her workplace. If he is still too young to be sent to the men, he is nonetheless old enough to be put to work, and spinning, at least, will be a useful skill for him later in learning to make rope. (We see boys regularly employed in those scenes also.) The women's workshop thus serves as both a "day-care" center and a sort of vocational school. White as opposed to red paint for the skin (the common Egyptian painter's convention for women versus men) proves some of the working children to be girls; one has been set up on a high platform so she will be tall enough for her spindle to drop a good distance.

To weave, one must first make the warp—a set of threads to be tied onto the loom to form the foundation for the future cloth (see Chapter 1). We see that one or two women of the workshop might do this job, taking the thread straight from the spindles or from prepared balls. Sometimes they measured out the thread on a large stand with upright posts for the purpose; one of the hieroglyphs depicts such a frame. But a cheaper warping board consisted simply of pegs stuck into a wall. We find this in one of the wooden models and once in real life.

Around 1350 B.C., the heretic king Akhenaton moved the Egyptian capital to a brand-new site on the edge of the desert. This site, now known as Amarna, was abruptly abandoned after Akhenaton died. Everyone moved back to Thebes, leaving the houses to the desert sands, where the ruins have endured like time capsules.

In the remains of a small workmen's village on the outskirts of Amarna, the modern visitor encounters such homely devices as warping pegs still stuck fast in the wall of an alley opposite the doors of some of the houses. In the trash round about were found many broken spindles and a few weaving tools. In this case the women—dependents on the men who carved the royal tombs— were probably weaving necessities for their own households rather than for an estate. Any woman in the little walled village who needed a warp for her loom could have walked over to this convenient spot to make it.

Where she then set up her loom is a more difficult question. Her Amarna village house, set in a long, monotonous row, typically had an entry room through which family and friends immediately passed to the all-purpose main room behind, with its stove, wall benches, and cupboards. Here the wife cooked the food and did her chores; here the family worked, ate, and chatted. Steep stairs led up and over the corner cupboard to a story above, perhaps no more than a flat roof with palm fronds set up as a sun shelter. Such a rooftop provided a cool place to sleep at night and a shady spot for the woman to peg out her loom for weaving during the day. (Rain was not a problem; recently it rained in Cairo for the first time in decades.) Most of the weaving equipment found by the excavators appeared to have fallen down the stairs. Even today in the Near East the rooftops are the province of women, places to talk with and signal to one another, havens from which to view events in the street without being seen.

Making the warp for huge cloths must have been tedious in the

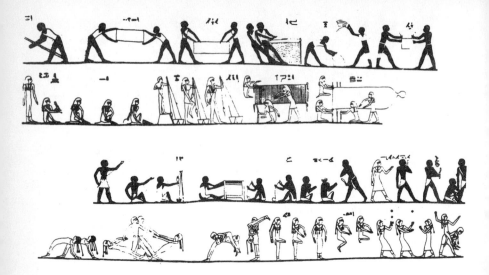

Figure 8.4. Friezes from the Middle Kingdom Egyptian tombs of a father and son, Baqt and Khety (at Beni Hasan), showing men spinning cord and laundering, while women spin thread and weave. Among the spinners in Baqt's tomb is a little girl, while in Khety's tomb a young boy helps with the spinning; day-care seems to have included vocational training. The women are also shown playing a variety of acrobatic games.

extreme. We have Egyptian linens as much as 9 feet wide and 75 feet long. At a mere hundred threads to the inch, that's more than 153 miles of yarn to measure out—the distance from New York to Providence, or Seattle to Portland. But the Egyptians were an ingenious lot. Perhaps the stability of their civilization allowed good ideas to be passed around easily. And so we see in one painting that a woman is measuring a dozen threads out at once, pulling them simultaneously from twelve balls of yarn lying in as many compartments in a big box—a real work saver.

Once the warp was made, helpers transferred it to the loom for weaving; "binding on the warp," says the legend. The shop might

have one or two looms pegged out on the floor, and each was attended by at least two women, who crouched at either side and sped the weaving by passing the weft bobbin back and forth between them.[2] One woman was also responsible for the beater that packed the weft in tight, and the other was in charge of the heddle bar that raised the alternate warp threads for the weft to pass under (see Chapter 1). Sometimes an extra girl helped out by attending to tangles or other problems with the unwoven part of the warp.

Somewhere on the cloth the women might weave in an extra thread in a little design or logo that functioned as a weaver mark—probably that of the workshop, but possibly of the estate. (Not until Classical Greek times did individual artisans begin to sign

[2] One must be careful, in interpreting the weaving scenes, to pay attention to the Egyptian way of presenting objects. They did not choose to use ocular perspective, the way we do, because that angle would often hide some important part of the object or person that needed to arrive in the next world intact. So the looms are shown as if from above, to make everything visible, whereas the operators are shown side view for the same reason. See fig. 3.5 for the true form of the Egyptian loom; then compare fig. 8.2.

their products.) The keeper of the linens would later ink onto it a little hieroglyphic notation indicating the quality, such as "good" or "best quality."

Virtually all of the Old and Middle Kingdom linen we have is plain white. (By contrast, in an Egyptian marketplace today, almost everyone wears black.) A few pieces were dyed as whole cloth, usually red or yellow, and the dyes were not colorfast, so the dyeing may have been carried out for funerals only. But not all of the cloth is totally plain. Most pieces were fringed, and a few pieces from the Middle Kingdom have simple patterns made with short tufts of extra weft, looking not unlike a modern chenille bedspread. Garments, moreover, were often pleated with row upon row of tiny pleats, to give them a snug but elastic fit. Our earliest preserved garment, from about 3100 B.C., already has this feature (fig. 5.3).

Who added the pleats or how, we don't know; but the men, not the women, did the laundering. Sometimes they boiled the cloth, and sometimes they stomped it in the river. This was heavy and sometimes dangerous work, as we learn from the scribes:

> The washerman washes on the shore
> With the crocodile as neighbor . . .
> His food is mixed with dirt,
> No limb of his is clean.
> He is given women's cloths . . .
> One says to him, "Soiled linen for you."

Crocodiles pose a real danger in Africa even today, but one has to take the text as a whole with a grain of salt. Middle Kingdom scribes gave their pupils literature to copy for practice. A particular favorite, the source of this excerpt, was a long tongue-in-cheek poem that extolled the virtues of becoming a scribe and exaggerated the horrors of taking up any other line of work, the moral being that scribes had cushy lives, were well fed, and were honored by everyone, so that the schoolchild would do well to study hard and learn the fiercely difficult hieroglyphics. These little stories served as carrots to entice the mulish students forward, but the stick was not far behind—as in the schoolrooms of Europe and America up into this century. Another verse describes the lot of the mat weavers (who were men) and at the same time puts to rest any thoughts that women's work might be enviable:

> The [mat]weaver in the workshop,
> He is worse off than a woman;
> With knees against his chest,
> He cannot breathe air.
> If he skips a day of weaving,
> He is beaten fifty strokes;
> He gives food to the doorkeeper,
> To let him see the light of day.

(These "satires of the trades" were composed with the assumption that all scribes were men, but we now have direct evidence for four or five women who were scribes in the Middle Kingdom.)

When the linen was quite clean, despite the snapping crocodiles, the men wrung it out by twisting it between two sticks (fig. 8.4), laid it out to dry, pressed it with weights, folded it, and returned it to the keeper of the linens, who stored it in large woven hampers or in big chests of wood or terra-cotta. Some of these storage chests have survived from the Middle Kingdom. Others—fancy wooden ones from the New Kingdom—are gaily painted to represent the lord and lady sipping cool refreshments in a cloth-covered outdoor pavilion, while a small serving girl attends their wants, like English gentry taking tea at Ascot (fig. 6.2).

Middle Kingdom pavilions, like those pictured in the Old Kingdom, were normally made of brightly colored reed mats rather than cloth. But the tomb of Hepzefa, a deputy who ruled the nome, or county, around Asyut in the Twelfth Dynasty, around 1900 B.C., displayed on its ceiling the designs of six cloths, mostly imported from the Aegean (see Chapter 4) and sewn together into a colorful canopy top. Only one pavilion cover has come down to us: that of Princess Isimkheb of the Twenty-first Dynasty. It is woven of strips of green leather with handsome figures appliquéd around the edges and was found tucked into a crevice in the tomb, where it had escaped the notice of ancient tomb robbers.

Linen was more than just clothing or decor. Sheets of woven linen, made and stored up in huge quantities, also counted as wealth and served as a sort of money for barter. (Coinage was another fifteen hundred years into the future.) No fewer than thirty-eight folded linen sheets, for instance, lay atop the mummy of the estate manager Wah, who lived and died during the Middle Kingdom, and a great many more sheets had been used to wrap the body. Some were marked with his name, and some with the names of others. Nor was Wah particularly wealthy. He was not the owner of the estate, and he died rather young. If this many linens went into *his* tomb, one of the rare ones to have been discovered intact, the tombs of the really wealthy must have been copiously supplied. In fact, we gather that linens, too, along with gold and jewels, were plundered from the tombs and sold. After all, not every household contained someone who wove, so basic cloth and also clothing sometimes had to be purchased (see Chapter 11).

The linen, once woven, had myriad uses. Plain lengths of it served as towels, bed sheets, and blankets, the blankets sometimes made with long loops of extra weft on one side, to insulate by trapping air (fig. 11.4). Egypt has a hot climate, but in winter the nights become chilly. Strips of linen provided bandages for wrapping the dead, and little pieces were drafted for wrapping all manner of things, much the way we use tissue paper. For example, a small wooden cosmetics casket found in a Middle Kingdom tomb and now in the Metropolitan Museum of Art was described by William Hayes, the curator there, as "containing a tiny alabaster vase tied up in a scrap of linen, and four alabaster jars, including two beakers for ointments, each wrapped or sealed with linen cloth."

Both women and men regularly kept small chests or lidded bas-

Figure 8.5. Egyptian woman applying face paint with one hand while she holds her mirror and paintpot in the other. From a pen-and-ink sketch on a New Kingdom papyrus.

kets with an array of cosmetics, the most important of which were ointments to soften the skin (dried out by heat, dust, and frequent washing) and eye paint, which was used not only for beauty but to help prevent eye infections and destroy parasites. Finely ground green malachite, a particular favorite from 4000 B.C. on, consists of oxide of copper—lethal to both bacteria and fly eggs. The exaggerated eye makeup that we associate with Queen Cleopatra in Hollywood spectaculars was originally of this nature. Ancient Egyptian women, however, clearly enjoyed the aesthetics of face paint, too (fig. 8.5).

Clothing was entirely of linen in this era. Men wore knee-length kilts, especially for active work, but might also possess sleeved shirts, long kilts, and mantles for other occasions. The garments were tied on with a square knot. Women typically wore slim, tubular jumpers reaching from the breasts (either above or below them) to the ankles and supported by shoulder straps. One exception is the costume of a woman named Sit Snefru and titled "nurse" (fig. 8.6). Her statue, found in Adana on the southeastern coast of Turkey, shows the archaeological usefulness of knowing about clothing styles. Hayes likens her ankle-length dress, a single large rectangle wrapped so that the right arm and shoulder are bare, to the mantles sometimes worn by Egyptian men. It is identical, however, to the wrapped tunics worn at this time by Sumerian and Semitic women of Mesopotamia and Syria. Hayes supposes that she "was attached to the household of an Egyptian official assigned to this remote station, and, before leaving home, had the statuette made to be placed in her tomb. . . ." Since the statue is otherwise "wholly characteristic of the best sculptural tradition of the Twelfth Dynasty," she must have had it made, instead, during a temporary return to Egypt, after she had adopted the native dress of her new country. We learn from this that at least a few Egyptian women traveled as great distances as some of the men.

Linen, with its slick-surfaced fibers, is difficult to dye, so colored thread was not easy to obtain. Furthermore, the Egyptians, priding themselves on cleanliness, constantly washed both themselves and their clothes. The linen was easier to bleach clean when it was plain white. Yet color is attractive to the human eye, and here and there on the statues and paintings one glimpses bright patterns on the clothes (fig. 8.7 left). These women are wearing skirts and even entire dresses of beaded nets, put on over the linen jumpers. One such bead dress survives from the Fifth Dynasty, so the custom already existed in the Old Kingdom. We also have Middle Kingdom bead skirts from burials at the southern outpost of Kerma in the Sudan, made with huge quantities of blue, white, and black faience beads and found along with such oddities as fluffy rugs woven with the long barbs from ostrich feathers as pile. Occasionally the net dresses were not linen, but cut from fine leather. One pharaoh on record got his fun, in fact, from watching his serving girls rowing up and down his pleasure lake wearing nothing else.

The Egyptians are famous, of course, for their huge beaded necklaces—pectorals, actually, covering the whole chest—which did a lot to dress up a clean white outfit. Fancy wooden boxes

Figure 8.6. Left: Stone statue of Sit Snefru, an Egyptian nurse of the Twelfth Dynasty (early second millennium B.C.), who accompanied the family she served all the way to Adana, at the northeastern corner of the Mediterranean. There she evidently adopted the local Near Eastern style of clothing; compare the typical wrapped tunic of the Mesopotamian woman on the right (this statue came from Tell Asmar, mid-third millennium B.C.), and contrast the sewn-up jumpers normally worn by Egyptian women (e.g., figs. 8.2, 8.4, and 8.7).

inlaid with precious materials like ivory held the necklaces and other jewelry owned by wealthy women and men, for men wore much jewelry, too, and particularly treasured the pectorals given out by the pharaoh as marks of honor. Both men and women might have among their jewelry a personal seal, in the form of a

Figure 8.7. Small sculpted models of women servants. One wears a bead dress over her linen tunic as she carries a basket of bread on her head and a bird in her hand (Middle Kingdom, ca. 2000 B.C.). The other kneels at the arduous task of grinding grain, the staple of life (Old Kingdom, ca. 2500 B.C.). In some areas of the ancient world the knee and toe bones of women are found deformed from spending so much time in this position (Chapter 3).

sacred scarab beetle with an inscription on the flat bottom and a hole pierced for a linen cord by which it could be worn. Upper-class women in the Middle Kingdom also developed a taste for huge wigs, the tresses of which were sometimes bound with ribbons of silver or linen and topped with still more jewelry, as fancy as any from the court of Marie Antoinette. We find these wigs carefully stowed in the tombs in large chests and see the servant girls in the paintings adjusting them for their mistresses. One female title carved onto the monuments of the time is "hairdresser."

If we judged only by the genre scenes painted on tomb walls and carved as little wooden models, we would have to conclude that most types of work were done by men. The women, instantly recognizable by the convention of painting their skins white (the men's are red), appear as laborers essentially only in the scenes of weaving and of grinding grain. But they also appear as attendants of wealthy mistresses—serving food, assisting the toilette, entertaining as singers, harpists, and dancers—and they turn up in an interesting sequence showing some rather acrobatic games (fig. 8.4). In one of these, two girls play ball while sitting astride the backs of two other girls, who have leaned over to make "horsie" and are supporting the weight with their hands on their knees. Each has her hair pulled back into two pigtails. Others perform flips, jumps, and backbends, while two girls try to keep a pair of balls in the air at once.

If we analyze the titles accorded to women on their monuments, however, we learn a few more details. In addition to weavers, we find a few women listed as overseers and "sealers" of storehouses. In one case the store held "royal linen" that seems to have belonged to a temple. More often the stores in question contained food, and a large number of the titles of women have to do with food, all the way from scullery maid through grinder (fig. 8.7 right), brewer, and table attendant up to a butler and the keeper of the dining hall. More unusual are a woman who helped with winnowing the grain and another who was a gardener. Elsewhere in the house we find housekeepers, nurses (including wet nurses—women who suckled other women's infants), hairdressers, cosmeticians, cleaning women, and just plain servants. We also encounter the dancers and various sorts of female musicians that we saw in the murals, both free citizens in the service of a deity and servants on a private estate. Not a few women were priestesses of some sort. Then, of course, we have the women who styled themselves the "lady of the house"—that is, a married woman whose job was to run her husband's household—and those who called themselves simply "townswoman" or "freewoman." The lady of the house often appears in the murals seated in an elegant chair, her pet goose or monkey crouching beneath it.

William Ward, in making a thorough study of Middle Kingdom women's titles, points out that "of all these professions, only the 'Gardener' and 'Winnower' worked outside the house and its subsidiary buildings. This points to the general observation that outside work in the fields, etc., was performed by men, including washing clothing. There would seem to be a division of labour on large, private estates: men worked outside (except for household servants) and women worked inside." The division would account for the convention that men were shown with dark skin and women with white. It also fits well with Judith Brown's thesis (Chapter 1) as elaborated within the peculiar Egyptian environment: In the blistering sun of Egypt, the cool of the house shade is the only reasonable place to tend small children, especially since, as the ancient satires tell us, the invitingly cool waters abounded with swift and lethal crocodiles. The analysis of one mummy has revealed that the deceased's legs had been torn off and the lungs showed signs of drowning.

Indoors, however, the women had all the work they could manage, preparing the food and turning flax into linen cloth, which, along with metal, was the very currency of Egypt. In the Middle Kingdom most of these women—weavers and grain grinders included—were not slaves but serfs of the estates or entirely free women, equal in either case in the eyes of the law to the men of that rank. Massive slavery came later, with the wars of conquest in the New Kingdom, and it changed the economic structure thoroughly, right down to who was doing the weaving. In Chapter 11 we will explore that changed world, when men moved into textile work to make luxury goods. For now we will leave the women of the Nile not only with their endless manufacture of linen but with their leisure activities—their ball games, dancing and acrobatics, pet geese, music, and cool drinks. The work of these women was not easy, but life had its pleasures.

9

The Golden
Spindle

Alkandre, the wife of Polybos, who lived in Thebes
of Egypt . . . bestowed on Helen beautiful gifts:
a golden spindle she gave, and a silver wool-basket
with wheels underneath and finished with gold on the rims.
— *Odyssey*, 4.125–26, 130–32

Gold and silver spindles may seem to us the stuff of fairy tales, as
when Sleeping Beauty hurt her finger on a golden spindle and fell
asleep for a century. After all, why should a woman rich enough
to own so much gold need to spin thread, the unending task of the
lowest servant girl? Yet archaeologists have actually found such
precious objects. The earliest golden spindles lay in opulent tombs
dating to the middle of the third millennium B.C., in the Early
Bronze Age, not long after the use of soft metals had become widespread.

The royal graves of Alaca Höyük in central Turkey, spectacu-
larly rich in precious metals, are the best documented of this
group. Each broad, flat tomb at Alaca contained a person laid out
on his or her side, surrounded by statuettes, religious or status
objects, jewelry, weapons, and tools of gold, silver, and copper. In
the grave that the excavators labeled Tomb L (fig. 9.1), for

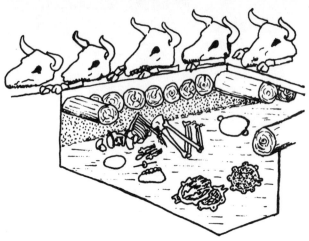

Figure 9.1. Burial of a rich and important woman at Alaca Höyük, in central Turkey (Tomb L), in the Early Bronze Age (mid-third millennium B.C.). Near her hands lay a gold and silver spindle, a large silver spoon, and religious paraphernalia. She wore much gold and silver jewelry. Bulls' heads and feet, probably the tokens of a massive funerary sacrifice, decorated the roof of the low log-built tomb.

instance, lay a woman wearing a golden diadem, necklaces of precious stones, a belt with a golden clasp, gold and silver bracelets, a silver pin, and buttons of stone and of gold. Near her face a variety of religious objects had been set out, but just beyond her hands lay two implements useful in normal living: a large silver spoon and a silver spindle with a golden head. It is tempting to say that this woman, obviously a figure of prominence, was symbolically equipped to deal with food and clothing, the two occupations most closely associated with women in the ancient world.

When I first began to work with this material fifteen years ago, I assumed that the Alaca lady's spoon and spindle were translations into precious metal of daily objects made of wood and had been made only for funerary purposes. The shape of the large, flat whorl in the middle of the spindle is not so different from wooden ones used today in Turkey and Greece. It is an easy shape to fashion in wood—certainly not a copy of a clay whorl, which needs to

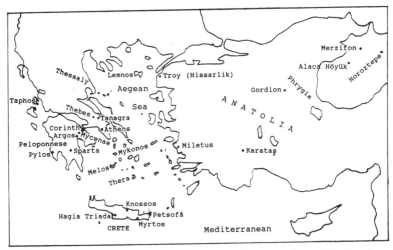

Figure 9.2. Map of Greece, the Aegean, and western Anatolia, showing Bronze Age and Classical sites mentioned.

be small and compact because of the greater density and greater fragility of clay. So, yes, the silver spindle probably does imitate a common wooden prototype.

But was a spindle so precious made only for show? By now we know of half a dozen more from the same Early Bronze era and the same region of Turkey (fig. 9.2): two from Horoztepe, two from Merzifon, at least one more from Alaca, and one from Karataş to the southwest, made variously of silver, bronze, gold, and electrum (a handsome alloy of gold and silver). That we have so many from so early an age suggests that constructing a precious metal spindle was not just the passing whim of one eccentric noblewoman. We also have Homer's description of gold and silver spinning gear being presented as gifts by one highborn lady to another, which suggests that they might have been part of a form of diplomacy akin to the presents that Mesopotamian kings and queens gave one another (see Chapter 7). Now, the garments and rugs that composed those gifts, no matter how ostentatiously ornate they might be, were directly useful. Were these spindles intended for use, too? If so, they would have been for the hands of rich queens and princesses only. But why would queens be spinning and weaving at all? There lies the crux of the matter.

The answer seems to be that royal ladies were indeed producing cloth themselves, ornate cloth woven from expensive yarns that other women could not afford: linen strung with precious beads, or skeins of wool colored with costly dyes such as the purple obtained from sea snails like the murex. Murex dye was later called Tyrian purple because it became the specialty of dyers from Tyre in Phoenicia or royal purple because it was so costly that in Rome, for example, only the emperor had the right to wear an entire garment dyed of it. Why was it so dear? Because each snail contained only a single drop of the dye and had to be destroyed to get it. The Minoans and Greeks had their own banks of purple snails, off the east end of Crete, which they fished until none was left.

In the scene quoted above, Homer goes on to show Helen of Troy sitting comfortably at home in Sparta in a chair, her foot on a footstool, chatting with visitors and using her golden spindle to spin the expensive purple wool which fills her silver wool basket with its gold-rimmed wheels. Again, were this scene unique, we could point the finger at poetic license. But over and over in the literature we hear of highborn ladies learning to spin and weave precisely in order to produce ornate cloth. For example, in Euripides' play *Ion*, Ion's mother, Kreusa, describes the cloth she wove as a girl and left in his baby basket when she abandoned him at birth:

> Not a finished piece, but a kind of sampler of weaves . . .
> A Gorgon is on the central warps of the robe . . .
> bordered with snakes like an aegis.

Nor would this be the only time in history that noblewomen worked at textiles. In the Middle Ages, for example, and in the eighteenth century, elegant ladies passed their time spinning and embroidering silks, not for sale but for conspicuous use at court.

Threads colored with expensive dyes that don't wash out make it possible to weave designs that won't disappear. The repetitive patterns that the Minoans wove (see Chapter 4) could be partially mechanized, but the elaborate fabrics that Helen and her noble friends wove may well have been pictorial, a kind of nonrepetitive weaving that takes enormous amounts of time. None but the rich had that kind of leisure. Says Homer of Helen, living at Troy:

> She was weaving a great warp,
> a purple double-layered cloak, and she was working into it
>   the many struggles
> of the horse-taming Trojans and bronze-clad Achaians.

Nor were such pictorial cloths for personal clothing, but for the rituals of the gods and kings. So, too, in medieval Europe, no textile was too expensive for the glorification of God and his servants.

The silver and gold spindles of the Early Bronze Age suggest that a tradition of noblewomen weaving may have sprung up quite early in Anatolia, fourteen hundred years before the Trojan War of around 1250 B.C. At Troy itself Heinrich Schliemann came upon quantities of gold fashioned into vessels and jewelry not unlike those at Alaca. Passionately fond of Homer and guided by ancient descriptions, Schliemann had arrived at the site of Hissarlik in northwestern Turkey to dig up what he hoped would be the legendary city of Troy. The year was 1870, archaeology was in its infancy, and Schliemann (a wealthy businessman in his sixties) had no clear concept of stratification—the principle that the debris from more recent periods is laid down on top of the residue of older periods, leaving a sort of layer cake from which one can deduce the relative ages of the remains. Assuming that Troy's mound was homogeneous, he and his hundred workmen started shoveling their way through the very middle of the great hill of debris, hunting for buildings and objects worthy of great King Priam and the other Homeric heroes. Although Schliemann was both curious and meticulous enough to save and record in his diary the artifacts he found, he destroyed irretrievably most of the architectural and stratigraphic history of this important site.

When the diggers finally came upon giant defense walls and a regal hoard of gold, they had burrowed right past Priam's Troy of 1250 B.C. (now identified as Level VII), all the way down to the Early Bronze Age (Level II), around 2600 B.C. This city, too, had clearly been sacked and burned, just like Homer's Troy, a finding that only confirmed Schliemann in his belief that he had finally found what he was looking for. By now it was June of 1873, and Schliemann had endured for too long the scorn and ridicule of European scholars who thought that both he and his scheme to find Troy were crazy. To enhance the small troves of gold he found stashed about the city by the frantic inhabitants of the burning city, he secretly sent his wife off to buy additional pieces of prehistoric gold from antiquities dealers round about, while partially falsifying his diaries about what was found when and where. Then he smuggled the whole lot out of Turkey to Athens and eventually to Berlin, carefully "leaking" spectacular news of his success to the press, once the treasure was safe, and soon thereafter writing two copiously illustrated books detailing the uncovering of Troy. A particularly famous lithograph portrays his wife, Sophia, dressed up in lavish Trojan jewelry—not that of Helen, Andromache, and Queen Hecuba, as they believed, but of nameless queens and princesses who had lived some fourteen hundred years earlier.

Among his finds from the burnt city (Level II), Schliemann describes a small round clay box or casket, within which nestled the remains of a linen fabric decorated with tiny blue-green faience beads and a spindle full of thread. Perhaps it was a noble lady's workbox. Elsewhere he mentions tiny gold beads. Where Schliemann had no posture to maintain, his books are apparently excellent records of what he found. But where gold is concerned, a more reliable source is his set of copious diaries (and even they have to be treated with discernment at times). While in Greece a few years ago, and curious about these beads, I called at the Gennadion Library in Athens, where Schliemann's diaries reside, and asked if it were possible to consult them. The next thing I knew, I was seated at a huge polished wooden table with three volumes of the diaries piled in front of me.

I confess that I spent the first hour in awe, leafing through the pages just to see what this great man, one of my childhood heroes, had been like in his private moments. The diaries are not easy to read since they are handwritten in four different alphabets and at least seven languages. In the volumes before me I found Greek (Greek alphabet), Turkish (Arabic script), Russian (Cyrillic alphabet), French, occasionally English, and most often his native German. Schliemann was an astounding polyglot, having taught himself to read, speak, and write more than a dozen modern languages as well as to read Classical Greek and Latin—often from the most meager resources. He tended to write in whichever language he was speaking most often at the moment. Fortunately for me, the days at Troy were recorded not in Turkish but in German, along with numerous sketches of the artifacts he was finding. At least one reason for choosing German was to keep the diary unintelligible to the local authorities! After much browsing, using the sketches as the quickest guide, I gradually located a few more references to small finds of gold and faience beads, but no others with a clear context of cloth decoration.

Much luckier, however, were the American archaeologists who reexcavated Troy in the 1930s in hopes of working out something of the stratigraphy. In an area missed by Schliemann's diggers, they discovered hundreds of tiny gold beads all through the dirt around the remains of a warp-weighted loom. This loom had been set up in the palace with a half-finished cloth on it on that fatal day when Troy II was sacked and burned. Given what we now know of bead-decorated cloth from other sites in Bronze Age Greece and Turkey, we can conclude that a most royal cloth beaded with gold was in the making. Troy II is contemporary with both Alaca Höyük and the other sites with gold or silver spindles; perhaps the royal ladies knew each other. At any rate the "common" women of Troy were busy with the cloth industry, too, for the Early Bronze Age levels at Troy disgorged some ten thousand clay spindle whorls, a truly phenomenal number.

What form such an extensive cloth industry took at that early date we can only guess. We see evidence for linen, for massive production of woolen cloth, and for luxury fabrics like those with the gold and faience beads, and we see considerable social stratification, with the leaders of the city commanding great wealth. But we know little of the women who made these textiles. On the other hand, we have rather more information about the Late Bronze Age and Early Iron Age on both sides of the Aegean—that is, information about some other palace-run societies that were equally appropriate settings for Homer's golden spindle.

The direct ancestors of the later Greeks that we so admire began to trickle into the Greek peninsula from the northeast sometime after 2000 B.C. They are hard to trace, but by 1600 B.C. they were numerous and powerful enough to build citadels and palaces in several key locations in the eastern half of Greece, especially on the previously uninhabited hilltop of Mycenae (see map, fig. 9.2). Mycenae overlooks the rich agricultural plain of Argos to the south, a fertile source of food. It also controls the pass through the hills from the north, just beyond which lies the narrow Isthmus of Corinth, the only way for northerners to reach the entire southern half of Greece by land. Truly a strategic position—so strategic that Mycenae became the capital of the loose federation of chiefdoms that ensued, giving its name to the era and to the people themselves. The Mycenaean Greeks were above all warriors and organizers, organizing everyone and everything they conquered so that they could keep efficient control, like the Romans in later times.

One way to keep order is to keep records of who is to do what

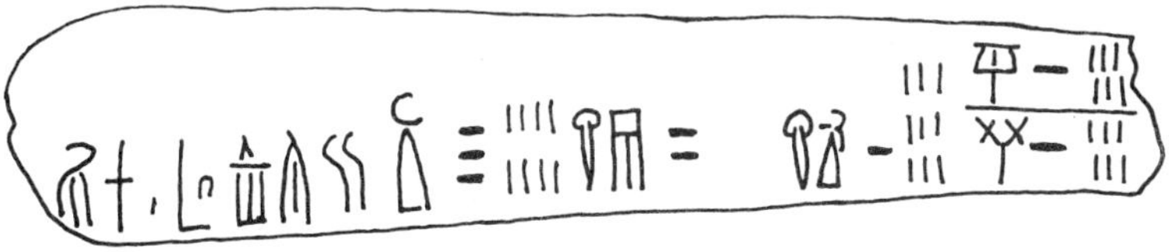

Figure 9.3. Clay tablet from Pylos, Greece, inscribed in Linear Script B and telling of rations sent to textile workers and their children. The signs read: "Pu-lo ra-pi-ti-rya: WOMEN 38, ko-wa 20, ko-wo 19. WHEAT 16, FIGS 16." That is, "Pylos seamstresses: 38 women, 20 girls, 19 boys. Wheat: 16 measures, figs: 16 measures." The sign for "woman" is a pictogram showing her head and long skirt.

and who owes what to whom. The Mycenaean Greeks, illiterate when they entered Greece, soon learned how to write from the Minoans or other Aegean peoples and began keeping palace accounts on small clay tablets, using a script that we call Linear Script B. Unfortunately Linear B was adapted from local scripts that were ill suited both to clay and to the sound structure of the Greek language (see below). To the extent that we can understand the contents, we can say that many of the tablets have to do with personnel, especially with rations issued and with work meted out and completed (fig. 9.3). It is interesting for our purposes that most of the workers listed are women; their named occupations include grinders of grain, water carriers, a wide variety of textile workers, priestesses, nurses (?), serving women, and new captives.

The last term is the key to the social structure: Most of these women, perhaps all except the top priestesses, seem to have been captured during the sorts of raids so frequent in Homer's epics, right from the opening of the *Iliad*, where Agamemnon, king of Mycenae, makes the following boasts:

> We went to Thebes, the sacred city of Eetion,
> and sacked it and brought everything here.
> And the sons of the Achaians divided it up among themselves,
> [including] the fair-cheeked Chryseis . . .

And I will not release [Chryseis], not before old age comes
    upon her
in our house in Argos, far from her father,
walking up and down at the loom and tending my bed.

When a town or settlement was overwhelmed and looted, the men who survived the fighting were typically slaughtered, while the women and children were hauled away to become captive laborers.

I hesitate to call them slaves. The general attitude seems to have been that women were relatively docile and did not have to be fettered or beaten, once co-opted. So the newly captured women were employed in the palaces and temples, where they could be kept track of and taught skills if necessary. But once they had a child or two, born of a local father, they were too encumbered and too tied to their new homes to run away. From then on they might live in suburbs or farmhouses, continuing to do piecework for the palace (like weaving garments) and perhaps tending orchards or gardens, while they raised their children. Such a life was more like serfdom than slavery. It is the census and supply lists for these dependent workers, both inside and outside the palace, and accounts of their products that constitute the bulk of our Linear B documents.

Not only do the women greatly outnumber the men, but the majority of the workingwomen labored in the textile industry. Indeed, textiles for export must have been a main source of Aegean wealth. At Knossos alone, records for a single season list at least seventy to eighty thousand sheep, the vast preponderance of them wethers (neutered males, which give the finest fleeces, but no milk and only tough meat). At upward of a pound and a half of wool per adult sheep, by the Myceneans' own reckoning, we come up with some sixty tons of wool—a count that checks well against the Knossos accounts of cloth made. For comparison, a bulky ski sweater today might contain a pound and a half of wool. Imagine spinning and knitting eighty thousand of them by hand in one season. This was no small industry. A single shepherd could run several hundred sheep, although fifty to a hundred was more normal. But to get enough women to spin and weave all the wool grown by those sheep, the palace warriors had to go out raiding for captive female labor, even when no war was afoot. Being carried off was a constant hazard for women and children during Mycenaean times, especially for those living near the sea. A servingwoman in the *Odyssey* reports her entry into bondage thus:

> Pirate men from Taphos [a Greek island] grabbed me
> as I was coming from the fields, and bringing me here they
>   sold me
> to the household of this man; and he paid a good price.

Quite a few of the women listed in the Linear B archives of Pylos, an important Mycenaean town on the west coast of Greece, came from such faraway places as Lemnos, Knidos, and Miletos on the east side of the Aegean.

Much of the populace, then, consisted of captive women manufacturing textiles. As usual, men lent a hand at each end of the textile production, in this case raising the fibers and disposing of the cloth, while the women handled the part in the middle—chiefly spinning and weaving.

A careful look at the accounts, however, reveals a marked difference in how the Mycenaean women were organized to make textiles, compared with the other systems we have looked at. Egyptian and Mesopotamian women, having obtained their fibers one way or another, made the cloth from start to finish, either alone or as a workshop team. Not so in the Mycenaean world. Here the palace controlled the means of production at each stage, manipulating the system from the center like an orb-spider in its web. The people who did the successive bits of work specialized in doing only that one task, living and working separately from those who did other parts of the job, connected as a production team chiefly via the palace. A system in which no one person or workshop alone could complete an entire piece of cloth from start to finish gives the central manipulator yet more control over a large captive populace.[1] The same sort of outworker system for cloth production, but run by private entrepreneurs for profit, is documented from the Netherlands and northern France in the Middle Ages and from the tiny Mediterranean island of Malta as recently as the last century.[2]

Linen was manufactured in the Aegean as well as wool, and considerable quantities of flax were raised in the western Peloponnesos, in the same area in which the Classical Greeks produced linen. But clearly wool ran the show. Let us, then, follow a pound of wool through the hands of the Mycenaean people who worked it, to get some glimpses of their daily lives.

First we catch and fleece a sheep, preferably in the spring. Men raised the sheep; the names of the shepherds are masculine. Who removed the wool from the sheep, however, is not clear. Scholars often assume that the wool was sheared off in a mass, as is done today, but archaeological, zoological, and linguistic evidence indi-

---

[1] Some of the Mesopotamian palaces, too, may have used this kind of outworker system. We have little information about the internal organization of the women textile workers to whom rations were issued there. But we do not seem to see these women divided a priori into such specialty groups as combers, spinners, weavers, seamstresses, etc., and the Mesopotamian form of agriculture, which required large numbers of people to band together to maintain the irrigation channels across great wide-open spaces, seems to have precluded the sort of scattered villages with cottage industries that were the norm in Europe for millennia. Security for workers in outlying districts would have been nil.

[2] Bowen-Jones et al. describes the Maltese system thus: "In 1861 there still remained almost 9000 workers occupationally described as spinners and weavers and some 200 beaters and dyers. Ninety-six percent. of the total were women, and male labour was generally used only in the final stages of cloth preparation. The industry included all processes from the growing of indigenous short staple annual cottons to the manufacture of cloth. The actual operations however were carried out almost entirely by individual workers in their own homes and were linked only by merchants specialising in this trade. In many cases merchants advanced seed to the farmers on a crop-sharing basis. In all cases they bought the picked lint and then distributed quantities by weight to 'out-work' spinners. These would return the yarn, . . . and were paid by weight and fineness of the yarn. The village merchant would store the yarn until he received an order for cloth and then would make similar contracts with domestic weavers."

cates that Bronze Age sheep still molted (shed) their wool and that wool for weaving was typically retrieved by combing it loose from the bristly kemp hairs that molted later in the spring than the wool itself. (Modern sheep have evolved to the place where they don't molt, and they don't have scratchy kemp in their coats either.) By combing the wool out, the Bronze Age people thus came away with a much finer, softer fleece to spin than shearing everything at once would have produced.[3] In the Mycenaean records we find some women listed as *pektriai,* meaning "combers." One can imagine the combers and shepherds working together at the task in molting season, when, as in most harvesting jobs, speed must have been essential so as not to lose the crop.

Then as now, and also as in Homer, the herdsmen lived most of the time with their flocks, in lonely huts out in the hills. The combers, on the contrary, lived in towns and villages, perhaps going out to the pastures only when it was time to fleece the sheep. One tablet records a monthly ration of wheat and figs for eight comber women and their children living at Pylos. They may have spent the rest of the year cleaning and combing tangles out of the harvested wool for spinning, for those were the next jobs to be done.

Before the women could touch it, however, our pound of wool had to be brought to the palace (or at least to the palace officials) and weighed in balance pans with the rest (see fig. 9.4), only then to be redistributed for processing. Lest moths spoil the uncleaned wool, it must have been sent out again just as fast as the textile workers could manage. We read of the weighed-out units of wool being dispatched to various work forces for various purposes, each

[3] Nor was it possible to invent an efficient pair of shears for a few more centuries, until the advent of iron. Iron has spring to it, so the shears (built much like old-fashioned grass clippers) will open automatically after each clip, but bronze will not do this. If the Mycenaeans cut the wool off their sheep, they would have to have done so with a straight knife, which is much slower and riskier. Worse yet for such a hard-driving economy, clipping a molting sheep wastes a lot of good wool—namely, the part between the cut and the root, which will soon fall out anyway and could have been used. The partnership between kempless sheep that no longer molt readily and efficient iron shears seems to have begun in the mid-first millennium B.C.

Figure 9.4. Greek women engaged in all phases of textile work: preparing wool, folding finished cloth, spinning, weaving, and weighing out unworked wool. From a Greek vase of ca. 560 B.C. (fig. 3.6 is a photograph of one side of this vase).

batch carefully sized for the job to be done, from little items like headbands to great cloaks and blankets. The palace bureaucrats intended to lose track of nothing.

After cleaning the allotted wool by removing the burs and other debris, the women needed to wash it. That it had not been washed previously is suggested by the fact that small amounts of raw wool from the inventory went directly to the ointment makers, presumably so they could extract the lanolin, an oil with skin-softening properties still in demand today. Sometimes the palace dispatched aromatic herbs along with the raw wool and olive oil. With such plants, these early "pharmacists" could have perfumed the ointments for the queen and her ladies. (*Pharmakon* is a Greek word, occurring already in Mycenaean texts, that denoted any substance that comes in small quantities and will do something useful for you. It includes drugs and remedies but also dyes, aromatics, spices, and miscellaneous chemicals like astringents and fixatives.) Perfumes and ointments may also have constituted important exports, as much in demand abroad as Chanel perfume is outside France today.

Once our pound of wool was clean, the women would have combed and rolled it into fluffy sausages of fiber (see fig. 9.4), and from these rolls the spinners spun the yarns required by the palace for the weavers. The spinners, like the weavers, functioned in groups, at least for administrative purposes, although spinning can easily be done alone. One group of spinners working for the palace at Pylos consisted of twenty-one women (along with their children: twenty-five girls and four boys); another contained thirty-seven women (with forty-two children). Many lived in outlying villages, others in the local capital itself. One member was put in charge, and supplies of wool and food were allocated to her to distribute to the other women in her group. For this extra responsibility (unlike her Mesopotamian counterparts) she received double rations.

Their food rations seem to us a strange diet: wheat and figs. Occasionally barley replaced wheat, and sometimes olives supplanted figs. Even in Classical Athens, meat was a rare treat for most people, available only after animals had been slaughtered for a religious sacrifice and the meat distributed to the populace. (The philosopher Socrates, in fact, complains of associating stomachaches with big festivals because of the unaccustomed feasting on meat.) As in Classical and later times, villagers could supplement the grain, figs, and olives by collecting tasty wild vegetables in season, such as members of the onion and celery families. The Linear B tablets list coriander, cumin, and fennel seeds—still among the basic spices in Greek cooking today—as condiments collected and stored for the palace kitchens, along with safflower and two types of mint (a word that we borrowed from the Greeks, after the Minoans had lent it to them).

When the spinners finished their work, half the yarn went to women who specialized in preparing the warp on a distinctive band loom—an entirely different piece of equipment from the large loom designed for making cloth.

Our only ancient European depiction of the key process of making the warp comes from Etruscan times, almost a thousand years later (fig. 9.5). Our ability to interpret this scene, however, comes from a Norwegian scholar, Marta Hoffmann, who discovered that

Figure 9.5. Etruscan women helping each other construct a warp, the threads of which are being stretched out to the proper length on the pegged stand at right. Yarn baskets sit on the floor. From a damaged bronze pendant of about 600 B.C., found at Bologna, Italy.

women in remote parts of northern Norway and Finland were still using the warp-weighted loom in 1964. She traveled around to the farms where families possessed these looms (usually stored away somewhere) and persuaded them to demonstrate the processes to her. Oddly, some of the women had modern floor looms as well, but they explained that only on the warp-weighted loom could they produce the large, heavy bedspreads needed for winter sleeping. Hauling the pieces out of storage, they set up the looms while Hoffmann took notes and pictures. From such firsthand evidence, it became possible to interpret many of the weaving scenes from ancient Europe. In fact, some of the Norwegian scholar's pictures of the women working at their looms look remarkably like the ancient ones.

The Etruscan (or Villanovan) scene engraved in bronze (fig. 9.5) shows two women working as a team to make the warp—the foundation for the cloth. One sits in front of a band loom weaving the starting band that will stabilize the warp as it is formed (see Chapter 1 for technical terms). She pushes a loop of warp yarn through the shed of the dozen threads on the band loom in front of her and hands the loop to her companion. As the weaver pays out yarn, the second woman takes the new loop and walks across the room with it until it is long enough to slip it over a peg on a specially constructed stand set up exactly as far away as the warp is to be in length. Then she walks back to fetch the next loop while the weaver changes the shed (to lock the last loop into place) and begins to form another loop.

Because of the starting band, which organizes it and holds it together, a warp for this sort of loom could be made up separately and carried from one workplace to another. We possess a warp from Norway dating to the Iron Age, when it was lost in a bog as it was being transported. The warp strings had been tied up in loose knots in groups, to keep everything neatly organized in transit.

Around 1400 B.C. some weaver discovered a simple trick for weaving brightly variegated starting bands rather than plain white ones, by dividing up two or four colors of thread in the right order on the band loom when setting up. Suddenly it became the height of fashion to wear these bright borders. We see a pattern of bars in alternating colors on many a fresco from this era and read of "cloths with white edges" versus "cloths with variegated edges" in the Mycenaean accounts. Lappish women weaving on warp-weighted looms in rural Scandinavia only thirty years ago were still using an identical pattern for their starting bands.

Once the entire warp was made, it could be turned over to the weavers, who also worked more efficiently in pairs. They would lash the starting band to the top beam of a big warp-weighted loom, divide the shed, add the clay weights to the bottom for tension, and begin to weave the cloth, using the other half of our pound of wool spun up into yarn for the weft. Weft yarn, incidentally, often differs considerably from warp thread. The warp has to be very strong and hard, to stand up under the tension and punishment of the weaving, but the weft can be of any quality desired— for instance, soft and fluffy so as to produce a warm cloth.

Weaving seems simple enough. Over, under, over, under, and soon you have a length of cloth. But in fact, learning to control everything so you come out with a *nice* piece of cloth, with the threads evenly spaced and the edges straight, takes a good deal of time and practice. It is not surprising, then, that we find Mycenaean women billed as apprentices. For example, one village near Knossos housed two supervisors, ten regular craftswomen, one woman who had just been trained, four older girls, and one little boy—these last five presumably the children of the grown women. The listing, as always, is in order of seniority. Other tablets distinguish between "new" trainees, set to work "this year," and "old" apprentices, who were assigned "last year" and are apparently about to assume full status. Training slave women was a regular part of the world Homer describes. Odysseus' elderly nurse and housekeeper, Eurykleia, refers to the other women in his house as "the servants, whom we taught to do their work, to comb the wool and to bear their slavery."

Linear B records are tantalizingly cryptic regarding the kinds of cloth the Mycenaeans would have made from our pound of wool. We learn much more from the frescoes depicting people and their clothes. And there we see radical changes from the earlier Minoan times (see Chapter 4), among both men and women. Minoan women had worn elaborate dresses fashioned from densely patterned textiles (figs. 4.5–7 and 6.3), while the men sported only skimpy loincloths with cinch belts and ornate footwear. With the advent of the Greeks, the tables turned. In Crete we suddenly see men wearing the intricate patterns formerly associated with women, but in the form of an ample kilt rather than a brief loincloth—a new form of dress worn also by the Hittites, the Indo-European cousins of the Greeks, next door in Anatolia. We also observe the cloth of the women's dresses suddenly becoming plain, with at most a decorative edging, as though the men had pre-empted for themselves the use of the fancy Minoan cloth. Soon the men's cloth becomes plain again, too, although still with fancy edgings sometimes.

It is not hard to reconstruct what was happening. In fact, the clothing provides an excellent mirror of the radical changes in economic and social structure brought by the Mycenaean Greeks. We have already seen that the Mycenaeans were organization men. Upon entering Crete, they quickly marshaled the defeated local populace into labor groups to produce quotas of cloth for the central palace at Knossos; the Linear B records list not only how many pieces of cloth a team of weavers finished but also how many they fell short of their quota. Apparently these conquerors requisitioned the existing supply of handsome local fabrics for their own clothing. But clothing soon wears out, and the new labor system was not geared to manufacturing such fancy cloth. So very soon the men's clothing became as plain as the disenfranchised women's.

Working within a quota system of production is not like weaving for oneself. It is no longer fun, nor does the weaver get the benefit of extra effort put in. Mass production is not at all like making single pieces at will; there isn't time to do a careful job. This economic principle is illustrated many times in history. For instance, in Mesopotamia, when people first figured out how to make pottery, they painted it with truly exquisite designs, but when the potter's wheel was invented and it suddenly became possible to mass-produce the pots, the designs rapidly degenerated into a quick swish of the brush for a little color. The same effect is visible in Cretan textiles made for the central palaces, under Mycenaean rule, as they rapidly became plain with at most a fancy edging. Elsewhere on Crete, however, in remote areas that the Mycenaeans failed to subjugate, the Minoan women continued to make their elaborate fabrics all the way down into the Iron Age.

Indeed, independently woven edgings suited Mycenaean parsimony very well: When the main cloth wears out, the good parts of the fancy border, which is more expensive than the cloth, can be removed and reused. (Many a European folk costume has been adorned in this way.) Linear B accounts mention several different kinds of band weavers and several styles of edgings.

We do not have the bookkeeping on the dyers who colored the thread for the pretty edgings. But we have ration lists for thirty-eight seamstresses at Pylos, together with their children. The seamstresses must have sewn on the edgings and stitched up the linen tunics listed. Elsewhere a few men who sew are mentioned, but they seem to be involved with stitching leather for harnesses and the like.

Once the cloth had been finished by the weavers and enhanced, if need be, by the band makers, seamstresses, and fullers, it was returned to the palace to be stored until needed. Some cloths were designated "royal" in quality, others as suitable for retainers, and yet others for guests. Again we catch a glimpse of diplomacy through the giving of textiles to honored visitors, a practice often seen in Homer. As the Phaiakians prepare to send Odysseus home, they present to him a new tunic and cloak and a chest full of clothing and other goods. We also see that the king was responsible for clothing his retainers as well as his servants and slaves, a common practice in the ancient Near East and in medieval Europe. Thus the cloth made by the captive women did not merely dress people but also functioned at the heart of the economy, both domestic and external.

At the other end of the social scale from the dependent workers in the Mycenaean accounts were those who ruled. As the result of reconstruction work done in the wake of archaeological excavation, we may now stroll through their frescoed halls, try out their contoured thrones for size, and admire their great hearths, pillared porticoes, and comfortable bathtubs, while we picture them living a lazy life on the labor of their captives.

But another Homeric example of textiles used as guest gifts furnishes us with a different perspective. While Menelaos prepares to give Odysseus' son, Telemachos, a silver cup and mixing bowl as guest gifts, his wife, Helen—she of the golden spindle—picks out a particularly beautiful robe from those in the storeroom, one "which she had made herself." She presents it to the young man "as a remembrance from the hands of Helen, for your bride to wear at the time of much-desired marriage; and until then let it lie at home in the care of your mother." We deduce from this and numerous other passages that queens, in Homer's view, were in the habit of spinning and weaving certain types of special cloths themselves and of keeping at least some track of the royal stores of cloth and clothing. Penelope and Hecuba are presented the same way.

In short, Mycenaean queens were remembered as busy ladies, just like their counterparts at Mari and Karana (Chapter 7), with many of the same duties in running the palaces. The large numbers of storerooms in the excavated palaces at Pylos, Tiryns, and Mycenae (Schliemann started in to dig at Mycenae just as soon as he had finished Troy) suggest that there was much to run.

Managing a palace is one thing, but actually spinning or weaving like the slaves, even with a spindle made of gold, is another. To understand what cloth was so special that it took a queen to make it, it helps to understand other aspects of early Greek and indeed Indo-European society (see Chapter 2).

Over and over, we find early Indo-European literature obsessed with renown—the renown of the individual, of the family or clan, and of the deities thought to protect that family. We find this as true in Germanic and Indic epics and sagas as in Greek and Roman, and we see the Hittites, when they become literate, creating a genre new to the ancient Near Eastern world: the long historical expositions that prefaced their treaties, cataloguing the deeds that led up to the event at hand. But how do you carry people's fame on down into future generations forever if you don't know how to read and write?

Technically Mycenaean society was literate: it had its syllabic Linear Script B, built on the model of such local Aegean scripts as Minoan Linear A. But Linear B is very poorly suited to writing Greek. Its models made no provision for clusters of consonants— Greek is chock-full of them—and they allowed little room for distinctions between many sounds that are critical to telling words apart in Greek. Thus the Greek word *khiton* "tunic" would be written with the syllable signs that we transliterate *ki-to*. But *ki* could theoretically represent *ki, khi, gi, ski, skhi; kin, khin, gin, skin, skhin; kis, khis, gis, skis, skhis; kir, khir, gir, skir,* or *skhir,* while *to* could represent either *to* or *tho,* with long or short *o* and with or without *n, s,* or *r* at the end of the syllable. Theoretically more than three hundred different words could end up written simply *ki-to,* with no way of distinguishing them.[4] In practice this all but intolerable ambiguity meant that Linear B could be used only for short-term, repetitive (i.e., very redundant) records that would probably be read only by the person who wrote them originally, as a memory aid soon discarded as obsolete. (The account tablets were not baked by the scribe to preserve them, as they often were in Mesopotamia, so they survive only when someone conveniently burned down the palace.) That is, the script was fit only for mundane and fleeting accounts, in which most of the information lay in the numerals rather than in the words—and that is just how we find it used. No complex confections here: no poetry, no history.

How intolerable it must have seemed that such glorious kings and queens as ruled Mycenae and Sparta should die unremembered! Epics there were, but even the bard needed a jog to his memory. It was for this express purpose that men toiled to raise huge funeral mounds—variously called barrows, kurgans, or tumuli—over the bodies of their heroes, from central Asia all the way to Greece and Britain. Achilles piled up one for his dead comrade Patroklos, on the shore near Troy, that all might see and remember, just as the friends of Beowulf raised one for that early

---

[4]Some languages, by contrast, are well suited to such a writing system because their words are built largely without consonant clusters. Japanese and Cherokee use syllabaries with no trouble, and Hawaiian could if it weren't already using the Roman alphabet. (Consider the sequences of consonants and vowels in Hawaiian words like *a-lo-ha, Ho-no-lu-lu, Ka-me-ha-me-ha,* and *hu-la.*) We are aware of one or two such languages having existed in the Aegean before the Greeks arrived. Presumably the speakers of one of them were responsible for inventing the first of these syllabic scripts, which later comers then took up without rethinking the structure. We do not know how well Minoan fitted the mold, but apparently it fitted it with less ambiguity than Greek, for we find many more kinds of inscriptions in Linear A than just accounts—on jewelry, on pottery, on walls, on religious objects. (Minoan Linear A is still undeciphered, but we can infer a good deal about its structure.)

Germanic king after his death: a great mound "on the headland, [built] so high and broad that seafarers might see it from afar." The largest one we know of was raised over the wooden tomb of King Midas of Phrygia—he whose touch was said to turn anything into gold—just after 680 B.C., at Gordion in central Turkey. One hundred and seventy feet high, the mound dominates the landscape, dwarfing the dozens of other tumuli in the neighborhood. (Ironically, Gordion had just been sacked by another warlike Indo-European tribe, so Midas' followers had not a scrap of gold left to put into their lord's tomb.)

Thus the Indo-European men raised mounds and composed oral epics to try to attain immortality for their names and deeds, during long periods when writing was not widespread. But the women turned to their textiles to portray the deeds of their families. We have already mentioned the women who made the Bayeux Tapestry to glorify William of Normandy's victory (Chapter 6), and from western Europe we could add the story found in the *Nibelungenlied* that Brünhilde depicted the exploits of Siegfried on her web, ripping the cloth in fury when he betrayed her (no more memory of him!). There is mounting evidence that noble Mycenaean ladies likewise recorded the deeds and/or myths of their clans in their weaving. Homer implies as much of Helen and Penelope, and in Classical times noble Athenian girls still carried on an ancient tradition (almost certainly from the Bronze Age) of weaving an important story cloth for Athena every year (Chapter 6). The stories were woven in friezes, using a supplementary weft technique perfected in Europe in the Neolithic and Bronze ages. We have many depictions of Iron Age Greek story cloths, and fragments of at least two have been discovered in Classical Greek tombs in the Crimea (fig. 9.6).

Captive women undoubtedly wove the mass of towels and bed sheets, cloaks and blankets, tunics and chemises used by the ruling household and its many dependents, plus extras for the guests and the export trade. The noble ladies may have chosen to make especially fancy clothing for themselves and their highborn friends as

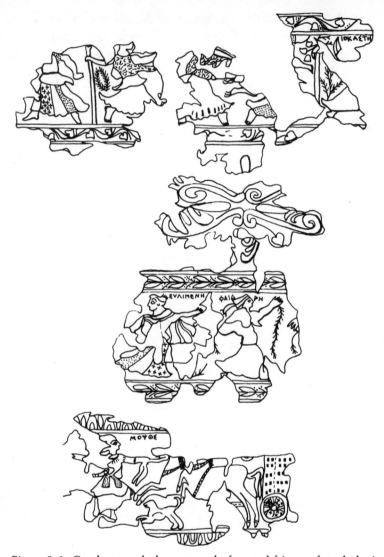

Figure 9.6. Greek story cloth composed of several friezes of mythological and quasi-historical figures, reserve-dyed in red, black, and white, from the fourth century B.C. Found in a tomb near the Greek colony at Kertch, on the north shore of the Black Sea. It was sufficiently precious that it had been carefully mended in antiquity.

well. But the recording of the mythohistory of the clan would have been a task so important that it could be entrusted only to the queens and princesses, with their gold and silver spindles and royal purple wool.

10

≫≫≫

Behind the Myths

> I will don a white dress
> and turn into a white swan;
> and then I will fly away
> to where my darling has gone.
> —Russian folk song

> White linen is the paper of [housewives], which
> must be on hand in great, well-ordered layers,
> and therein they write their entire philosophy
> of life, their woes and their joys.
> —Gottfried Keller, *Der grüne Heinrich* (1854)

Once upon a time an Athenian princess named Prokne was wed to Tereus, king of the barbarous Thracians of the north. When Prokne's unfortunate sister, Philomela, came for a visit, Tereus fell madly in love with the girl, locked her away and raped her, then cut out her tongue to prevent her from telling anyone of the crime. Philomela, however, wove into a cloth the story of her misfortune. When Prokne, receiving the cloth, understood what had befallen, she freed her sister, killed her own son, Itys, whom she had borne to Tereus, and served the child up to his father at a feast—the vilest revenge she could think of. When Tereus discovered the truth, in wrath he pursued the two sisters, thinking to kill them, but the gods transformed all three into birds: Tereus into the hoopoe (a large, crested bird with a daggerlike beak), Philomela into the swallow, which can only twitter unintelligibly, and Prokne into the nightingale, which spends the night singing "Itys, Itys!" in mourning for her dead son. All these birds have reddish spots, it is said, from getting spattered with the blood of the child.

So Ovid tells the tale for his jaded Roman audience, embroidering it more profusely than Philomela herself. (Aeschylus, five hundred years earlier, tells it in briefest outline.) Clearly we have here a "just so" story—the explanatory sort of tale found worldwide and polished to a modern art form by Rudyard Kipling. It is interesting for our purposes because it shows in yet another way the great importance that clothmaking had in women's lives, becoming central to their mythology as well.

In an increasing number of cases, archaeological understanding throws light on myths and their shaping. Consider the stories in which someone is poisoned by donning clothes dipped in dragon's blood—preposterous on the face of it, since we know that there is no such thing as a dragon.

There are at least two such stories in Greek mythology. In one, the sorceress Medea uses poisoned cloth to kill her rival, Kreusa, the young princess of Corinth, whom her longtime husband, Jason, has just arranged to marry behind Medea's back. She sends a beautiful dress steeped in dragon's blood as a royal bridal present and gloats over the lethal results. In the other, the centaur Nessos (half man, half horse) offers violence to Herakles' bride, Deianeira, for which offense Herakles mortally wounds him. As he dies, Nessos whispers to Deianeira to gather some of his blood—itself mixed with that of the Hydra, a water dragon—and to keep it, so that if she should ever doubt the hero's love she can color a garment with it and win him back through his wearing it. Deianeira falls for the trick and many years later uses the blood on a garment in an attempt to win Herakles back from a younger woman. The monster's blood turns out to be fatal poison, of course, not a love charm, and Nessos' revenge is complete.

Bits of evidence pieced together from archaeology, geology, and ancient texts now suggest that the soft mineral realgar, which is a dark purplish red (a favorite royal color), was one of several stones sometimes crushed and used as pigments—for cloth, among other things. Realgar also upon occasion was known as dragon's blood, as its bright color typically occurred splashed across the surface of harder rocks. But realgar has another property: It is the "arsenic ruby," sulfide of arsenic—a deadly poison if kept in prolonged contact with the skin. I have collected estimates that a month or so of wearing a garment colored royal purple with arsenic would be sufficient to do one in. Arsenic poisoning is not a fast and fiery death, as Euripides pictures it for dramatic purposes in his play *Medea* (written perhaps a millennium after the alleged events). But it kills just as dead, after (ironically) giving the victim an especially lovely skin complexion for a few days. And so we see that death by poisoning from cloth dipped in dragon's blood could be quite real, even without any dragons. Once the cause of death is handed down in story to a time or place where this pigment is unknown (realgar is not widely found), it becomes easy for fertile minds to supply the dragons.

Another example of the real turning fantastic when people don't understand it concerns magical shirts made from nettles, which occur in fairy tales from several parts of Europe. Everyone knows that nettles sting the skin painfully; therefore, to make a soft and handsome shirt from such a plant would clearly take nothing short of magic. Or at least so it must have seemed to peasants who were vaguely aware that such objects had once existed. Laboratory studies have shown that all the Scandinavian archaeological finds of fabric thought to be linen were in fact made of nettle fiber. The nettles had been picked in the wild, then retted (see Chapter 8), spun, and woven exactly like flax. Furthermore, the technology was practiced right up into this century. (During World War II, when domestic supplies of the common fibers were getting scarce, elderly peasant women who still knew how to prepare nettle fiber were set to work by the Germans.) It turns out that nettles can be picked comfortably if one is careful always to move the hand in the direction in which the stingers will lie flat (up the stalk), and the process of retting rots away the stingers, so there is no problem at all after that. The resulting fiber is finer and silkier than flax, giving a much nicer chemise. Magic indeed!

Many ancient myths that revolve around women's textile arts function on the basis of analogy. For example, fate, to the Greeks, was spun as a thread. Both thread and time were linear, both easily and arbitrarily broken. One could argue that, since women were the people who spun, the spinners of one's destiny would have to be women. These divine female spinners were called the Moirai, or Apportioners, and are often mentioned in Greek literature as being three in number: Klotho, "Spinner," who spun the thread of life, Lachesis, "Allotment," who measured it out, and Atropos, "Unturnable," who chose when to lop it off. Homer is less specific, and in both the *Iliad* and *Odyssey* he repeats a stock couplet probably passed down from bards much older than he:

> And then [the person] will suffer whatever Fate and the
>   heavy[-handed] Spinners
> spun into their linen [thread] for him, coming into being,
>   when his mother gave birth to him.[1]

The triple image of Klotho, Lachesis, and Atropos, however, has caught the popular imagination both then and now. In a modern clay sculpture of three peasant women, the Hungarian artist Mar-

[1] These lines occur in the *Odyssey,* Book 7 (197–98) and almost verbatim, for example, in the *Iliad,* Book 20 (127–28) and Book 24 (210). In each case the participle *gignomenōi*, which means "coming into being," is ambiguous in its reference, applying equally well in both sense and grammatical agreement to the thread and to "him," thus further emphasizing the parallelism perceived in the events.

git Kovacs has splendidly encapsulated this tradition of fate. Hungarian girls customarily learned to spin at about twelve to thirteen years of age, so the spinner is shown as a young girl, plying her task with a rather naïve and hopeful expression. A young matron beside her, now old enough to be mistress of her own household, measures out the thread between her hands in gentle self-importance. Beyond them an old woman, slightly stooped and eyeing her companions a bit enviously, wields the shears.[2]

The notion of female deities creating a life by spinning a thread is particularly Greek and runs through Greek mythological thinking at a very deep level. It may have begun from the association of childbirth with attendant women who did their spinning while waiting to act as midwives in the birthing room. The parallel between bringing forth new thread and new humans—both done by women—strengthened the image. The Romans, for their part, equated the Greek Moirai with their minor goddesses the Parcae, who presided at childbirth but were not necessarily spinners. Scholars also compare the Moirai to the Germanic Norns, of Wagnerian fame. These female deities had indeed to do with fate, but their function seems to have been to warn humans of impending doom by speaking out somehow—their name has etymologically to do with vocal noises—and sometimes to produce destinies by weaving cloth.

The Greeks associated another deity of procreation with spinning. Close analysis of the musculature of the famous Venus de Milo—the ancient Greek statue of Aphrodite found on the island of Melos in 1820 and now in the Louvre—shows that she couldn't hold on to her drapery even before the statue lost its arms. Why? She was holding both arms out (fig. 10.1). One, the left, she held high and a little back, counterbalancing its weight by curving her

---

[2] This sculpture and many other celebrations in clay of women and their work are on display in the museum made from Margit Kovacs's house in Szentendre, just north of Budapest. Male subjects, though fewer, are equally powerfully portrayed. Visitors to Hungary who enjoy the visual arts will find it well worth their while to make a sidetrip up the Danube to Szentendre.

Figure 10.1. Venus de Milo, the famous marble statue of Aphrodite
(Roman name: Venus), goddess of love and procreation, found on the
Aegean island of Melos. The musculature of what is left of her arms
suggests that she stood in the typical position for spinning thread in the
Greek manner. Spinning was a common symbol for the creation of new
life in Greece and elsewhere.

body. The other she held out in front of herself at about chest level; her gaze rests about where the hand would be. In those positions lies a story. Modern art critics are not often aware of it, but this was a pose painfully familiar to women in ancient Greek society. They spent many hours holding a distaff loaded with fiber high in the left while working the thread and spindle with the more "dexterous" right, out in front where it could be watched. This Aphrodite (or Venus, as the Romans called her) was spinning.

We have other statues of Aphrodite with the arms similarly placed, although the distaff and spindle, which would have been sculpted from more perishable materials, are not preserved. We also possess several vase paintings of women spinning that show a similar positioning of the implements (cf. figs. 1.3 and 9.4).

Why should the goddess of love and procreation be a spinner? For the same reason, ultimately, that the Moirai who attend the birth are spinning. Something new is coming into being where before there was at most an amorphous mass. Listen to the description of a naïve onlooker; the scene happens to be laid in Africa:

> The woman ... took a few handfuls of goats' hair and beat them with a whippy stick so that the hairs became separated. Then, taking a stiff piece of dried grass stem in her right hand she twisted some hair round it and continued to twist, while a thread as if by magic grew out of the mass of hair continually fed into it by her left hand.

The analogy of a person's life-span to a thread goes beyond length and fragility to the very act of creation. Women *create* thread; they somehow pull it out of nowhere, just as they produce babies out of nowhere. The same image is latent in our own term *life-span*. *Span* is from the verb *spin*, which originally meant "draw out, stretch long" and only later shifted to mean "turn, whirl" as people refocused on the whirling spindle that stretched the newly forming thread.

The analogy between women's making thread and bringing souls into (or back into) the world finds expression in another famous Greek myth. According to the tale, the Athenian hero Theseus went to Crete to bring down King Minos by confronting his powerful beast, the Minotaur. There Minos' daughter, Ariadne, fell in love with Theseus and gave him a ball of thread that would lead him back out of the Labyrinth if he succeeded in killing the fearsome bull-monster. (Linguists have argued that *Labyrinth* was actually the name of the palace at Knossos. Its hundreds of rambling rooms in at least three stories would have been bewildering to a mainland Greek accustomed to houses with two rooms and a porch. Bull-jumping games were apparently held in the huge courtyard in the center of this palace.)

A nice story—and perhaps the original purpose of the thread was indeed to lead Theseus to safety. But at some point a cult of "Aphrodite Ariadne" sprang up on some of the Greek islands. There Theseus was said to have abandoned the princess Ariadne on his way home to Athens after killing the Minotaur. This cult—of Ariadne and Aphrodite combined—included the peculiar custom of having a young man imitate the sounds and motions of a woman going through labor.[3] Thus we find Ariadne, the girl with the thread, tied simultaneously to the bringing back of souls (Theseus and his companions) from death's door, to the birthing of new lives, and to Aphrodite, goddess of procreation.

Weaving, as opposed to thread making, was the special province of Athena. Wherever divine weaving was to be done, ancient Greek storytellers looked to Athena. In Hesiod's tale of Pandora ("All-gifts") and her infamous box—a box filled with all the evils

---

[3] Mock labor by a man is well known in other parts of the world—for example, in Guyana and among the Ainu of northern Japan—as a way of deluding and diverting the attention of evil spirits who might harm the newborn child. (It is known in the literature by the French term *couvade*.) The woman who is undergoing parturition elsewhere, meanwhile, is supposed to keep quiet and try to look as though nothing were happening to her. Couvade has been reported fairly recently in Europe, too, in Corsica and Albania.

of the world, including hope (no better than delusion, to the Greek mind)—Zeus orders Hephaistos to make the image of a beautiful girl out of clay. Aphrodite is to "shed grace on her head" and "Athena to teach her skills—to weave a complex warp." As the various gods busy themselves in tricking Pandora out,

> The owl-eyed goddess Athena girdled her, and bedecked her
> with a shining garment, and on her head a fancy veil
> she spread with her hands, a wonder to behold.[4]

Thus Athena provides for the young bride both her clothing and her instruction in weaving, the basic household craft.

Perhaps the most famous story of Athena's weaving is that of Arachne. This uppity girl boasted that she could weave better than Athena, the patron goddess of weaving. Not a wise thing to do: Athena heard and challenged her to a weaving contest. According to Ovid, again embroidering his tale to the utmost, Arachne boldly wove into her web the stories of the most scandalous love affairs of the gods: how Zeus, the king of the gods, repeatedly was unfaithful to his wife as he disguised himself to rape or seduce a dozen women—appearing to Leda as a swan, to Europa as a bull, to Danaë as a shower of gold, and, most treacherously of all, to Alkmene as her own absent husband, Amphitryon. Not content with that, Arachne depicted Poseidon, Apollo, Bacchus, and Hades as they also assumed false forms to take advantage of various hapless maidens. Athena, for her part, grimly wove stories of mortals who had lost contests with the gods and been soundly punished. (We have a representation of this weaving contest on a little oil flask from Corinth, from about 600 B.C.—fig. 10.2. Athena, a divine being, is so much taller than the human women

---

[4]Note that the first and apparently most important garment for this young woman is the girdle, as everywhere else in the early Greek texts. I suspect that this is some traditional form of the ancient string skirt, with all its significance for mating (see Chapter 2). Unfortunately we are seldom told more, because everyone at *that* time, of course, knew all about it and didn't need to have it explained.

Figure 10.2. Design on a small Greek perfume flask from Corinth showing the contest between the goddess Athena and the mortal Arachne. Arachne unwisely boasted that she could weave better than the goddess of weaving herself. After the contest Athena (recognizable here as taller than the humans) turned the unfortunate girl into a spider to weave webs forever. The Greek word for *spider* is *arakhnē*, from which we get our scientific name for spiders, arachnids.

that her head scrapes the top of the picture.) Gods always win, of course. When the cloths were finished, in wrath Athena turned Arachne into the Spider, doomed to weave in dark corners for the rest of time.[5]

But Athena's purview is much wider than just the making of cloth and clothing. Athenians worshiped her also as the one who brings fertility to the crops and protection to the city, as the inventor of the cultivated olive (one of the central crops in the Aegean), as the patroness of shipbuilders and other handcrafters, as a goddess of war, and so on. In fact, she is the goddess of so many things that modern commentators lose sight of her central nature.

That nature is most clearly seen by looking at what she is not, at what opposes her. Her traditional opponent is Poseidon, with whom she strove first for possession of Athens. As a sign of supremacy, Poseidon hit the rock with his trident and a salt spring gushed forth, but Athena produced the first olive tree. (Both the

---

[5] The English word for spider means "spinner"; our culture has fastened on to a different aspect of the spider's repertoire. Biologists, on the other hand, call all spiders by the name *arachnids*.

trident mark and the "original" olive tree were proudly shown to visitors at the Erechtheum, on the Athenian Acropolis, in Classical times.) The citizens of the new state judged that Athena's gift was going to be much more useful to them than a salt spring and awarded her the prize. But Poseidon was a poor loser and in revenge sent a tidal flood, which Athena barely halted at the foot of the Acropolis, protecting her people. (Bad tidal waves did occur in the Aegean.)

This whole tale, despite its anchors in reality, is obviously another packet of "just so" stories to explain origins, but the nature of the opposition shows us that Athena is the beneficent deity that protects humans and makes them prosper, pushing back the untamed forces of nature represented by Poseidon.[6] More exactly, she represents everything that human skill and know-how (*tekhnē*, whence our word *technology*) can accomplish; she is goddess of "civilization" itself. Exactly this same opposition motivates the *Odyssey*, where Athena helps Odysseus by means of clever stratagems and skills (including building a seagoing raft) to escape the wrath of Poseidon, who for his part throws an endless barrage of storms, gales, and wild seas at the poor mortal. Homer treats Athena in both epics as the goddess of good advice and clever plans. Hence she functions as the embodiment of one's "conscience" and bright ideas.

If human skill and cunning are personified by Athena, and the central womanly skill is weaving, then weaving can itself become a metaphor for human resourcefulness. One's life-span was conceived by the Greeks as a thread, formed by the Fates at birth, but the act of weaving the thread symbolized what one did with that

---

[6] Modern scholarship has made it clear that Poseidon is a local Aegean deity of earthquakes and tidal waves, who got grafted onto the pantheon of the incoming Greeks in the spot where the Indo-European god of fresh water belongs (Roman Neptune, etc.). "Raging waters" are the point of crossover. Big rivers were major forces to Indo-Europeans living around the Volga, Don, Danube, etc., but there are no such enormous rivers in Greece. The most fearsome body of water there is the sea, especially when seismic activity whips it up into a killer tidal wave.

life, the choices of the individual. Thus throughout the *Odyssey* Athena and "the wily Odysseus" (her favorite devotee) are constantly hatching ingenious plots to escape one tight situation or another, rallying with the words "Come, let us weave a plan!"

Odysseus' clever wife, Penelope, is from the same mold. Not only does she, too, use this phrase, but she actually attempts to weave her way out of trouble, telling the suitors who pester her in Odysseus' prolonged absence that she cannot marry until she finishes an important funeral cloth for her aged father-in-law. For three years she tricks these men by unraveling at night what she has woven during the daytime. Truly she was a worthy wife for the trickiest of all the Greeks.

Good evidence exists that the basis of Athena's mythology lies far back in Aegean prehistory, long before the Greeks themselves arrived. The names of Athena and Athens are not Greek or Indo-European names but come from an earlier linguistic layer. Furthermore, most of the Greek weaving vocabulary is not Indo-European. The proto-Indo-Europeans (see Chapter 2) seem to have had scant knowledge of weaving, their women knowing only how to weave narrow belts and bands. Probably they were ignorant even of heddles, which mechanize the weaving process and make it efficient (see Chapter 1). The Greeks clearly learned how to use the large European warp-weighted loom *after* they broke off and moved away from the proto-Indo-European community since all their terms for using a large loom (as opposed to a small band loom) have been borrowed. The people who taught the Greeks this technology, vocabulary, and associated mythical lore must have been the "indigenous" inhabitants of the Balkans (skilled in weaving since the middle of the Neolithic, perhaps even 5000 B.C.). The Athenians referred to these natives as "autochthonous"—born of the land itself—and Athena must belong originally to them. After all, no one develops a major deity around a technology one doesn't even know yet.

The antiquity of Athena as a local, non-Indo-European deity is

Figure 10.3. Greek loom weight showing an owl spinning wool. The reference is to the goddess Athena, patroness of spinning and weaving, whose sacred bird was the owl. Several such weights are known, dating to the fourth century B.C.

hinted at further by her frequent representation as an owl, that wise-looking bird so common in parts of Greece. In Classical times, after money had been invented, the Athenians chose Athena's owl to stamp on their silver coins. But we also have, from the same period, loom weights stamped with the owl of their favorite goddess. A particularly charming weight shows the owl with human hands, spinning wool from a wool basket at its feet as it looks cockily out at the spectator (fig. 10.3). It gives a new image to Homer's stock epithet, "owl-eyed Athena,"[7] and it underscores once again the importance of this deity to the women on whose textiles so much of Aegean commerce and social interaction was built.

[7] This much-disputed epithet, *glauk-opis,* is often translated "bright-eyed" or "gray-eyed," which is etymologically a possibility, but the term has good company in Hera's epithet *bo-opis,* which can only mean "cow-eyed." (The word for *owl* is *glauks.*) Such animal forms for deities are common in the layers of European culture that preceded the classically Indo-European populace, persisting here and there in dark corners even up to the present.

The fairy tales of the rest of Europe frequently involve spinning and sometimes weaving and sewing. Most of these tales were first written down long after Classical Greek times, and they often show the influence of that important culture. But often, too, they go their own way.

In late Roman times the neuter plural word *fata*—"those things which have been spoken" (therefore equated with destiny)—was reanalyzed as a feminine singular noun (both end in *a*) and consequently personified as a woman. This divine lady Fate then eveloped a host of identical sisters (the Fates) and took over the duties and attributes of the Parcae, the birth goddesses who determined a person's destiny. English *fairy* comes from a derivative of French *fée*, which itself comes directly from the Latin *fata*.[8] In France and other countries that developed from Roman culture, a fairy is popularly viewed as a female spirit who turns up at birth to bestow good or evil on the child's life. She need not have a spindle—a simple wand is more likely—but occasionally she does.

The tale of Sleeping Beauty illustrates the type well. To celebrate the birth of their child, the king and queen of a mythical land throw a magnificent party, inviting among others the birth fairies. One fairy is not invited—either because she is evil or because she is the thirteenth fairy on the list (which in Christian lore amounts to evil, since the thirteenth person at the Last Supper—counting Jesus as the first—betrayed the Savior). Enraged, the uninvited one crashes the party and curses the baby princess, saying the child will die when she reaches fifteen (some versions say sixteen), upon

[8] Neuter plural and feminine singular sounded the same, both ending in -*a: fata*. The switch to feminine singular was further helped by the Parcae (singular: Parca), who had the same function, and Fama, meaning "Rumor," who had the same kind of name. The Italian word *fata* still preserves both the form and the meaning, whereas the French *fée* (whence English *fee-rie, fairy*) and the Spanish *hada* (both meaning "fairy") have undergone changes in the sounds that are normal in each of these languages.

pricking her finger on a spindle. All seems lost. A good fairy who has not yet made *her* wish, however, commutes the sentence to a century-long sleep instead of death. As a precaution, the king banishes all spindles from the kingdom, but to no avail, for on the girl's fifteenth birthday, the evil fairy in the guise of an old woman brings the fateful spindle into the castle. Entranced by the spindle's dancing motion, the princess reaches for it, pricks her finger, and she and the entire court fall asleep for a hundred years. An enormous hedge of thorny roses grows up around the castle to protect it (in the version collected by the Grimm brothers, she is named Dornröschen, meaning "Little Thorn Rose"). One hundred years pass. At the end of them the princess is aroused by the kiss of a handsome and valiant prince, who has found his way through the thicket to her side.

The old elements of birth Fates are still there, but their purposes are only hazily remembered. No longer does the thread carry the child's destiny. That function has moved to the spindle itself, even though one would be hard put to find a European spindle sharp enough to prick one's finger. Spindles are typically made with rather rounded ends and polished smooth so as not to catch on the thread. The finger prick seems almost to have wandered over from the rose thorns, which have the very real and ancient job of protecting the innocent (see Chapter 6).

Most European fairy tales to do with spinning concern the plight of some poor woman left to carry out this endless task. For example, supernatural creatures may transform roomfuls of flax or even worthless straw into the finest of spun gold—hence instant wealth—as in the tale of Rumpelstiltskin. (The source of the image is not far to seek. Flax that has been retted in standing or running water turns golden; flax retted in the nightly dew is pale silver.) Or they may simply spin prodigious amounts.

In one of the Grimms' tales, called "The Three Spinsters," a lazy girl who hates spinning is forced to spin impossible amounts for the queen. Three deformed women turn up in the nick of time, one with a huge foot, the second with a huge lower lip, the third with an enormous thumb. They offer to spin it all for the lazy girl if she will promise to invite them to the head table at her wedding. She agrees, and in no time they spin all the thread. The queen, amazed at what she thinks is the girl's skill and industry, marries her to the crown prince. But the girl does not forget her promise and seats the three women at the bridal table. The curious prince asks each one how she got her deformity. The woman with the large foot allows that it came from treadling a spinning wheel all the time, the one with the enormous lip says she got it from always wetting the flax, and she of the huge thumb blames her problem on constantly drafting the fibers into the yarn. Horrified, the bridegroom decrees that his beautiful new wife is never to spin again.[9]

More than a little wishful thinking lurks in both these tales!

The Slavic women of eastern Europe took a slightly different approach to getting help, one that seems to go very far back. In the north the Slavic women preserved memory of a pagan goddess named Mokosh or Mokusha, possibly Finnic in origin, who walked at night spinning wool and to whom one might pray for help both with spinning and with doing the laundry. If the sheep were losing their wool, the saying was: "Mokosh has sheared the sheep." The eastern and central Europeans also paid attention to female spirits known as *rusalki* or *vily* (mentioned in Chapter 6), thought to be the souls of girls who had died before having any children—that is, cut off from living on through their offspring. As such a *vila (rusalka)* had the power to bestow her unused fertility on the crops, livestock, and families of others. In the cold and infertile north these deities were portrayed as ugly and unkempt, and of vicious temper, but farther south, in Ukraine, they were imagined as beautiful young nymphs with long hair, who hid in the water and made it rain by combing their wet tresses. If properly treated, they might help out during the night with such female tasks as spinning. But if surprised during their nightly dances, especially by a man, they would surround the poor unfortunate

[9] Note that the tale as it stands is no earlier than late medieval because that is when the spinning wheel was introduced into Europe.

a.   b.   c.

Figure 10.4. Slavic representations of *vily (rusalki)*, female fertility spirits who appeared typically as birds ([a], from a medieval wedding earring of gold) or fish ([b], from an eighteenth-century windowsill carving). In ancient times women danced in their honor, using their long sleeves to imitate the *vila*'s wings ([c], from a twelfth century wedding bracelet of silver).

and dance him to death. (Someone who "has the willies" has just been terrified by a forbidden glimpse of them.) Images of the *vily,* usually half girl and half bird or fish, adorned the women's distaffs and wedding jewelry as well as the window frames and barnyard gates, in perpetual silent appeal for their protection and fertility (fig. 10.4 a and b).

Since the *vily* were conceived as bird-women—beings that could take either womanly or avian shape, especially that of white water birds like swans—the women performed dances in their honor at certain festivals by loosening the tremendously long white sleeves of their chemises and waving them about like wings (fig. 10.4 c). Some of these dance figures survive, as do several representations of the women dancing with loosened sleeves—both in a medieval manuscript and on ancient wedding bracelets dug up in Ukraine. (The bracelets normally held the sleeves up at the wrists so the woman could use her hands.) These dancers of the summer Rusalii festivals were vehemently taken to task by the proselytizing Christian priests, newly arrived from Byzantium, who considered the whole business utterly anti-Christian. We wish they had told us more details in their railings, however, so we could understand the ritual more clearly. But knowing even this much will allow us to interpret better one of the most famous Russian fairy tales, that of the Frog Princess.

"In ancient years, in times of yore," a king of a far-off kingdom demanded that his three sons shoot their arrows into the air and then marry whoever retrieved and returned them. The arrows of the two older princes were brought back by highborn ladies, but Ivan's was retrieved and presented by a female frog, which he was obliged to marry anyway. Soon, to test their skill, the king requested his daughters-in-law to make shirts for him. Ivan was in despair. His wife was a frog. How could she weave? But during the night, as he slept, the frog-bride shed her green skin, turned into a beautiful girl for a short while, and procured from her *rusalka*-handmaids a shirt so fine that the king chose it as best by far.

Next the king ordered the three brides to bake bread for him— the second household skill requisite in a good wife. This time, suspecting that the frog was magical, the brides of the older princes spied on the frog to learn her recipe. Aware of their presence, the frog set about making bread in preposterous ways so that when the brides went off and imitated what they had seen their bread fell and tasted terrible. Then, in the middle of the night when everyone slept, the frog called her servants to bring her the finest loaf ever tasted, decorated, moreover, with figures of birds, animals, and trees.[10]

Finally the king announced a great ball at the palace, to judge which of the three brides danced the best. The frog told her

---

[10] In villages in parts of Russia to this day the bride brings bread decorated in exactly this way to the groom's house for the wedding. It is the traditional wedding loaf. In fact, the entire story of the Frog Princess embodies step by step the ancient Slavic wedding customs, starting with locating a prospective bride, testing her abilities to make clothing and food (traditionally in that order), testing her strength and endurance through dancing (is she strong enough to do the farmwork?), all the way down to presenting her to the family in a golden dress the morning after the wedding has been consummated. The groom, too, was tested, but those rites are harder to decipher in this text.

dejected husband to go on ahead, that she would follow in an hour. Then she shed her frog skin, dressed, and went to the banquet hall to join him. He was overjoyed at her great beauty, but her sisters-in-law were dismayed, since the Frog Princess was clearly a magician. Again they decided to imitate whatever she did, in hopes of learning to do magical things too. When they saw her put the bones from her swan-meat supper into one sleeve and the dregs of her drink into the other, they did likewise.

It came time to dance; the tsar called on the older daughters-in-law, but they deferred to the frog. She immediately took hold of Prince Ivan and came forward: how she danced and danced, spun and turned—everything a marvel! She waved her right arm—forests and waters appeared; she waved her left—all sorts of birds began to fly. Everyone was astonished. She finished dancing and all disappeared. The other daughters-in-law went to dance, and tried to do the same: but when one waved her right arm, the bones flew out, right among the guests, and from her left sleeve water was flung about, also all over people. The tsar was not pleased.

Entranced by his wife's new form, the prince rushed home, seized the frog skin, and burned it so his beautiful bride would have to keep her human shape. The princess, upon reaching home, was horrified. Mournfully she told him that if only he had waited three more days, the evil spell that had made her a frog would have been broken. Now she must return whence she came, and he would have to seek for her "beyond the thrice ninth kingdom." At that she vanished.

Eventually the prince learned from an old witch that Elena the Beautiful (as she was called) was living with this witch's eldest sister. The younger witch then gave him the following advice: "As you begin to come close, they will become aware of it. Elena will turn into a spindle, and her dress will become gold. My sister will start to spin the gold; when she finishes with the spindle and puts it in a box and locks up the box, you must find the key, open the box, break the spindle, throw the top behind you and the ase in front of you—and she will spring up before you." Prince Ivan followed her instructions and finally regained his wife. They flew away home, where they continued to "live and feast wonderfully."

It is clear from what we know of the *rusalki* that the princess's dance involving waving the long white sleeves was intended to symbolize not just birds and countryside but the magical creation of nature itself—the plants, waters, and creatures (especially the white water birds) over which the *vily / rusalki* presided and among whom they lived. The mysterious and powerful nature of the egg, and with it the birds, frogs, fish, and snakes that produce eggs, is the central image of Slavic creation lore. (In one version of this story Prince Ivan must also feed the princess an egg at the witch's house before she can recognize him again.) In the Slavic *rusalka* dance, the woman arranges the color, form, and use of her clothing to *imitate* the life-giving deities in their form of swan-maidens, thus sharing their magic "sympathetically." This is quite a different image from the Greek one of creating by spinning thread, although even more intimately tied to females. By contrast, the spinning that occurs at the end of the tale equates the golden thread on the spindle with the girl's golden dress. The thread is merely the source of clothing, and the woman the tool that makes the thread.[11]

---

[11] In fact, another layer of symbolism involved the spindle itself. Traditional Russian wedding songs often speak of the young hero finding his bride by shooting his arrow into the maiden's tower—a simple phallic image. The lock plates of storerooms and wedding chests were traditionally made in the form of a lozenge (a simple female sexual image, but often painted to be quite graphic). Inserting the key into the hole in the center thus symbolically opened the way to nature's riches. Here the spindle functions the same way since the part Ivan is to throw away behind him is the shaft (which is not his), and the part that he throws in front of him that becomes his wife is the spindle whorl at the bottom—a disk with a hole in it (fig. 8.3).

When Adam delved and Eve span,
Who was then a gentleman?
    —John Ball, at Wat Tyler's Rebellion, 1381

Lay not up for yourselves treasures upon earth,
where moth and rust doth corrupt. . . .
    —Matthew 6:19

Biblical references to spinning, weaving, and other aspects of textile making are rather few, compared with those in early European texts, but popular culture draws upon them constantly. While staying with friends in the hill country of Wales recently, I was taken to see a flock of sheep that were considered remarkable because they were all speckled and spotted, instead of the usual white with black face and feet. "Jacob's sheep" they were called. The reference is to Genesis 30–31, where Jacob performs a bit of sympathetic magic by placing speckled rods in front of the mating animals so that the offspring will be speckled. This he does in order to increase his pay, since he is to receive all the spotted animals from his master's flock.

The lack of references to spinning and weaving is surely not because these crafts were unknown in the days of Genesis and Exodus. From the point of view of Abraham and his family the textile arts were very old; Eve had consigned herself and all womankind to an eternity of spinning and weaving the moment she ate of the Tree of Knowledge and realized that she and Adam were naked. The Patriarchs, in fact, were primarily shepherds and had lots of wool at their disposal. Moreover, they used it for modes of clothing that the Egyptians who came in contact with them found quite distinctive. Joseph's "coat of many colors" answers nicely to Egyptian tomb paintings of their well-to-do neighbors in Palestine (fig. 10.5), depicted from their visits to the Nile in the Twelfth Dynasty (the early second)—probably not far from the time of Joseph's arrival. There we see both men and women wearing

Figure 10.5. Egyptian depiction of Aamu visitors from Palestine, bringing eye paint to trade to the Egyptians. Like the biblical Joseph, they wear "coats of many colors." From the Middle Kingdom tomb of Khnemhotep at Beni Hasan, early second millennium B.C. (cf. fig. 8.2).

gaily striped and patterned tunics, some of them fringed, that look very heavy compared with the Egyptians' thin linen garments. Color plus thickness, in light of what we know about ancient cloth, almost guarantees that the foreigners are wearing wool. They are driving donkeys laden with their children and their goods, much the way Joseph's family must have looked when it moved to Egypt.

Philologists still dispute the exact technical meaning of the Hebrew word translated by the phrase "of many colors" in the King James Bible—whether it means "striped" or simply "patterned."[12] One scholar, however, provides a slightly more sinister slant to the whole story by pointing out that, whatever it means, the same term is used of some princesses in 2 Samuel 13:18, where we are told that this was the special dress of the ruling class. No wonder Joseph's older brothers, already enraged at him for telling them his dreams that he would become their ruler, stripped him of his ruler's garment!

In Exodus we begin to hear a bit more of textile arts. When Moses rallies the people to furnish the new tabernacle, as they settle in their new lands, he asks them to bring all the necessaries,

[12] Or perhaps "pattern-woven" (Genesis 37:3). The Hebrew of the Septuagint is *ktoneth pasim,* the first word meaning "tunic" (see Chapter 5) and the second word something like "striped" (to judge from other passages and from the Latin Vulgate's choice of translation).

including cloth of various sorts: "And all the women that were wise hearted did spin with their hands, and brought that which they had spun, both of blue, and of purple, and of scarlet, and of fine linen. And all the women whose heart stirred them up in wisdom spun goats' hair." From these offerings were made great "curtains of fine twined linen, and blue, and purple, and scarlet [wool]." The distinction made in the verbs between the spinning of the colored wool *(tavah)* and the "twining" of the linen thread *(shazar)* shows us that these women, who had just come from Egypt, had learned to splice and twist linen in the peculiar Egyptian manner while living there (see Chapter 8). In the early layers of the Late Bronze Age sites in Israel, moreover, we suddenly begin to find locally made clay imitations of Egyptian fiber-wetting bowls (fig. 4.2), developed for just this purpose. The appearance of these humble textile tools, used only by women, alerts us that this is a time when *women* had just arrived in Palestine from Egypt in considerable numbers and settled there—and there is no other such time that we have found. Thus, out of the several points in Egyptian history that scholars have suggested for the date of the Exodus, the women's artifacts tell us that this one (around 1500 to 1450 B.C.) is the archaeologically most probable layer to equate with their Exodus from Egypt.[13]

In later books of the Old Testament we see further references to weaving that are elucidated by excavation. The next major change in textile technology visible in the archaeology of this area occurs around the start of the Iron Age, shortly after 1200 B.C., when we see loom weights of the sort long used in Anatolia and the Balkans suddenly flooding into parts of Israel. By 1000 B.C. they are turning up in great numbers in special weavers' shops—that is, men now seem to be weaving on a large scale for commerce, at Gezer, Lachish, and Tell Beit Mirsim, to name a few (see map, fig. 8.1). Equally abruptly we begin to find metaphors to do with this indus-

[13] The chief contenders have been that the Exodus took place in the thirteenth century B.C., under the long reign of Rameses II, or around 1500 to 1450, during the reigns of Hatshepsut and Thutmose III.

try used among *men's* affairs. The most intimidating spears, for example, are now said to be thick as a weaver's beam. Goliath's was among them. Indeed, Goliath was a Philistine champion, and the material remains of the Philistines—loom weights, pottery, and all—show strong connections with the Mycenaeans and other northerners from warp-weighted loom territory. (For that matter, the bones in the royal burials at Mycenae from a slightly earlier age showed that those warrior-kings stood over six feet tall—veritable giants in comparison with the five-foot men of the eastern Mediterranean.) Once again the textile remains help glue the fragmentary data back into a more coherent picture.

By New Testament times the weaving technology was shifting once again, to the more advanced looms and methods gathered together by the Roman Empire. One of the new techniques, known directly from Coptic Egypt, was that of dividing the warp into two layers and weaving with a circular weft, so as to produce a seamless tube big enough for a tunic. Judicious manipulation of the weft at the sides and top make it possible to build in armholes and a neckhole without any cutting or stitching: the sort of "coat without seam" mentioned in John 19:23 as belonging to Jesus. Wool still dominated the economy, as we see from references to moths as the corrupters of earthly treasure.

The final (though not the only other) mention in the Bible of a matter of textile interest comes with the reference, toward the end of Revelation, to an apocalyptic battle to be fought "at the place called in the Hebrew tongue Armageddon." There is some memory here of another devastating battle fought at this spot shortly after 1500 B.C., when Thutmose III set forth from the Nile into Palestine with his troops, determined to push far away from his borders the enemy that had harassed Egypt for centuries. In one of his bloodiest frays he captured and sacked the walled city of Armageddon (now known as Megiddo; a shadow of the old name still lurks). It must have been a terrible catastrophe for the people there—the end of the world as they knew it. In his annals the pharaoh records that he not only took home masses of booty in the form of beautiful textiles but also carried off the craftworkers into bondage in Egypt, after killing the soldiers. Shortly thereafter we find the Egyptian textile industry, which before this had produced nothing but white linen, undergoing a thorough revolution: new type of loom, new techniques of patterning, and increasingly lavish use of colored thread. All these techniques had been developed much farther north, in Syria or the Caucasus, in the third millennium B.C., and were finally transmitted to Egypt via such men and women as the poor captives from Armageddon.

All these stories and many more, tucked away throughout early literature, contain references to women's work—to spinning, to weaving, and to the clothes the women made. Most of the myths and legends about women, in fact, hover around the craft that was of such central importance to their lives. Archaeology and the technology of clothmaking help us understand these stories. But the latter, in turn, add details about cloth and clothing that are not recoverable directly from the archaeology and—better yet—details about women's lives. In truth, cloth for thousands of years was the notebook that recorded the woes and joys, hopes, visions, and aspirations of women.

11

⫷⫷

Plain or Fancy,
New or Tried and True

For people praise that song the most
that is the newest to those listening.
　　　　　—Homer, *Odyssey*, 1.351–52

We are more ready to try the untried
when what we do is inconsequential.
—Eric Hoffer, *The Ordeal of Change* (1964)

Cloth and clothing, once upon a time novelties in themselves, rapidly became essentials of living in the ancient world, locked into
the fabric of society at every level—social, economic, and religious. Those members of society responsible for making these new
necessities soon found themselves on the proverbial squirrel wheel,
always running just to keep up with daily demand.

Early on, because of the easy compatibility of clothmaking with
child care, women had almost total responsibility for producing
the cloth and clothing in their societies. But toward the end of the
Bronze Age and in the Iron Age, references to male weavers turn
up in increasing numbers. What has changed?

First, the connections between societies.

The men, in contrast with the women, appear linked with new

types of cloth, new techniques, new equipment, all brought in from elsewhere. Nor do they weave for their own households. Wherever we get a good glimpse of them, they are weaving for cash profit, for prestige, or (and here the women join them) for a slave master's profit.

Novelty, prestige, and cash are remarkably closely intertwined.

"Cash"—not in the sense of coinage but of surplus commodities available to pay for things—had grown increasingly available during the Neolithic and Bronze ages (probably from about 4000 B.C. on), as specialization flowered. People came to have extra goods—more than they needed to live—goods they could trade for things not essential to daily life: items to indulge one's fancy, to make life easier (including slave labor as well as better tools), or to enhance one's prestige and position in society.

What is novel catches our interest; the purveyor of the new is looked upon as special. Fashion thrives on this principle, and what is so responsive to "fashion" as clothing? What are the top movie stars wearing? The royal family? There is prestige to be had from copying new fashions—despite the sometimes considerable danger. Indeed, textile history is as full of people fearing novelty as it is of those obsessed with it. For instance, when the East India Company began importing cotton prints from India in the seventeenth century, this colorful cloth swept over Europe. It waxed so popular that European spinners and weavers, threatened by the competition, had stringent laws enacted against its importation. When people wore it still, stories have it that in parts of France women caught wearing the cotton prints were stripped and men selling them were sentenced to hard labor in the galleys.

Those who can produce imitations of new objects of prestige will, of course, turn a fat profit. But who can take up this enterprise? Not those running on the squirrel wheel of providing daily necessities; they are too busy. The only people who have the leisure to experiment with how to make new articles, or how to use new tools, are those *not* locked into basic subsistence production—people with time and / or cash to spare. So not only is spare cash needed to buy the prestigious new things, but cash or its equivalent in time is required to develop and produce them as well.

Loose "cash" had been available for some time already when men finally entered the textile business in a big way in the late second and early first millennia B.C. But now access to the new was easier, apparently as a result of the vast searches for metal ores begun in the Early Bronze Age and the massive trade that developed in the wake of this search. Until about 1500 B.C. textile tools and techniques were developing in several areas of the Old World in virtual isolation of each other. Egypt, for instance, used flax and the ground loom, and decorated its cloth one way; Meso-potamia and the Levant wove wool as well as flax on the ground loom but decorated its cloth by a different technique; Europe wove both flax and wool on the warp-weighted loom and pat-terned it yet a third way. Significant differences also separated the spinning methods.

After 1500 B.C., however, such distinctions fade. The techniques and even the tools for making patterned cloth were being passed from one area to the next, not to mention the cloth itself and the ideas for decoration. And this is when we begin to see male weav-ers turning up in significant numbers, starting with Egypt.

Shortly after Thutmose III sacked Armageddon (see Chapter 10), a new type of loom, new types of weavers, and a prestigious new kind of fancy cloth appeared in Egypt. The first manifestation comes from a wall painting in the tomb of Thutnofer, a nobleman of the Eighteenth Dynasty (Table 11.1, fig. 11.2). Thutnofer held the highly prestigious post of "royal scribe" at the court of Thut-mose III's son, Amenhotep II, or his grandson, Thutmose IV, late in the fifteenth century B.C. On one wall of his tomb this scribe proudly presents a view of his townhouse in the royal city of Thebes—not painted from a picturesque distance, as we might do, but shown in cutaway cross section so that all its important inter-nal activities could be preserved for the eternal afterlife.

In the main hall the master is being served a cooling drink as he

Pharaoh	Length of Rule
Hatshepsut (wife, half sister)	2 year regency + 20 years
Thutmose III (stepson, nephew)	32 years after Hatshepsut
Amenhotep II (son)	30 years
Thutmose IV (son)	9 years
Amenhotep III (son)	38 years
Akhenaton (= Amenhotep IV) (son)	17 years
Tutankhamon (son-in-law, cousin)	9 years

Table 11.1. Succession of late Eighteenth Dynasty pharaohs mentioned in the text. In parentheses is given the family relationship of that pharaoh to the preceding one. Absolute dates are still argued by the experts, but the period covers roughly 1500–1350 B.C.

sits in his great chair in perpetuity. (He is rendered as far bigger than anyone else because he is the most important.) Upstairs another attendant fans the mistress. Despite the heat, servants busily run up and down the stairs, carting supplies to the attic, where yet other servants store them away. Below the master's feet, in the basement—the dampest place in the house—some men sit twisting fiber for rope while others weave linen at two great looms. Linen is more tractable when damp, and keeping it that way must have been a constant problem in hot, dry Egypt. The basement was ideal for such work.

Men weaving: That's new. Moreover, the two looms shown here differ completely from the horizontal ground looms with a woman squatting on either side invariably depicted in the Middle Kingdom and earlier (figs. 3.5, 8.2, and 8.4). Thutnofer's looms are vertical, with a double frame to adjust for tension. The male weavers sit on low stools in front of the warp, so close that their knees have to stick out to either side. One loom is large enough that two weavers work side by side; the other, rather smaller, is manned by a single operator. Thutnofer seems to have been as proud of his unusual looms as of his well-appointed house.

Another detailed picture of the new upright looms occurs in the

Figure 11.2. The Theban townhouse of the Egyptian nobleman Thut-nofer, as he had it drawn in his tomb in the late fifteenth century B.C. The master sits in the main room at left, accepting a cool drink and flowers from his servants, while another servant fans the mistress above. Male servants in the basement weave cloth on newly imported vertical looms and spin rope; other servants run up and down the stairs, stowing supplies into the attic.

tomb of Neferronpet (fig. 11.3), who styled himself "Chief of the weavers in the Ramesseum in the Estate of Amun on the west of Thebes." This nobleman served Rameses II of the Nineteenth Dynasty (thirteenth century B.C.). In the preserved part of the painting we see five weavers working at four large looms, as well as two warpers and two spinners(?). The looms are much the same in their design as Thutnofer's, two centuries earlier, but one of the weavers is now a woman, who has to sit with both knees twisted to one side because of her tight skirt. All are guarded by a door-keeper—a hint that we are looking at slave labor. One is reminded

Figure 11.3. A Nineteenth Dynasty Egyptian weaving shop containing vertical looms. The male weavers sit on low stools with one knee to each side, in order to get close to their work, while the female weaver sits with both knees to one side. To their left, women measure out warps on vertical stands; two other (damaged) figures are probably making thread. Next to the door on the far right sits an irate guard chasing away two impish little boys (above) from the door. The workers are probably slaves. Painting from the tomb of Neferronpet at Thebes, thirteenth century B.C.

of the trade satire (quoted in Chapter 8) describing the poor weaver sitting with his knees under his chin, who must bribe the doorkeeper "to let him see the light of day." This particular doorman, however, busies himself at the moment keeping people out rather than in, as he shakes a stick and gesticulates at two impish little boys running away as fast as they can. (Egyptians relished an occasional humorous "slice of life" among the formal drawings, and guards—probably hated by all—come in for more than their share. In another tomb, servants bringing home the new wine pound in vain on the door of the cellar because the doorman inside has been sampling too much and has fallen asleep drunk.)

The third known depiction of an upright loom occurred in the tomb of one Neferhotep, from the late fourteenth century B.C. Badly damaged, the painting nonetheless shows us one noteworthy feature: The cloth being woven was partly colored, unlike the traditional white linen. In short, the men were weaving new patterned fabrics on the new vertical weaving frame that we today call a tapestry loom. It is no accident that textiles with colored designs also begin to turn up in Egypt at this time, mostly executed in a new technique, weft-faced tapestry.[1]

The earliest well-dated cloths with colored design that we have from Egypt come from the tomb of Thutmose IV, the short-reigned grandson of the illustrious and energetic Thutmose III (see Table 11.1). There are four linen fragments, belonging probably to three cloths. The simplest has rows of pink and green rosettes set off by a thin stripe, woven in a technique that combines rather tentatively a basic idea of tapestry weaving with the antique Egyptian method of inlaying a bit of thicker weft. (The inlay method was used previously only for such things as fringes and weavers' marks, not for an organized all-over pattern.)

The next cloth, now in two pieces, has multicolored hieroglyphs woven in true tapestry technique on a white linen ground. But there are two peculiar details. First, whoever wove the glyphs was a very competent weaver but had not yet made some very basic decisions about how to weave tapestry and so kept vacillating between methods, as though this were an entirely new technique full of unfamiliar problems. The second peculiarity is that the hieroglyphs on it spell out the name of Thutmose III, not of his grandson, Thutmose IV. The glyphs on the third piece, moreover, belong to Thutmose IV's father, Amenhotep II, son of Thutmose III. As a matter of fact, Thutmose IV's tomb was remarkably full of heirlooms—five of the vases had belonged to his father and one to his grandfather—as though the best this pharaoh could do was rest on the laurels of his predecessors. It seems that tapestry technique entered Egypt at just the same time as the new vertical "tapestry loom." And no wonder! Can you imagine squatting for hours over a ground loom to do the detailed work of a tapestry pattern? Sitting upright with the work at a comfortable and well-

---

[1] In tapestry the weft completely hides the warp, and each color of weft is used only where that color is needed for the design. As a result, a single weft thread usually goes back and forth across a compact area rather than across the entire width of the cloth. Structural problems frequently arise because of this, in making the cloth hang together—see Note 2, below.

lit height near one's face is infinitely more practical. The two-beam vertical loom is to this day the tool of choice for tapestry weavers, although it can also be used for other techniques.

By the end of the long and prosperous reign of Amenhotep III, son and successor of Thutmose IV, both the new looms and the fancy new cloth had trickled down from the pharaohs to the nobility. Tapestry, however, is a particularly costly way of decorating cloth, and we see signs that the nobles of not so great means were hitting upon ways of *looking* as elegant as their betters without quite the expense. "Keeping up with the Joneses" has at least a forty-five-hundred-year history.

In the unplundered tomb of the royal architect Kha, Italian excavators found several handsomely painted linen chests with colossal numbers of linen sheets and tunics stowed for the next world. Among the linens were two large tapestry-woven bed-spreads or coverlets (fig. 11.4). Broad bands of large, simple buds and leaves on stems occupy the four edges, while the plain white center is tufted underneath to insulate the sleeper. The design seems innocent enough, but weavers will notice that the flowers have been cleverly oriented in a direction that makes them as cheap and easy to weave as possible—far less costly than the pharaoh's tapestries.[2]

Another prestige-seeking noble of less than adequate means owned a tapestry of the Nine Bows and Captives (fig. 11.5). In this traditional design a series of bound captives represent by their dress and skin color the nine parts of the "known world" and alternate in the composition with a strung Egyptian bow, symbol of their (wished-for) subjugation. For this cloth, the red and black parts of the design were woven in with tapestry technique, but the other colored parts (blue, green, and probably yellow) were painted on afterward—an infinitely cheaper method! Unfortu-

---

[2] Lines parallel to the warp are difficult to negotiate in tapestry and cause the weaver a multitude of structural problems, whereas those in the other direction—parallel to the weft—are quick and easy. Kha's stems and petals are all carefully arranged to lie in the "easy" direction.

Figure 11.4. One of two tapestry spreads from the Theban tomb of the Egyptian nobleman Kha (mid-Eighteenth Dynasty, ca. 1450–1400 B.C.). The ends of the warp threads have been braided into an ornamental fringe. Note that the tapestry designs run as much as possible in lines *across* the cloth—that is, in the weft direction—which is by far the easiest and cheapest way to weave tapestry. The blank area in the middle is worked with long white loops of thread on the back side, probably to insulate the sleeper.

nately we do not know just which tomb this fragment came from, so we can say no more about the owner.[3] But clearly tapestry cloth was becoming important to a nobleman's social standing if people went to such lengths to imitate it.

[3] Enormous amounts of information, the presence of which is little suspected by the casual observer, can be deduced from the context in which an object is found—even so simple a context as which tomb it was in. This principle has been illustrated many times in this book and is the reason why the scholarly community is so set against nonscientific digging of tombs (and against inadequate publication by those who pass as scholars). It is not, as dealers in antiquities keep telling the public, because scholars are "selfish" and want it all to themselves but because the riches of *information* about our human past, which should be the legacy of everyone, are hopelessly destroyed to feed the monetary greed—and need for prestige through novelty—of a few.

Figure 11.5. Fragment of tapestry cloth woven in a favorite and traditional Egyptian design, the Nine Bows and Captives. Each captive (the legs and torso of one can be seen here) appears in the regional dress of one of the nine areas that the Egyptians thought constituted the world outside Egypt. Between captives appears an Egyptian-style bow, symbol of Egypt's wished-for domination of its enemies. All of one bow and part of another have survived, as well as some very elaborate edge patterns typical of Egyptian tomb paintings of the time (mid-Eighteenth Dynasty, ca. 1400 B.C.).

Others were getting into the colored cloth business, too. After Amenhotep III came the heretic king Amenhotep IV, who soon renamed himself Akhenaton (or Ikhenaten—the exact pronunciation of the vowels is uncertain). Among the ruins of his capital city at Amarna, which he built from the ground up and which was abandoned after his death (see Chapter 8), excavators found a handful of cut ends from a warp—that is, the wasted part left on the loom after the cloth has been finished and cut free. These ends are remarkable because they are not linen but wool, almost certainly imported, and dyed: mostly blue, with some red and green yarns as well. There would be no reason to find weaver's waste here unless somebody at Amarna had actually been weaving a colored woolen cloth, another novelty textile apparently fashionable at that time and one that almost certainly involved foreigners.

The fact that a European-style spindle was found in a woman's grave elsewhere in Egypt during the late Eighteenth Dynasty (at Gurob in the Faiyum, known from other data to be full of foreigners—fig. 8.3 c) suggests that alien women living in Egypt may have found an adequate living making colorful textiles in their native styles. The spindle by its very design was unsuited to spinning linen and must have been used for imported wool, the easily dyed fiber. This woman, in fact, had a predilection for color, for the other noteworthy find in her simple grave was a pair of red slippers.

Akhenaton was followed presently by the short-lived but now world-famous Tutankhamon. Enthroned at the age of eight or nine and dead by nineteen, this young and inconsequential pharaoh was bundled away into a small and hastily built tomb with his basic household and otherworldly furniture and clothing, probably a mere fraction of what a big and important king took with him. The tomb survived chiefly because another nobleman soon undertook to hollow out a huge tomb slightly higher up the slope in the Valley of the Kings and so totally buried the boy king's doorway in an avalanche of rock chips that it was not seen again until 1922.

For twenty years archaeologists had been hunting for the tomb of Tutankhamon. Almost every other New Kingdom pharaoh's burial site was known. Two caches of objects clearly taken from Tutankhamon's tomb had turned up right in the center of the Valley of the Kings at Thebes. Near those, in 1908, someone discovered behind a boulder a blue faience cup with Tutankhamon's name on it. Clearly an ancient robber had stashed it there in haste and never gotten back to fetch his prize. Now it lay as a tantalizing signpost without an arrow. The tomb was close by. In which direction should one look?

Howard Carter and Lord Carnarvon took up the search after World War I, but they dug in vain, year after year. Finally in 1922, Lord Carnarvon, who financed the expeditions, was about to call a halt, but Carter begged for a bit more time in which to dig one last spot: under the path he had courteously left for tourists visiting the tomb of Rameses VI. On the fourth day his workmen hit the top of a staircase cut into the bedrock, and quickly they cleared enough steps to reach the top of a sealed tomb door. Whose? Mindful of his long-suffering sponsor, Carter refilled the passage, cabled Lord Carnarvon in England to come at once, and sat down to guard the tomb and wait.

The three-week journey must have seemed like eternity both to him who waited and to the travellers, Lord Carnarvon and his daughter (and assistant) Lady Evelyn Herbert. Meanwhile, offers of technical help poured in from every side as news of the find spread. Finally the time came to open the tomb. The first door at the bottom of the steps proved to have the long-anticipated seal of Tutankhamon—but also, at the top, a resealing by the official guards of the royal necropolis. This 18th-Dynasty tomb had indeed been robbed before the 19th-Dynasty rock chips buried it, but not robbed again. How much remained? Laboriously the excavators emptied the long, rubble-filled passage to the second sealed door, and bored a small hole through the top corner of the barrier to the room beyond. Carter wrote:

"I inserted the candle and peered in, Lord Carnarvon, Lady Evelyn and Callender [Carter's chief assistant] standing anxiously beside me to hear the verdict. At first I could see nothing . . . , but as my eyes grew accustomed to the light, details of the room emerged slowly from the mist, strange animals, statues, and gold—everywhere the glint of gold. For the moment—an eternity it must have seemed to the others standing by—I was struck dumb with amazement, and when Lord Carnarvon, unable to stand the suspense any longer, inquired anxiously, "Can you see anything?" it was all I could do to get out the words, "Yes, wonderful things."

Ancient tomb robbers had indeed gotten in, but they must have been surprised in mid-robbery by the valley guards. One thief in his flight had stashed the blue cup; another, the other objects that had been found. The robbers had made a terrific mess, yanking open boxes and packages as fast as possible to find the most valuable contents. The guards hastily tidied up before they resealed the tomb, shoving things into containers that didn't fit and piling everything hodgepodge into the corners. It was this disorganized but glorious heap of royal belongings that Carter now saw.

The ancient robbers' loss was our gain. Even so insignificant a pharaoh's tomb was full of an astonishing array of articles that almost never survive for us to see. Gold—that untarnishable prize—makes headlines any day, and the amount in Tutankhamon's tomb was prodigious. Carter soon learned that the robbers had not reached the inner chamber where the king lay encased in gold. Yet the most precious treasure in some ways was not the gold but the perishables: elegant wooden furniture—carved beds, tables, chests, stools, and chairs (one the right size for a child king)—and sumptuous royal clothing, including tunics, tapestry gloves, and sandals painted with bound captives so the king could tread on his enemies with every step.

Two of Tutankhamon's tunics interest us in particular. One is done entirely in tapestry weave, which the king's weavers by this time handled with consummate ease and sophistication. The other tunic is a puzzle. First, it has sleeves—a rarity in Eighteenth Dynasty Egypt. Fancy bands adorn it—tapes that were woven separately and sewn over the side seams and around the neck. The neck was designed in the shape of an Egyptian ankh hieroglyph (the looped cross meaning "long life" that modern occultists still use), with Tutankhamon's name embroidered at the crossing point. Thus the garment was created specifically for Tutankhamon by people who understood Egyptian beliefs. Around the bottom, however, the designers sewed on a series of panels embroidered with typically Syrian motifs. Not only are the designs foreign, but true embroidery is otherwise virtually unknown in Egypt. Furthermore, the panels don't fit around the hemline; there is a small gap toward the back where things didn't come out quite even. Everything points to the panels' having been made by foreigners in a technique preferred by them—namely, embroidery—and produced separately from the tunic. The ensemble may have been made in Syria and sent to the young king as a royal gift (we have seen plenty of that kind of activity in Syria—see Chapter 7). Or it may have been put together in Egypt by foreigners in the service of the royal family. We know that Thutmose III had brought back captive craftworkers from his campaigns in Palestine and southern Syria, women and men who had presumably helped introduce the vertical loom and tapestry weaving into Egypt. But that had been a hundred and fifty years earlier.

Thutmose IV, however, had broken Egyptian tradition by marrying a foreign princess, from the kingdom of the Mitanni (which extended over parts of eastern Syria and northern Mesopotamia), and his son, Amenhotep III, had followed suit. To the total amazement of the Egyptians, this second Mitanni lady arrived with an entourage of 317 handmaidens. We hear nothing more of them, but we can surmise that they spent their days doing *something*—most likely fine textile work. Back in Syria and Mesopotamia (as we saw in Chapter 7) a queen's women were mostly trained to make cloth, the fancier the better. Did the survivors of these 318 Mitanni women still live and work in Tutankhamon's palace?

All in all, the making of prestigious patterned textiles in Egypt seems to have been developed in the New Kingdom by royal captives, where the captives in the early stages of this revolution were teaching the Egyptians. Many of the new-style Egyptian weavers were clearly men. Meanwhile, the native Egyptian women continued to weave the household linens much as before, as we learn from the glimpses we have of a chap named Paneb.

Paneb was without doubt a rascal and an evil-tempered bully. He worked as a stonecutter and headed a gang of workmen carving out and decorating noblemen's tombs at Thebes at the end of the Nineteenth Dynasty. These workmen and their wives, children, and servants lived near the tomb sites in a village. There they received, prepared, and ate their government rations of grain, vegetables, and occasional meat; there they kept house, slept, occasionally partied, and worked out their lives of hard labor.

Some of the inhabitants were slave women assigned by the government to several stonemasons in common. A given workman might "own" a few days a month of a particular slave woman's work at grinding grain and whatever else was needed. Most of the weaving, however, was done by the workmen's wives, as we gather from a short papyrus in the British Museum listing the charges brought against Paneb by an irate fellow workman. Paneb had long ago usurped this unfortunate man's rightful position as head of the work gang by bribing a high official and then had gone on to other outrages.

The charges begin with an account of the official's bribery, followed by charges of thievery from the royal tombs, sacrilege in a temple, and perjury when confronted with same. Rape and robbery of a woman come next, then "debauchment" of at least three other women, harassment of the former chief workman, and battery of nine men who came to protect this man when Paneb threatened to murder him. Next comes a charge of frequent personal conscription of labor to which Paneb was not entitled, including making the other workmen's wives weave for him: "Charge concerning his ordering to the workmen to work on the plaited bed of the deputy of the temple of Amun, while their wives wove clothes for him. And he made Nebnufer, son of Wazmose, feeder of his ox for two whole months." Then follow allegations of more murder threats, the cursing of tombs, more battery, throwing bricks at the workmen, stealing tools, more perjury, throwing stones at the servants of the village, and finally murdering some people who were on their way to tell the pharaoh.

A rascal indeed! If you go to Egypt, you can visit at Deir el-Medinah the village where he lived—excavated over many years by the French—and see both Paneb's house and the place where he broke down the door of his former overseer. Fortunately you won't have to tangle with Paneb himself. His tomb is nearby and is decorated in part—if we may believe the charges, at least some of which we *can* substantiate from excavated evidence—with things stolen from other tombs!

From such circumstantial details as these we see that, despite the introduction of a new loom and new types of cloth, the women of ordinary families such as those in Paneb's village continued to weave household linens much as before. And apparently they did so on the traditional ground loom. One reason for this claim is that the new vertical loom required large, heavy beams for the frame. But wood, especially big, strong pieces, was exceedingly expensive in Egypt because it had to be imported. It was probably bad enough for a lower-class family to afford the few thin sticks and pegs needed for a ground loom; four thick beams would have been out of the question. Nor have any of the excavators yet published good evidence for upright looms in the working-class houses that have been excavated.

Plain white linens (which did not *need* a fancy new loom for their efficient manufacture) also continued to be a mainstay of Egyptian civilization for another two millennia. Women were thus not disenfranchised of their main product and continued to enjoy equal status with men in the eyes of Egyptian law—both for protection and for punishment.

Another Nineteenth Dynasty lawsuit of which we have record concerns a woman named Erenofre, accused of using some goods that belonged to another woman as part of the price for two slaves. The objects used for payment included various bronze vessels, some beaten copper, and a large quantity of linen: a shroud, a blanket, five garments of some sort, and ten shirts. From this we learn that linen, like metal, was still a major form of currency, that women could make their own commercial deals, purchase slaves for themselves, and, of course, sometimes be as crooked as men. Such slaves performed mostly housework, especially the constant and laborious task of grinding grain for the family. But occasionally, especially in later times, they were set to work enlarging a free woman's textile production. For women's strong position in Egyptian society eventually enabled them to go into business for themselves. One of the last interesting textile records to come out of ancient Egypt, some fifteen hundred years later, A.D. 298, concerns a woman named Apollonia who bought a large and complicated secondhand loom for the high price of more than three hundred troy ounces of silver. The only possible reason for spending so much money was that she expected to recoup her capital by producing expensive textiles in her own weaving shop.

Arriving in the land of Euelthon, Pheretima requested of him an army which she could lead against Kyrene. But Euelthon gave her anything and everything other than an army, while she, accepting each present, said that this was nice but giving her the army she needed would be even better. Since she replied this way to every gift, finally Euelthon sent her as a present a golden spindle and distaff, and some wool besides. And when Pheretima again made the same remark, Euelthon answered that he honored women with these kinds of presents, not with armies.

—Herodotus, 4.162

Athenian women, unlike Egyptian ones, lost their social equality during the transition from the Bronze Age to the Iron Age. We learn from various texts that by the dawn of the Classical age the married women of Athens, like their Mesopotamian sisters, were held in haremlike seclusion and scarcely allowed out of the house except for major rituals and festivals. Their duties were to take care of the food and the servants (if any), to spin and weave the wool needed for clothing and other household uses, to bear and care for the children, and to obey their husbands.

We see this arrangement, for example, in the unusually intimate glimpses of Athenian married life that we catch in Lysias' legal oration on the killing of Eratosthenes, a man caught in bed with another man's wife and killed on the spot by the incensed husband. Lysias presents the unnamed husband's side of the case as a justifiable homicide.

The wife almost never left the house; a maidservant did the shopping. Trouble began, the husband says, when his wife walked in the procession for his mother's funeral and the roving rake Eratosthenes saw her there. This lover could get at the wife to woo her, however, only by finding the maid at the market and persuading her to carry notes secretly into the house. Eventually the husband was tipped off by the servant of yet another mistress of Eratosthenes; she was miffed that he wasn't coming to see *her* anymore. Suddenly the husband remembered that one night, when he had come home unexpectedly early from the countryside, his wife had had face paint on, although she should have had no reason for it; in fact, with her brother dead not thirty days before, she should still have been properly mourning. And later in the night he had heard the outer door shutting. Alerted, the husband then forced his slave girl, by threat of torture and a life sentence of working in the grain mills, to tell him the whole story and to let him know when Eratosthenes next paid a secret visit. The visits were made easier by the fact that the husband had allowed the wife to sleep downstairs instead of upstairs (the usual sequestered arrangement for women) once their first child was born, so she would be closer to the washing facilities during the night. Four or five days later the maid woke him to say that Eratosthenes was paying a call. The husband lost no time. "In silence I slipped out, went to this and that neighbor, . . . and found those who were home. Gathering as many as possible . . . and fetching torches from the nearest tavern, we returned home, where the outer door had been opened and kept ready by the maid. As we forced the door of the bedroom, those who rushed in first saw him still lying beside the woman, and those who got there last saw him standing naked on the bed." They grabbed and bound his hands. Eratosthenes admitted his guilt and begged to be allowed to pay damages with money instead of his life. The enraged husband replied, "It is not I who kills you but the law of the city," and, acting on his legal right to slay *on the spot* an adulterer caught in the act, cut him down.

From this story we learn various details about the life of a "free" woman of Athens—to name a few: the heavy restrictions on her movements, her use of cosmetics, and some typical and atypical arrangements of her living quarters. We also see something of a slave girl's life and treatment. Note that whereas the husband killed the lover, he gave immunity to the slave girl in return for her help (after roughing her up a bit), and whatever he did to punish his wife was not thought worth mentioning—although if he didn't kill her outright, her marriage can hardly have been a pleasant one after that.

A similar picture of how Athenian women lived, with many more details about domestic work, emerges from a long conversation that Xenophon records between a wealthy and rather self-satisfied Athenian gentleman named Isomachos and his fourteen-year-old bride, as reported to Socrates years later. The description begins when Socrates inquires whether Isomachos trained his young wife himself. Of course, says the gentleman, for being a girl of good breeding, she had spent her first fourteen years seeing, hearing, and saying "as little as possible." It was therefore not astonishing that she knew no more than "how by taking wool to produce cloaks, and she had seen how woolworking was allotted to the maidservants." (Cf. figs. 11.6 and 11.7.) Her chief virtue was that she had been taught self-control and modesty.

Isomachos' lessons to his wife began with teaching her that marriage has three purposes. Only the first of these is shared by the animals: to have offspring. These children then function as an insurance policy, supporting the parents in their old age. Marriage also helps maintain a shelter for both the family and its acquisitions. (Note how similar these goals are to the Neolithic ethic described in Chapter 3.) It is the woman's job, he explains, to keep the shelter in good order, since she is the weaker and more timid and needs to nurse the infants. The man, for his part, goes out to acquire the things with which to fill the storerooms, since he is

Figure 11.6. Young woman at her loom, accosted by suitors who offer her jewelry from a fancy box. From a Greek vase found in Italy, early fifth century B.C.

stronger and more courageous—and less tolerant of children. In all this Isomachos likens the wife's job to that of a queen bee.

> "And what sorts of jobs," said she, "does the queen of the bees have that are like those which I'm supposed to do?"
>
> "In this," I said: "she stays in the hive and doesn't let the bees be idle, but the ones who have to work outside she sends out to their duties, and what each of them brings in she receives and saves up until it is needed for use. And when the time comes for it to be used, she measures out to each bee the proper amount. And she has authority over weaving the honeycomb inside, so that it gets woven well and quickly, and she takes care of the offspring born, and nourishes them. And when they've been raised, and the young have grown ready to work, she sends them out. . . ."

Her wifely duties, he explains, are parallel to these:

> You will have to remain inside and to send out those of the servants whose work is outside; and you will need to oversee

those who have to work inside and to receive what is brought in; and what must be doled out from them, this you must distribute, and what must be stored away, this must be cared for and guarded, so that what is to last a year is not spent in a month. And when you are brought wool, you must deal with it so that there are cloaks for those who need them. And you must see to it that the dry grain is properly edible.

(This picture tallies well with that from Lysias' speech; but children are not discussed, as Isomachos tells Socrates, because the girl was still too young for them.) He then admonishes her to take care of the servants when they fall sick and to teach them skills: "Other duties, pleasant ones, will fall to you also, Wife, as when, taking a servant girl ignorant of wool-working, you make her knowledgeable and she doubles in worth to you. . . ." Basically the wife is to stay at home and work.

With women thus sequestered, the development of commercial textiles understandably was taken up chiefly by men. Whereas the women in their homes did every step from preparing the raw wool to weaving and sewing the cloth, the men typically broke the work up by specialties. Thus there were wool combers, flax preparers, spinners, weavers, tailors, and two kinds of experts whose services the housewives also sometimes employed—dyers and fullers—both of whose work tended to be very smelly and hence unsuitable for an urban home. (Many dyes had to be fermented, while other dyes and certain cleaning processes required uric acid and ammonia, obtained in those days from stale urine. In ancient Pompeii fullers and dyers even set urns out on their front sidewalk with a sign requesting passersby to contribute then and there to the supply!) Some of the men seem to have been in business alone, whereas others employed slaves to help them—in a few cases even sizable numbers of slaves (perhaps forty), a portion of whom may have been women. The products, generally clothing and blankets, were then sold for cash. Who bought them is not clear, but apparently more people than just a few bachelors with no women to weave for them.

At least two classes of women, however, sometimes did do textile work for cash: those who were not properly married or not properly Athenian. We have a record of at least one foreign woman, named Andria, who made wool cloth to support herself for a while. In the lists of freed slaves that have come down to us, 77 women are listed (along with 115 men), and of the 57 women whose occupations are given, 44 were involved in textile work. The scholar who analyzed these lists, A. W. Gomme, remarks that "where the occupation is given, it should be descriptive of the trade proposed to be taken, not just of past activity." Most likely they had learned the necessary skills as domestic servants and would now use them to stay alive. The other 13 ex-slave women included mostly shopkeepers, plus 2 cobblers and a musician. Gomme estimates that "in the most prosperous times of the fifth century" there may have been "35–40,000 female slaves in domestic service" in Athens.

In addition we gather that the prostitutes, or *hetairai* (literally "companions") as they were called, supplemented their income in their spare time by making small textiles such as the stretchy headbands with which Athenian ladies tied up their curls. Widows, too, were sometimes forced to support themselves with textile work. Homer portrays a pitiful woman of this sort in a simile for evenhandedness:

> Thus an honest woman, a handspinner,
> holds up the weights and the wool on either side of her
> balance
> keeping them even, so as to earn a miserable wage for her
> children.

The idea that "free" women of good families should work commercially, on the other hand, was viewed as very strange, as we see from a little tale related by Xenophon about Socrates' customary helpfulness and concern.

One day Socrates sees that his friend Aristarchos is looking very gloomy and asks him if he can help. Aristarchos explains that during a recent political upheaval in the city, many had fled to the Piraeus (the port of Athens, then as now), and a crowd of stranded female relatives had come to live with him for protection, "so that now there are fourteen freeborns in the house." He has no idea, he says, how he can feed them all, much as he would like to.

Socrates begins to question, asking how it is that a well-known man named Keramon manages to feed that many and get rich besides.

"Why of course," said he, "because he is taking care of slaves and I of free people."

"And which do you think are better—the free people at your house or the slaves at his?"

"I myself think," he replied, "the free people at my house."

"Then isn't it disgraceful that he, because of his people, should be doing so well, while you, having much better ones, should be in dire straits?"

"Of course! But he is taking care of craftspeople, whereas I am caring for people with a liberal education."

"So aren't craftspeople those who know how to make something useful?"

"Absolutely."

"And isn't barley-meal useful?"

"Very."

"What about bread-loaves?"

"No less."

"What about cloaks for men and women, and shirts and mantles and half-tunics?"

"Very," he replied; "all these things are useful."

"Then," said [Socrates], "don't the people at your house know how to make any of these?"

"Indeed, *all* of these, I would think."

Socrates then enumerates at length all sorts of people who make good livings manufacturing one or another of these commodities, to which Aristarchos impatiently replies that they can do this because they have bought foreign slaves and can force them to work, whereas he, poor man, is saddled with free people, and relatives at that. (One can guess that part of his resistance stems from the knowledge that the only women he knows who work for commerce are slaves, ex-slaves, and whores.)

Socrates expounds at length about the relative benefits to the human psyche of idleness versus useful employment, then suggests that if the gentleman were to order the gentlewomen to get to work and support themselves within the protection of his house, they would soon come to love him as well because they would no longer feel a burden to him.

Sufficiently convinced, Aristarchos vows to borrow enough money to get started, saying that he was unwilling to borrow money before, because he would have no way to repay it. The narrator continues: "As a result, resources were found, and wool was bought. The women ate their noon meal while they worked, and quit working only at suppertime; and they were cheerful instead of gloomy." Presently Aristarchos returns to tell Socrates how splendidly everything is working out. But, he adds, the ladies are displeased at one thing—namely, that he himself is still idle. The story ends with Socrates suggesting that Aristarchos tell them that he is like the apparently idle sheepdog, who gets better treatment than the sheep because his protection is what allows them all to prosper.

We do not hear how that fable went over with the women, but we know how it would be received today.

Elsewhere in the Classical Greek world (see map, fig. 9.2), the situation was often rather different from that in Athens. Spartan women were not hidden away but participated in civic life much more fully right from childhood, for as youngsters they were given strenuous physical training alongside the boys. This training, according to Plutarch, "instilled in them the habit of a simple life" that even today we call "Spartan living." They cultivated simple and direct speech, too, a trait we still name "laconic" after Lakonia, the southern Greek province that Sparta ruled. But Spartan women did not spin or weave. The plain homespuns for their clothing were made by the serfs or bought in the marketplace since the elite were supposed to occupy their time entirely with serving the state.

"Respectable" ladies in Ionia, by contrast, prided themselves on weaving ornate fabrics, and even did so for profit, as we deduce from the following anecdote told by Plutarch in his *Moralia:* "When an Ionian woman was showing great pride in one of her own weavings (which was very costly), a Lakonian woman, pointing out her four sons (who were very well bred), said, 'Such should be the products of the fair and virtuous woman, and over these should be her elation and her boasts.' " The Ionian women's tradition of making elaborate textiles was one of many customs coming down from the Bronze Age that were preserved in Ionia but lost elsewhere in the Aegean area. Another was the relative freedom of these women to come and go from the house, if the poems of the irrepressible Sappho and the other island writers are a fair sample. In one surviving fragment (No. 114), for example, Sappho complains that she cannot weave because Aphrodite, the love goddess, has thoroughly smitten her with desire for a certain young person she has met. Furthermore, the names of several different objects of her passion occur in her poems. The young women of Lysias' and Xenophon's accounts seldom had the occasion to meet and fall in love with even one person, let alone several.

The Athenians, for their part, viewed both these Greek subcultures—the Spartan and the Ionian—as strange. Athenian women knew how to do elaborate weaving but did it chiefly in the service of their patron goddess, Athena. Each year the entire city and its outlying districts celebrated Athena's birthday with huge sacrifices, processions, and games, at a festival called the Panathenaia. The meat from the sacrificed animals was distributed to the populace, so it was a festive time indeed. As part of these celebrations, the women wove and presented to the goddess a new dress for her statue. The dress was in the form of a *peplos,* a rather heavy rectangle of woven wool that was wrapped once around the body, pinned at the shoulders, and belted in the middle. We see from representations that the drape hung fairly straight, so it was probably about four feet by six. The peplos was no longer fashionable among mortal Athenian ladies by the fifth century. It had been outlawed a bit earlier (so the story goes) after a group of irate Athenian women used their long, straight dress-pins to stab to death a messenger bearing bad news of a battle in which the women's menfolk had been killed. But it was the traditional dress of the goddess, and so it remained.

People made special trips to Athens to see the newest peplos, so splendid was it. Its lavish ornamentation depicted the battle of the gods and the giants, a horrific contest (described at length by the poet Hesiod in his *Theogony*) in which Athena and her father, Zeus, king of the gods, were said to have led the gods to victory. The garment celebrated Athena's powers and gave yearly thanks to the goddess for saving her city.

Such an ornate cloth, an especially appropriate gift for the goddess of weaving, took great time and skill to produce, but of course, nothing was too good for the great patroness. The freeborn women of Athens viewed it as a privilege to help spin the colored yarns. Saffron yellow, long associated with women's rituals in the Aegean (fig. 4.7), and sea purple provided the dominant hues for ground and figure. A full nine months before the festival, the loom was set up, the warp made and hung upon it, and the weaving begun. To weave an elaborate tapestrylike cloth of some twenty-four square feet covered with friezes of mythological figures would take that long. Priestesses known as *ergastinai,* meaning "workers," did the actual weaving, aided by two half-grown girls called *arrephoroi,* who seem to have been chosen from among the aristocratic Athenian families to live on the Acropolis and serve the goddess for a year. When the sacred dress was finally presented to Athena and the sacred Panathenaic procession wound its way through the city streets, Athenian women obtained one of their rare excuses to leave the house.

The ancient European weaving technology, color associations, and mythology of the peplos all connect the robe with the Bronze Age, as do the offices of the the priestesses who produced it. Athenian women thus preserved as a largely religious tradition what the freer Ionian women to the east pursued for more secular (and profitable) ends. But the loss of fancy textiles as a major source of secular economic wealth undoubtedly went hand in hand with the decline of women's status in Athenian society. With no independent way of generating wealth, they lost their political clout and, like Aristarchos' female relatives, could at best envy the freedom of the watchdog while they toiled at endless household work, locked up at home (fig. 11.7).

Our twenty-thousand-year odyssey has shown us women working under a wide variety of conditions. Their social status and economic production have varied together, reaching lowest ebb when people valued least the contributions that women could make while rearing children.

When we picked up the story of women's work back in the Palaeolithic, we saw that women could conveniently combine certain crafts with the necessities of child raising. The fiber arts—spinning, sewing, netting, basketry, and eventually weaving—suited the purpose particularly well because these tasks posed no dangers or hardships to toddlers. Clothing, too, was already becoming the human race's next language after speech—unique in its ability to convey important (if simple) information continuously and relatively permanently.

Then the world changed. With the advent of settled life and food production, people began to acquire objects in quantity. Cloth and clothing became increasingly integrated into social customs, and the making of cloth shifted from a merely useful art to an essential of cultural life. With the shift came a mounting

Figure 11.7. Young girl biting knots out of the wool in her thread as she spins. From the center of an early fifth century B.C. Greek cup, showing girls and their suitors.

demand on women's time and labor to provide this commodity.

As commerce gradually rose in importance, women were able to keep up for a while in supplying cloth to their increasingly demanding societies, under a variety of economic systems—some more favorable to women's freedom and economic standing than others. (None of this says anything about women's *happiness,* of course. Some individuals feel lost when no one tells them what to do and blossom when integrated into a tightly tied position in society. Others are the opposite. Furthermore, women as a whole have seldom complained so loudly as today, when we have more freedom than ever before—just as the loudest complainers in eighteenth-century Europe, the organizers of the French Revolution, were the richest peasants around. Happiness is a different and very personal issue.)

By the start of the Late Bronze Age (mid-second millennium B.C.), however, the flood of new technological changes related to prestige demands began to overwhelm the traditional textile workers in certain societies. Women lost economic ground, sometimes enormous ground, to those who could afford to specialize in the new and different—to those men with some free time to experiment. Mothers were still too busy with uncontrolled pregnancy and children to play around with novel ideas. Only to the extent that the women's cloth recorded religious or historical information, as with the sacred dress woven for Athena, did the women then reap prestige for their work.

And so matters remained, within the vicissitudes of social structure and customs, until the medically researched birth control methods of the last few decades. Now we see a strong movement in medically rich societies to reopen wide varieties of work, knowledge, and legal rights to women. Where women's work will go from here, the future will tell.

12

Postscript:
Finding the Invisible

A tough wedge must be sought for a tough log.
—Publilius Syrus, *Sententiae*

Past scholars have generally dismissed the history of easily perishable commodities like cloth as unreconstructable, on the ground that there was no evidence. By tracking down a great deal of evidence from unusual sources, however, we have reconstructed much about ancient textiles and the people and societies that made them.

Women's work consisted largely of making perishables—especially food and clothing. So if we are to retrieve significant amounts of women's history, or of the history of any evanescent occupation in particular (and I am thinking of such things as music and dance as well as food and clothing), we need better evidence than just that which falls into our laps. We need the skill to glean all surviving evidence and to wring out of it every last drop of information and useful analysis. A hypothesis, after all, is no better than the evidence that supports it, and hypotheses without evidence are mere wishful thinking. A tall order? Perhaps, but also a delightful challenge to those who, like Agatha Christie's immortal Poirot, enjoy "exercising the little grey cells" in the chase.

Let us start by asking: What are the general directions from which the evidence for such ancient objects and activities might come? The conventional sources are archaeology and surviving texts. But the problem with archaeological remains is that what we want to study in our case may not survive directly or in a recognizable form. Cloth itself, for example, seldom makes it through the millennia except in tiny, hardly recognizable shreds. Until recently excavators tended to throw even those away, assuming they were of no value. Loom weights, on the contrary, survived in great quantities but were also assumed to hold little information, so their fate was just as bad. It didn't occur to either diggers or scholars how much these unprepossessing blobs of clay could reveal about the development of the looms needed to weave the cloth and about the users of the looms.

The problem with texts, moreover, is twofold. They may not discuss what we wish to learn—for example, few ancient texts talk about women's lives, partly because very few women wrote or dictated texts—and even when they do touch the subject we want, they may not tell us what we need to know. Thus the economic texts that discuss clothing use so many unknown technical terms that we learn next to nothing about clothing from them. The *scribes* knew what they meant. Why should they think of explaining the details to us, three or four millennia later and half a world away?

Archaeology, however, has gone through revolutions in the last century. For a long while it was little more than a branch of art history, its task being to fill up art museums and private collections with handsome curiosities. (Those whose acquaintance with archaeology comes only from films like *Raiders of the Lost Ark* may think it is still that way; the film may be great entertainment, but it is terrible archaeology.) Around the turn of the century, however, archaeology began to pull itself up to the level of an investigative science, through the efforts of a few individuals who wanted to learn how ancient people lived. Scholars such as the great Egyptologist Sir W. M. F. Petrie were realizing that in removing an antiquity from its context the finder (whether "scientist" or "treasure hunter") destroyed forever any *social* information recoverable from the find group. The taker therefore had a duty to humanity to record everything about that context, no matter how small.

This new view leapt to international fame through the notorious act of a French specialist in the Coptic period (the early centuries A.D.), named Émile Amélineau. From 1894 to 1898 he obtained permission to excavate the incomparable tombs of the earliest Egyptian pharaohs at Abydos, who flourished around 3000 B.C. After ransacking them of their contents, keeping little record of what was found where, Amélineau deliberately burned or smashed to bits any and every object that he chose not to take back to France, so as to make those he took more valuable, because unique. The burning lasted for days. A horrified Petrie rushed in as soon as Amélineau had left, to glean "a rich harvest of history . . . from the site which was said to be exhausted," by carefully sifting through the rubble and putting back together what he could of the five hundred years of pivotal human history that the treasure hunters had wantonly shattered. (This was, after all, the dawn of human writing and civilization.) If it did nothing else, *l'affaire Amélineau* (as it came to be called) finally got people's attention, and a more responsible archaeology began to develop, characterized by the sort of exhaustive recording that Petrie specialized in.

Such changes in basic approach took time, however, and Petrie ended up putting into his own collection (now in the Petrie Museum at University College London) many types of artifacts that no one else considered of value yet. Thus it was that in the 1970s two women, an Egyptologist and a textile conservationist, found treasure in "a tumbled heap of dirty linens" among the masses of labeled items stored in the Petrie collection: the earliest complete garment that has come down to us (see fig. 5.3). It is a fine off-white linen shirt of the First Dynasty. Its seams, fringes, and elaborate pleating are intact and still show the creases at the elbows that remained when its owner last stripped it off over his head, five thousand years ago. Petrie had seen the value in this linen shirt and trusted that eventually textile history would come into its own.

Even at its blindest, when diggers of the mid-twentieth century were dutifully recording facts of no known use just because they were there, the new method of trying hard to preserve all objects and information found has proved its worth magnificently. In 1961 Emmett Bennett was able to reconstruct the filing system of the Mycenean scribes, hence a great deal about their economic practices and even the geography of the kingdom, because the excavators of the Pylos archives decades before had meticulously recorded the exact three-dimensional findspot of every as-yet-undeciphered tablet scattered through the fill.[1] We relied on some of this information in reconstructing the Mycenaean textile industry in Chapter 9.

But a second revolution was coming, too, one that radically increased the amount of information recoverable from what was dug up. After World War II a wide range of military technology and scientific knowledge that had accrued during the great struggle gradually became available for other uses, including the interpretation of archaeological data. Radiocarbon dating, infrared photography for seeing through unremovable dirt, isotope "fingerprinting" for tracing sources of raw materials like stone and ore, thin-layer chromatography for analyzing dyes, and a hundred other methods were and still are being worked out. Thus we have appealed over and over in this book to archaeological information that has been further interpreted through the natural sciences, from chemical analysis of the Lascaux string fragments to palaeo-

---

[1] As it happened, the baskets of clay tablets, filed by subject, had fallen off their wooden shelves one by one as the palace, and the shelves, burned. Each basketful was thus scattered in a characteristic fan across the accruing rubble as the destruction progressed, back on that terrible day around 1200 B.C.

The excavations took place in 1939 and the early 1950s, mostly before the decipherment of Linear B, which was worked out largely between 1952 and 1956. Until the tablets were readable, and until Bennett realized that different scribes could be recognized by their handwriting and that each scribe typically handled only one or a few types of accounts, no one had any inkling how useful the exact findspots would turn out to be. Recording them all was just "good excavation method." What greater triumph can one ask of it?

biological reconstruction of the era when sheep became woolly. Among the innovations have been a number of improved means for finding sites and artifacts. Thus magnetometers and other devices for finding metals, stone walls, and other anomalies have helped with archaeological prospecting, while new techniques of flotation and sieving have allowed excavators to find the tiny seeds, leaves, bone fragments, and so forth that tell us worlds about ancient environments. We learn what ancient climates were like, that ancient grain supplies were plagued by mice and weeds, and that hemp, a favorite fiber plant, was in use in Europe in the fifth millennium B.C., four thousand years before the narcotic subvariety (marijuana) was brought in from southern Asia. Improved methods of microscopic analysis, special photography, spectrometry, and other nondestructive techniques have added to our knowledge. For example, careful microscopic probing of an Iron Age woolen vest found in the salt mines at Hallstatt, Austria, showed that the ancient owner had been pestered by lice; the garment's seams were full of lice eggs. Textiles and other readily perishable objects are, as a result of all this, much easier to study now than they were twenty years ago, right within the discipline of archaeology and its scientific helpers.

But we need all the help we can get. What else is out there?

In this book we have often appealed to language itself via linguistic science, in addition to looking at such texts as have come our way. For example, we have used such revealing etymologies as *tunic, shirt,* and *to ret* to throw light on the history of clothing and the processes of preparing fibers. (We even added that the English word *robe* comes from *rob* because clothing was one of the most frequent forms of plunder in the Middle Ages, as in many another time and place.) The discussion in Chapter 9 of the stages of Mycenaean textile manufacture, too, was based on a careful linguistic analysis of the names of female professions in the Linear B tablets, worked out in detail elsewhere. We also combined archaeological with linguistic arguments to interpret the layering of vocabulary found in Greek, in which only the most primitive aspects of weaving show Indo-European names, the rest having been borrowed later. Since the technology for which they borrowed these terms—weaving on the great warp-weighted loom—is known from the loom weights to have developed in central and southern Europe in the Neolithic, the prehistoric Greeks must have learned the craft fairly late, as they were moving into Greece from farther east.

Another tool we have used in a particularly novel way is the comparative method of reconstruction. This method was gradually worked out in the nineteenth century by linguists interested in determining the historical relationships between languages. They began to realize that many languages were changed later forms of a common ancestor language (like French, Spanish, and Italian, all of which are simply later forms of Latin, each having changed gradually in its own way during many centuries) and that the parent could be reconstructed to a fair extent by meticulous comparison of the structures—especially the sound structures—of the daughter languages. The method works best when the structures used are both arbitrary cultural conventions (as language is) and so habitual that people don't think about them much. When we talk, we are worrying principally about framing our sentences well enough to get our message through to the other person, not whether our tongue is hitting this or that little spot in the mouth. What gymnastics the tongue has to go through to produce the needed words is *its* problem, as it were; the tongue is on automatic. The sounds of language are thus excellent fodder for the comparative method. But we have the same sort of dichotomy in the cultural conventions of clothing. On the conscious level we worry about fashion and momentary social messages, but we take for granted and scarcely, if ever, think about the basic notions of what constitutes dress within our culture, including (depending on the culture) what is appropriate for certain social classes, sexes, etc. These "automatic" aspects of clothing yield to comparative reconstruction back into prehistory. Very conservative forms of decoration (see Chapter 6) turn out to be partly reconstructable in this way also, and ancient music and dance may, too. One of the checks we have on such work comes in collecting the most archaic vocabulary connected with these fields and comparing its recon-struction to the reconstructions of the costumes, decoration, dances, etc.[2]

Other sources of evidence include mythology—a difficult field not widely understood as a potential helpmate for archaeological problems since, having been roundly abused by some, it has been rejected by most.[3] Then there is ethnology. Its particular virtue is to suggest possible solutions to archaeological problems by show-ing parallel behavior in other human cultures. That is, ethno-graphic studies can help determine the range of possibility and likelihood for what people did, especially if the researchers will take the time and courage to get a firsthand knowledge of what-ever they are trying to study. Besides, it could even be fun!

For a century or more, pottery has been the mainstay of archae-ological chronologies. It is central to the field. But few archaeolo-gists have ever made a pot—ever kneaded the clay (let alone found it and dug it out), built up the vessel, dried it, decorated it, fired it . . . and watched it come out of the kiln in shattered pieces the first time because as novices they hadn't gotten all the air out of the clay during the kneading. One learns just what the ancients faced by trying to do what they did, and overnight one's theories become a great deal more realistic. The same, of course, is true of spinning,

---

[2] A word of warning: This is not an easy task that one can whip off in a few days or weeks. Linguistic reconstruction of sounds and of the words that ride on them, although very simple in principle, is extremely complex in practice because there are so many intricately interlocking details to consider. Similarly, to do these other types of comparative reconstruction well requires enormous amounts of time, patience, and accuracy.

[3] But for at least one pair of archaeologists who grasped the subject at its core, and wrote about it splendidly, see Henri and Mrs. H. A. Frankfort, "Myth and Reality," in *Before Philosophy*, ed. H. and H. A. Frankfort, John A. Wilson, and Thorkild Jacobsen (Harmondsworth, 1949), 11–36. More recently, see also Paul Barber, *Vampires, Burial, and Death: Folklore and Reality* (New Haven, 1988). Mythology, too, is susceptible in part to the comparative method of reconstruc-tion. See, e.g., C. Scott Littleton, *The New Comparative Mythology*, 2d. ed. (Berkeley / Los Angeles / London, 1973).

weaving, cooking, woodworking, and any other craft.

Avigail Sheffer tells of worrying whether the soft, crumbly, doughnut-shaped weights she was digging up by the dozens at Iron Age sites in Israel could really function as loom weights, as everyone assumed. She thought they would break as they swung around on the loom. So she and her colleagues made up a stack of unbaked clay doughnuts, strung up a makeshift warp-weighted loom with wool hand-spun for them by some local Bedouin women, and began to weave. She reports: "The weaving was very easy and quick, taking less than an hour to produce a piece of material one metre long. No damage occurred to the weights even when the loom had to be moved from place to place." She learned a lot by trying it out—even more than she had set out to learn—such as how quickly one could weave on such a loom.

Pottery "experts" for a long time could get away with knowing little about how pottery was made, because there was so much else to study among the wealth of potsherds. (Today some scholars are also learning to make pots.) But with the study of perishable objects, we do well to *start* by learning the craft firsthand and to keep experimenting at every turn as we go along. We need all the practical help we can get because if we take a wrong turn somewhere in the logic of our theories, we don't have piles of other evidence lying around to warn us of our mistake. I have found that the considerable time it takes to replicate ancient practices is always amply rewarded, as when I rewove the Hallstatt plaid (figs. 0.1 and 0.2). Theories are kept on a sounder footing and new information gathered about the problems and limitations people faced in those days. And there is the pleasure of doing something different, something so old that it is new again.[4]

Yet another way to get evidence—and most difficult of all—is

---

[4] Another type of perishable commodity where the experimental approach has been invaluable is in the very important industry of making salt from brine. Beatrice Hopkinson, who has done much of the work, has found that many of the most intractable questions about the artifacts received answers as soon as she began trying to make salt in the ancient way.

to develop entirely new sources by looking carefully at the nature of the problem to be studied. For example, archaeologists have long been perplexed by evidence that new groups of people have infiltrated or overrun an area. How to tell whether whole families have arrived or just bands of men—traders, warriors, or the like? The problem diminishes, however, once we have discovered what women were doing that men weren't and then ask what traces these activities may have left. We have seen that women spent most of their time raising young children and preparing the daily food and household cloth and clothing. We can follow the evidence for those to find the women.

One thing that women typically impart to their children is the first elements of language, including the vocabulary of highest frequency, and we have seen some of the value in analyzing the linguistic inheritance. Second, spinning and weaving were almost always women's work (except in a few cases of urban specialization; see Chapter 11). In this case we can trace the women by tracking their tools. The job is made easier because the textile tools were mostly very humble—a few sticks, clay spindle whorls, and perhaps clay weights, with no intrinsic value for trade. So when we find Avigail Sheffer's crumbly clay doughnut weights, well known in Europe and western Anatolia, suddenly turning up in Israel in the Iron Age, far outside the homeland of the warp-weighted loom, we have every right to suspect that a group of women had moved in, along with their families, from rather far to the northwest. One may even suspect a connection with the biblical Philistines, whose pottery (as we said in Chapter 10) is related somehow to that of the Mycenaean Greeks and whom the Egyptians show arriving at the gates of Egypt around 1200 B.C., with husbands, wives, children, and baggage piled on oxcarts and in boats, looking for a home. Fought off and turned back by the Egyptians (who wrote the attackers' name, consonants only, as *P-l-s-t*), they settled around Gaza and gave their name to the whole area—Palestine.

On the other hand (as an apparent counterexample that serves to prove the rule), we have no right to assume migration of women when we find fancy little Syrian spindles carved of local ivory turning up occasionally in Mycenaean settlements in Greece in the Late Bronze Age. Themselves handsome, these objects must have sold for a good price—a wonderful trinket for a merchant or sailor to take home to his sweetheart.

Once we have located good sources of evidence, we need to sharpen our ability to make the most of what is there.

The first step, in my experience, is to trick oneself into focusing on every part of the data. *Draw it, count it, map it, chart it,* and if necessary (or possible) *re-create it.*

For example—a personal one—I inspected photographs of the Venus of Lespugue a dozen times, but it was not until I made my own tracing (fig. 2.1) that I noticed the marks showing that the strings of her string skirt were fraying out at the bottom, telling me that the sculptor knew of string made from twisted fibers twenty thousand years ago. The act of drawing forced me to pay minute attention to every tiny detail of the statuette for the first time. Similarly, it was not until I decided to color by hand my photocopies of all the known Mycenaean frescoes showing clothing that I began to appreciate how frequently a particular border pattern occurred on the frescoes as well as on the clothes and how easy it would be to weave it. That, in turn, prompted me to try to weave it, and during the relatively slow, step-by-step process of doing so I realized that I was making just the sort of band that I had seen—but not thought about—in black-and-white photos of rural women of this century starting their cloth on a warp-weighted loom in the traditional way. Except for color, the designs were the same between the modern Norwegians and the ancient Mycenaeans.

Mapping and charting help, too. Even after I had worked for ten years collecting the descriptions of every fragment of prehistoric cloth and textile tools that I could find in the archaeological literature of Europe and the Near East, I had no idea that these data separated into three main zones of development—until in desperation I sat down to map the evidence. To my astonishment, the distribution of fiber use and loom types exactly correlated with the types of pattern weaving for which I had data (see Chapter 11).

The acquisition of facts in a tough subject seldom goes in a straight line—that is, it seldom goes where you think *you* want to go with it. I often have data I don't know how to use, on the one hand, and on the other hand, I am always missing lots of data I'd like to have. Faced with a pile of opaque evidence, one can usefully ask, *"What are all the individual things I can deduce here?"* Thus we deduced from the bare bones of a lawsuit against a New Kingdom Egyptian woman (accused of using another woman's linens to help pay for two slaves; see Chapter 11) that linen could be used as a sort of currency, that women could themselves make such commercial deals as buying slaves, and that women were directly responsible in a court of law. We could also have learned about the price of slaves and the workings of the legal system had we wished. Once the details are systematically chipped loose from the matrix, it is often easier to figure out where they can be usefully filed—these under textile studies, those under women's rights, and so forth.

On the other hand, the problem of missing data may respond to the query "If I can't get at it by the straight path, *how else can I get at it?*" This takes us back to the question of creative use of sources, already discussed. For example, when I began working on textiles, I wanted to know about those specifically from Greece. But textiles don't survive in Greece. Eventually it became apparent that one could deduce information about Greek cloth from the textile tools left there, from the vocabulary, and from mapping the development of cloth and other related artifacts in neighboring areas.

Finally, we need the best possible methods of analysis for our hard-won evidence. Methods of working from the internal structure of the data and those based on logical deduction are well known. Thus, for example, allover designs can be classed not just randomly by motif but exhaustively according to symmetry types.

Studies also show that our sense of symmetry operates on a far less conscious level than our awareness of motifs and use of color. So when we see that the early Minoans use only Symmetry Type A but presently add to it the use of Symmetry Type B, which happens to be the Mycenaeans' favorite kind, we can deduce that a much more intimate contact than casual trade has started to occur between the two cultures. In fact, the use of the new symmetry type begins just about when we get evidence for the Mycenaeans' taking over part of Crete, and the decorative change can be used to help date that take-over.

The pursuit of the perishable, however, requires careful attention to a variety of invisible factors as well, factors that most people forget to consider because in some sense they "aren't": The factors aren't said, or aren't conscious, or aren't seen. It is their *absence* that is the problem, precisely because they don't obtrude on our attention.

For example, one difficulty in working with texts is that ancient scribes didn't think to tell us much of what we most need to know. *They* already knew all about it. (We moderns are no wiser. When I first went to Greece, no one thought to explain to me that in that country when you nod your head down, it means "yes," but when you nod your head up, it means "no." I got on several wrong buses before I began to suspect that Greek head nodding was even a problem to me.) Among our textile discussions in Chapter 11 we investigated the dress that the Athenian women made for Athena's festival. But working out the problem has been greatly hampered by the fact that Athenian writers never bother to mention which of Athena's statues on the Acropolis, the big or the small one, was to be clothed in the new peplos. We are stranded to deduce it as best we can.

On the other hand, silent assumptions come quite as often from ourselves. (I had assumed I knew what head nodding meant, just as my Greek friends had assumed that I knew what head nodding meant.) In making their deductions about Athena's dress, several scholars assumed that, since it took nine months to make, the dress must have been very *big* and therefore must have adorned the huge statue. The assumption that large size is the only reasonable cause for a long manufacturing time is unwarranted, however, as we see when we explore the technology thoroughly. Statistics of various sorts about weaving show that exactly that kind of time would have been needed to make a storytelling cloth big enough for the small statue. Furthermore, we are told of the setting up of a single weighted warp nine months before the festival. A Greek warp-weighted loom was not equipped to make a cloth much larger than that needed for the small statue.

Finding one's own unwarranted assumptions is one of the most difficult things to wrestle with, precisely because they are so hard to recognize. Trying simply to *state all one's assumptions explicitly* is the first major step. Thus, in the example of Athena's dress, it helps to say, "I am assuming that the long time needed to make the cloth is due to its size. Is that the only possible cause for lengthy time in weaving?" Put that way, one can begin to see some other possibilities: A small Persian carpet may take years to weave because the method is slow.

Another type of "missing data" can be found by systematic comparison. I had been working for years with the Egyptian material on spinning before I realized that nowhere was there a picture of a distaff in use, and nowhere among the thousands of textile artifacts a surviving distaff. So how were they draft-spinning a fiber that is typically longer than one's arm? (A distaff holds the unspun fibers and acts basically as an arm extender when the fibers are very long, so that a little group of fibers can be pulled or "drafted" most of the way past the next group, and so forth, to make a continuously long, thin thread.) The answer, I gradually discovered, was that they were not draft-spinning (unwarranted assumption discovered). Instead of *pulling* the fibers past each other, the Egyptians were separating them entirely and splicing them end to end (see Chapter 8). All the phases of the work were represented in the tomb paintings, but I was not ready to understand the details of what I saw until I had been forced to discard my wrong assumptions. This occurred when I noticed that a crucial element for my theory was *missing,* as the result of careful comparison to well-known examples of how people spin in most other parts of the world.

The principle is powerful: *the hardest thing to notice is what isn't there*—yet it may be every bit as important as what *is* there, and it takes the most careful of methods to ferret it out. Sherlock Holmes, master of methodical deduction, solves the mystery of the missing racehorse, in "The Adventure of Silver Blaze," precisely when he realizes that the dog *didn't* bark the night the wicked deed was done, hence the villain must have been very well known to the dog.

Finally, none of these methods will be of use unless the researcher is willing to learn what the subject has to say about itself instead of trying to make the topic come out in some predetermined way.

One of the most remarkable scholars I have studied with was Professor Albrecht Goetze of Yale University. Before I met him, I had heard that when his comprehensive book on the archaeology of ancient Anatolia was updated and republished some twenty years after it was first written the revisions consisted mostly of adding references to newly excavated material that further demonstrated the conclusions he had drawn the first time. I wanted to find out how a scholar could become so sensitive to the data as that. At first I felt very frustrated in this because he didn't talk much about method. But gradually I began to realize that the key was on the wall of his office, in a little hand-lettered sign to which he would often refer, laughing uproariously. It said, in German, "What do I care about my garbage from yesterday?" Each new fact discovered made the picture necessarily look a little different, and he was quite happy to let go of old, outmoded views—the garbage—and move on to a new vision with a joyful laugh of discovery. He never let his ego get in the way of learning, by hanging on to an idea simply because it was his.

We women do not need to conjure a history for ourselves. Facts

about women, their work, and their place in society in early times
have survived in considerable quantity, if we know how to look
for them. Far from being dull and in need of fanciful paint to make
it more interesting, this truth is sometimes (as the saying goes)
stranger than fiction, a fascinating tale in itself.

Illustration and Credit List

etching reprinted in P. V. Glob, *The Mound People* (Ithaca, N.Y., 1974), 44, fig. 15

2.8 Four string skirts from ethnic costumes: Mordvin, Walachian, Macedonian, Albanian

2.9 Sash from Drenok, Yugoslav Macedonia. Collection of P. Hempstead

2.10 Tree of Indo-European languages

3.1 Map of Neolithic and other early sites

3.2 Neolithic relief of pregnant woman, Çatal Hüyük. After Mellaart

3.3 Neolithic figurine of woman giving birth, Çatal Hüyük

3.4 Neolithic figurine of reclining woman, Hal Saflieni, Malta

3.5 Wooden model of Egyptian weaving shop, tomb of Meketre. Egyptian Museum, Cairo. Photography by the Egyptian Expedition, 1919–1920; Metropolitan Museum of Art

3.6 Greek vase, ca. 560 B.C., showing women weaving on a warp-weighted loom. Attic lekythos, attributed to the Amasis Painter. Courtesy of the Metropolitan Museum of Art; Fletcher Fund, 1931: no. 31.11.10

3.7 Reconstruction of Neolithic house, Tiszajenő, Hungary. After Tringham

3.8 Hallstatt-era urn with weaving scene, from Sopron. Drawing by A. Eibner-Persy; courtesy of Natural History Museum, Vienna

3.9 Hungarian village girls. After anonymous travel photo taken ca. 1950

3.10 Reweaving of Neolithic linen "brocade" from Irgenhausen. Photograph courtesy of the Swiss National Museum, Zurich (5752.P)

4.1 Cretan orchard and vineyard. Photo by author, 1962

4.2 Diagram of fiber-wetting bowl

4.3 Village of Mykonos. Drawing from photo by author, 1962

4.4 Minoan heart-spirals from tomb of Wahka II at Qau, and kilt in tomb of Menkheperraseneb at Thebes. After Petrie and Vercoutter

4.5 Clay figurine of Minoan woman, Petsofá, Crete. After Myres

4.6 Fresco of Minoan woman, Hagia Triada. F. Halbherr, "Resti dell' Età Micenea: Scoperti ad Hagia Triada . . . ," *Monumenti Antichi* 13 (1903), pl. 10

tan Museum of Art: Norman de Garis Davies, "The Townhouse in Ancient Egypt," *Metropolitan Museum Studies* 1.2 (1928–29), 233–34, fig. 1

11.3 Weaving shop with vertical looms, tomb of Neferronpet, Thebes. After Davies

11.4 Tapestry coverlet, tomb of Kha, Thebes. After Schiaparelli

11.5 Egyptian Nine Bows and Captives design in tapestry. After Daressy

11.6 Young woman at her loom, accosted by suitors, on Greek vase. Q. Quagliati, "Pisticci: tombe lucane con ceramiche greche" *Notizie degli Scavi di Antichità* 1 (1904), 199, fig. 4

11.7 Young girl spinning, on Greek vase. Hugo Blümner, "Denkmäler-Nachlese zur Technologie," *Archäologische Zeitung* 35 (1877), pl. 6

Sources

All translations were done by the author unless otherwise specified. All line numbers for Greek texts are given according to the Oxford editions.

INTRODUCTION

The plaid fragment from Hallstatt was published by H.-J. Hundt as No. 74 (p. 52) in "Vorgeschichtliche Gewebe aus dem Hallstätter Salzberg," *Jahrbuch des römisch-germanischen Zentralmuseums Mainz* 14 (1967), 38–67.

The technical details of the actual remains of ancient cloth and textile tools mentioned throughout this book are discussed, with full references, in E. J. W. Barber, *Prehistoric Textiles: The Development of Cloth in Europe and the Near East with Special Reference to the Aegean* (Princeton, 1991), hereafter referred to as "Barber 1991."

CHAPTER 1: A TRADITION WITH A REASON

The quotations come from Judith Brown, "Note on the Division of Labor by Sex," in *American Anthropologist* 72 (1970), 1075–76; George Foster, "Sociology of Pottery," in *Man in Adaptation: The Biosocial Background*, ed. Yehudi A. Cohen (Chicago, 1968), 323; Elise Boulding, *The Underside of History* (Boulder, Colo., 1976), 147.

The story of Hargreaves is collected with other such by Bette

Hochberg in her booklet *Spin Span Spun: Fact and Folklore for Spinners* (Santa Cruz, Calif., 1979), 46 and 62.

CHAPTER 2: THE STRING REVOLUTION

Concerning the spread of the Gravettian culture and the radio-carbon dates for it, see Grahame Clark and Stuart Piggott, *Prehistoric Societies* (New York, 1965), 71, and Grahame Clark, *World Prehistory in New Perspective,* 3d ed. (Cambridge, 1977), 96–97.

The double interment is described by René Verneau in *Les Grottes de Grimaldi* (Monaco, 1906), vol. 2, 29, and illustrated in pl. II.

For Uralic words, see Björn Collinder, *Fenno-Ugric Vocabulary* (Hamburg, 1977).

Quotation (translated from French) from A. Glory, "Débris de corde paléolithique à la Grotte de Lascaux," *Mémoires de la Société préhistorique française* 5 (1959), 137–38; drawing interpreted from fig. 2.

The quotation about camel pullers comes from Gösta Montell, "Spinning Tools and Methods in Asia," in Vivi Sylwan, *Woollen Textiles of the Lou-lan People* (Stockholm, 1941), 114.

For a summary of early New World textile remains, see Mary Elizabeth King, "The Prehistoric Textile Industry of Mesoamerica," in *Junius B. Bird Pre-Columbian Textile Conference,* ed. A. P. Rowe, E. P. Benson and A. L. Schaffer (Washington, D.C., 1979), 265–78.

The "clothed" figurines from Gagarino and Kostienki, respectively, were originally published by L. M. Tarasov, "Paleoliticheskaja Stojanka Gagarino," *Materialy i Issledovanija po Arkheologii SSSR* 131 (1965), 132–38 and figs. 14–16, and by P. P. Efimenko, *Kostenki I* (Moscow and Leningrad, 1958), figs. 140–42, pls. 14–17 and 20. The drawing of the Venus of Gagarino is based on Tarasov, fig. 16. The drawings of figurines from Šipintsi, Vinča, and Crnokalačka Bara are based on photos by the author and on Marija Gimbutas, *Goddesses and Gods of Old Europe* (Berkeley, 1982), 46, photo 13; 49, fig. 8; 52, fig. 21.

Details of the string skirt from Egtved are taken from Elisabeth Munksgaard, *Oldtidsdragter* (Copenhagen, 1974), 71.

For a rather strongly drawn picture of theories of early mating strategies, see Pierre van den Berghe, *Human Family Systems: An Evolutionary View* (New York, 1979). I am personally grateful to Terrence Deacon for pointing out to me how important this problem may have been for the evolution of language itself.

The seduction scene from the *Iliad* occurs in Book 14, lines 153–351; the quotations are lines 181, 214–17, and 220–21. Ildikó Lehtinen discusses Mordvin and Slavic aprons in *Naisten Korut: Keski-Venäjällä ja Länsi-Sipiriassa* (Helsinki, 1979); quotation from the English synopsis, p. 208.

A thorough discussion of Romanian folk costumes, including pictures of the details mentioned here, can be found in Elena Secosan and Paul Petrescu, *Portul Popular de Sărbătoare din România* (Bucharest, 1984). Illustrations of such aprons also occur in Max Tilke, *Kostümschnitte und Gewandformen* (Tübingen, 1945), pl. 43; the drawing is based on one of these.

Slavic lozenge symbols are discussed at length by A. K. Ambroz, "On the Symbolism of Russian Peasant Embroidery of Archaic Type," *Soviet Anthropology and Archaeology* 6.2 (1967), 22–36. Early phallic keys are mentioned in *Stepi evropejskoj chasti SSSR v skifo-sarmatskoje vremja*, ed. A. I. Meljukova (Moscow, 1989), 136.

The Macedonian costume with string skirts came from the village of Drenok; I am grateful to Peggy Hempstead for bringing it to show me from her collection.

Andromaqi Gjergji illustrates Albanian string skirts in *Veshjet Shqiptare në Shekuj* (Tiranë, 1988), 163 and among the unnumbered color plates; the drawing is based on one of these.

A discussion of the Bronze Age textile fragments that might represent magical belts can be found in Barber 1991, 184. All the ancient string, textiles, and clothed figurines from Europe that are mentioned in this chapter receive technical discussion (and often illustration) in that publication.

A brief description of the netted girdles from the Argolid occurs in the *Peloponnesian Folklore Foundation Catalogue* (Nafplion, 1981), 20–21, whence the quotation.

CHAPTER 3: COURTYARD SISTERHOOD

Statistics on early populations and growth are discussed by Paul and Anne Ehrlich in *Population, Resources, Environment,* 2d ed. (San Francisco, 1972), 5–12.

The early settlement of Ain Mallaha (Eynan) is discussed, with illustrations, by James Mellaart in *The Neolithic of the Near East* (New York, 1975), 31–38. This book comprises a thorough compilation of all the data we have (or had in 1975) on the development of the Neolithic in that area. Much shorter but almost equally broad is James Mellaart's *Earliest Civilizations of the Near East* (New York / London, 1965), with copious illustrations. More specific information on the peculiar village of Suberde is given by Dexter Perkins, Jr., and Patricia Daly, "A Hunters' Village in Neolithic Turkey," *Scientific American* 219 (November 1968), 96–106. Jarmo was initially published by Robert J. Braidwood and B. Howe in *Prehistoric Investigations in Iraqi Kurdistan* (Chicago, 1960), and its textile impressions by J. M. Adovasio: "The Textile and Basketry Impressions from Jarmo," *Paleorient* 3 (1975–77), 223–30, and "Appendix: Notes on the Textile and Basketry Impressions from Jarmo" in Linda S. Braidwood et al., *Prehistoric Archaeology along the Zagros Flanks* (Chicago, 1983), 425–26. For Çatal Hüyük and Hacılar in detail, see respectively James Mellaart's books *Çatal Hüyük, a Neolithic Town in Anatolia* (London / New York, 1967) and *Excavations at Hacılar* (Edinburgh, 1970).

Information about birth spacings is found in Albert J. Ammerman and L. L. Cavalli-Sforza, *The Neolithic Transition and the Genetics of Populations in Europe* (Princeton, 1984), 63–67.

The early stone sculptures from Malta are collected and shown by J. D. Evans in *The Prehistoric Antiquities of the Maltese Islands* (London, 1971), the famous recumbent ones from Hal Saflieni being on pl. 36, No. 6–11.

Quotations from Homer's *Odyssey:* Laistrygonian woman—Book 10, lines 112–13; Calypso—Book 5, lines 61–62.

The chief work on the warp-weighted loom is Marta Hoffmann's carefully researched book, *The Warp-Weighted Loom* (Oslo, 1964/74).

Ruth Tringham discusses and gives an artist's reconstruction of the Neolithic house at Tiszajenő in her book *Hunters, Farmers, and Fishers of Eastern Europe, 6000–3000 B.C.* (London, 1971), 84–87 and fig. 14 (upon which the drawing is based).

The original analysis of the crossing wefts is found in H. C. Broholm and Margrethe Hald, "Danske Bronzealders Dragter," *Nordiske Fortidsminder* 2.5/6 (Copenhagen, 1935), 215–347; see especially 242, fig. 31. Reprinted and discussed in Barber 1991, 178.

For a general account of how the Swiss pile dwellers' culture is now reconstructed, see Hansjürgen Müller-Beck, "Prehistoric Swiss

Lake Dwellers," *Scientific American* 205 (December 1961), 138–47. A complete analysis of all the textiles and basketry was done by Emil Vogt, *Geflechte und Gewebe der Steinzeit* (Basel, 1937).

The Neolithic textiles found in East Germany were finally published as well as possible by Karl Schlabow, "Beitrage zur Erforschung der jungsteinzeitlichen und bronzezeitlichen Gewebetechnik ...," *Jahresschrift für mitteldeutsche Vorgeschichte* 43 (1959), 101–20.

A thorough (if controversial) analysis of the symbols on the Neolithic art of southeastern Europe has been done by Marija Gimbutas, *The Goddesses and Gods of Old Europe* (Berkeley, 1982). B. A. Rybakov has drawn some very similar conclusions by other methods in *Jazychestvo drevnikh Slavjan* (Moscow, 1981).

Many details of Hopi society can be found in Fred Eggan's classic book *Social Organization of the Western Pueblos* (Chicago, 1950).

The peculiar evidence for bones deformed by too much grain grinding is given by Theya Molleson, "Seed Preparation in the Mesolithic: The Osteological Evidence," *Antiquity* 63 (1989), 356–62.

The notion of a "secondary products revolution" was first proposed at length by Andrew Sherratt, "Plough and Pastoralism: Aspects of the Secondary Products Revolution," in *Pattern of the Past: Studies in Honour of David Clarke,* ed. I. Hodder, G. Isaac, and N. Hammond (Cambridge, England, 1981), 261–305.

Concerning Çayönü Tepesi and early Neolithic metalworking, see Halet Çambel and Robert J. Braidwood, "An Early Farming Village in Turkey," *Scientific American* 222 (March 1970), 50–56.

CHAPTER 4: ISLAND FEVER

For an up-to-date and very readable account of Aegean archaeology (including the site of Myrtos), see Peter Warren, *The Aegean Civilizations,* 2d ed. (New York, 1989).

Details of the excavation of Myrtos appear in Peter Warren, *Myrtos: An Early Bronze Age Settlement in Crete* (Oxford, 1972), the tubs, loom weights, etc. on pp. 26–27, 52–54, 64–65, 75, 153, 207, 209, 243, 262–63.

The data for reconstructing the Minoan textile patterns are compiled in Barber 1991, 311–57; the zigzag belt is described on p. 197, and the ancient technology of dyeing on pp. 223–43.

The drawings of Minoan heart spirals are based on W. M. F.

Petrie, *Antaeopolis: The Tombs of Qau* (London, 1930), pl. 1, and Jean Vercoutter, *L'Égypte et le monde égéen préhellénique* (Paris, 1956), pl. 26, No. 188. That of the clay figurine from Petsofá is based on John L. Myres, "Excavations at Palaikastro. II.13: The Sanctuary-Site of Petsofá," *Annual of the British School at Athens* 9 (1902–1903), pl. 8.

Fragments of the fresco of the saffron gatherers were first published (in color) by the excavator, Spiridon Marinatos, in *Excavations at Thera VII* (Athens, 1976). More of the fresco plus interpretative data (such as medicinal use today) can be found in Nanno Marinatos, *Art and Religion in Thera* (Athens, 1984), especially 61–72.

For discussion of yellow as a women's color see E. J. W. Barber, "The Peplos of Athena," in *Goddess and Polis: The Panathenaic Festival in Ancient Athens*, ed. J. Neils (Princeton, 1992), 116–17. For Aristophanes' jokes, see most particularly his play *The Thesmophoriazousai.*

A lengthy discussion of the matrilineal vestiges found in Greek mythohistory can be found in Kenneth Atchity and E. J. W. Barber, "Greek Princes and Aegean Princesses" in *Critical Essays on Homer,* ed. K. Atchity (Boston, 1987), 15–36.

A major work on the interpretation of the archaic Cretan law code found at Gortyna is Ronald F. Willetts, *The Law Code of Gortyn* (Berlin, 1967).

A classic description of Hopi society is found in Fred Eggan, *Social Organization of the Western Pueblos* (Chicago, 1950).

Some of the Tanagra sarcophagi are illustrated by T. Spyropoulos, "Terracotta Sarcophagi," *Archaeology* 25 (1972), 206–09.

CHAPTER 5: MORE THAN HEARTS ON OUR SLEEVES
The net cap and other early textile finds at Naḥal Ḥemar in the Judean Desert were published by Tamar Schick, "Perishable Remains from the Naḥal Ḥemar Cave," *Journal of the Israel Prehistoric Society* 19 (1986), 84–86 and 95*–97*. More of the finds are to be found in the exhibit catalog by Ofer Bar-Yosef, *A Cave in the Desert: Naḥal Ḥemar* (Jerusalem, 1985).

Most of the Neolithic statuettes from central Europe, along with the symbolism of their decoration, have been treated at length by Marija Gimbutas, *The Goddesses and Gods of Old Europe* (Berkeley, 1982).

The frozen tombs of Pazyryk (including the boots and the tattoos) are nicely described and illustrated by M. I. Artamonov, "Frozen Tombs of the Scythians," *Scientific American* 212.5 (May 1965), 100–09. Full treatment of the site and its rich finds can be found in S. I. Rudenko, *Frozen Tombs of Siberia,* tr. M. W. Thompson (Berkeley, 1970).

Perhaps the most complete picture book of Sumerian art, including a number of statues of women (and presently men) wearing wrapped tunics, is André Parrot's magnificent volume *Sumer: The Dawn of Art* (New York, 1961), the best-known statuette of this type being one from Tell Asmar, shown on pp. 101 and 107.

The earliest complete garment known from Egypt was retrieved and published by Sheila Landi and Rosalind Hall, "The Discovery and Conservation of an Ancient Egyptian Linen Tunic," *Studies in Conservation* 24 (1979), 141–51.

The early Greek funerary urn containing a shaggy linen tunic and its belt was described by Mervyn Popham, Evi Touloupa, and L. H. Sackett, "The Hero of Lefkandi," *Antiquity* 56 (1982), 169–74.

N. I. Veselovskij originally published the discovery of the Kuban chieftain and his clothing in the 1898 report of the Imperial Russian Archaeological Commission (29–39). His photograph of the plaid cloth has been reprinted, together with a partial translation and synopsis of Veselovskij's report, in Barber 1991, 168–69. The comparative reconstruction of costumes of this era is discussed in Barber 1991, 295, note 6, and in E. J. W. Barber, "The Proto-Indo-European Notion of Cloth and Clothing," *Journal of Indo-European Studies* 3 (1975), 294–320.

Perhaps the best source currently for Russian regional folk dress is the photo book *Russkij Narodnyj Kostjum,* meaning "Russian Folk Costume" (Leningrad, 1984), published by the State Ethnographic Museum in St. Petersburg from the costumes in its collection.

The Iron Age plaid skirt from Huldremose, Denmark, is illustrated in Elisabeth Munksgaard's pictorial history of ancient Scandinavian dress, *Oldtidsdragter* (Copenhagen, 1974), figs. 97–98.

The Bronze Age statuettes from Cîrna, Romania, are published in V. Dumitrescu, *Necropola de Incineraţie din Epoca Bronzului de la Cîrna* (Bucharest, 1961); the drawing is of statue No. 3.

For the ancient Chinese historian Ssu-ma Ch'ien's account of the Hsiung-Nu and other nomads, see section 110 of his book *Shih*

Chi. The quotations given are from Burton Watson's translation, *Records of the Grand Historian of China* (New York, 1961), vol. II, 159, 170.

CHAPTER 6: ELEMENTS OF THE CODE

Roman coding of clothes by rank is explained in some detail in the *Oxford Companion to Classical Literature,* ed. Sir Paul Harvey (Oxford, England, 1969 edition), 110–11.

The quotations from Mary Kahlenberg come from her book *Textile Traditions of Indonesia* (Los Angeles, 1977), 28.

The passage in Euripides' *Ion* in which Ion builds the pavilion occurs in lines 1133–65, although the whole play revolves around textiles and is well worth reading for the insights it gives.

Discussion of Helen, Penelope, and the whole question of Greek story cloths and funeral cloths, along with reproductions of parts of the Black Sea ones, can be found in Barber 1991, 358–82 and figs. 7.11–13 and 16.15.

Fuller discussion of Athena's dress is found in Barber 1991, 380–82, and in E. J. W. Barber, "The Peplos of Athena," in the exhibition catalog *Goddess and Polis: The Panathenaic Festival in Ancient Athens,* ed. J. Neils (Princeton, 1992), 102–17.

National Geographic published a new set of color photographs of the entire Bayeux Tapestry on the nine hundredth anniversary of the Battle of Hastings (August 1966), 206–51.

George Melville Bolling presents his case for Andromache's rose magic in *"Poikilos* and *Throna," American Journal of Philology* 79 (1958), 275–82.

Marija Gimbutas's treatment of Neolithic egg and bird motifs (along with snakes, frogs, and fish) occurs in her book *Goddesses and Gods of Old Europe* (Berkeley, 1982).

A prehistoric bird-shaped ladle and much other related Slavic folk art are illustrated in Tamara Talbot Rice, *A Concise History of Russian Art* (New York, 1963), No. 61, etc.

Mary Kelly has collected material on Berehinia, her festivals, and the associated textiles in "Embroidery for the Goddess," *Threads Magazine* (June–July 1987), 26–29, and in her book *Goddess Embroideries of Eastern Europe* (Winona, Minn., 1989). Further material, also with copious illustration, can be found in A. K. Ambroz, "On the Symbolism of Russian Peasant Embroidery of Archaic Type," *Soviet Anthropology and Archaeology* 6.2 (1967),

SOURCES

22–36. The drawing is based on material from V. V. Stasov, *Russkij narodnyj ornament* (St. Petersburg, 1872), part 1.

Tutankhamon's tunic is reproduced with discussion in Barber 1991, fig. 5.10.

The first quotation on Batak textiles comes from Harley Harris Bartlett, *The Labors of the Datoe and Other Essays on the Bataks of Asahan (North Sumatra)* (Ann Arbor, 1973), 138, note 7; the others are from pp. 22–23 of Mattiebelle Gittinger's article "Selected Batak Textiles: Technique and Function," *Textile Museum Journal* 4.2 (1975), 13–26.

CHAPTER 7: CLOTH FOR THE CARAVANS

The Old Assyrian correspondence between women of Ashur and their husbands in Anatolia is largely published and analyzed by Klaas R. Veenhof, *Aspects of Old Assyrian Trade and its Terminology* (Leiden, 1972). The opening quotation is from BIN 6,7, translated on p. 113; the remaining quotations come respectively from pp. 114 ("Kuluma . . ."), 104 ("let . . . ," "if . . ."), 110 ("but . . . ," "in . . ."), 115 ("About . . . ," "Lamassi . . ."). Material concerning the packing of donkeys is on pp. 70, 26–27; Akkadian cloths are on p. 98; Lamassi's letters on pp. 113–15. The cuneiform transcription is based on Ferris J. Stephens, *Old Assyrian Letters and Business Documents: Babylonian Inscriptions in the Collection of James B. Nies, Yale University*, VI (New Haven, 1944), pl. 2, No. 7.

Concerning milk, see Andrew Sherratt, "Plough and Pastoralism: Aspects of the Secondary Products Revolution" in *Pattern of the Past: Studies in Honour of David Clarke,* ed. I. Hodder, G. Isaac, and N. Hammond (Cambridge, England 1981), 261–305; also Margaret Ehrenberg, *Women in Prehistory* (London, 1989), 101–02 for milkers.

The women's workrooms at Gordion were published by Keith de Vries, "The Greeks and Phrygians in the Early Iron Age," in *From Athens to Gordion: the Papers of a Memorial Symposium for Rodney S. Young,* ed. Keith de Vries (Philadelphia, 1980), 33–49.

Çatal Hüyük is described in full by James Mellaart, *Çatal Hüyük, a Neolithic Town in Anatolia* (London / New York, 1967).

The material on women's dowries in Mesopotamia is culled from Stephanie Dalley, "Old Babylonian Dowries," *Iraq* 42 (1980), 53–74, the quotations being from pp. 61 and (in the note) 57.

The archives of Queen Iltani of Karana and the rulers of Mari are extensively discussed by Stephanie Dalley in *Mari and Karana* (London, 1984), an extremely readable and graphic re-creation of the world of nineteenth-century-B.C. Mesopotamia. The direct quotations are from pp. 40 ("I . . ."), 103 ("some . . . ," "which . . ."), 82 ("The . . ."), 70 ("begs"), 109 ("the . . ."), 102 ("Now . . ."), 43 ("The . . ."), and 53 ("Send . . .") respectively. The historical background is on pp. 37–40, the palace on 26, Iltani's workers on 53 and 103, blind workers on 72, slave singers and children's rations on 99, giving away slaves on 70 and 102, women's jobs on 72–74, 93, 104, 109–10, Iltani's sisters on 103, the dispute on 72, and the carpet on 52. Zimri-Lim's letter to Shibtu is quoted from B. F. Batto, *Studies on Women at Mari* (Baltimore, 1974), 27. Men who dyed and finished cloth are discussed by H. Waetzoldt, *Die Neo-Sumerische Textilindustrie* (Rome, 1972), 153–54, while felt making is treated by P. Steinkeller, "Mattresses and Felt in Early Mesopotamia," *Oriens Antiquus* 19 (1980), 79–100, and Mesopotamian rug techniques by Barber 1991, 170–71.

Cylinder seals with representations of spinning and weaving (from Susa, Choga Mish, and unknown sites) are discussed and illustrated with references in Barber 1991, 56–57, 84.

The information on the workers of the two kings of Lagash was collated and analyzed by M. Lambert, "Recherches sur la vie ouvrière: Les ateliers de tissage de Lagash," *Archiv Orientalni* 29 (1961), 422–43.

The quotations from Sir Leonard Woolley were taken from *Ur Excavations,* 2 (London, 1934), 238–40.

CHAPTER 8: LAND OF LINEN

Herodotus relates his memoirs of Egypt in Book 2 of his *Histories,* including sheep in section 37 and wool in 81.

For the Egyptian way of donning a kilt, see William Kelly Simpson, "A Protocol of Dress: The Royal and Private Fold of the Kilt," *Journal of Egyptian Archaeology* 74 (1988), 203–04.

Miriam Lichtheim has published highly readable translations of many interesting texts in her paperback book *Ancient Egyptian Literature,* Vol. 1, *The Old and Middle Kingdoms* (Berkeley, 1975). Quotations were taken as follows: the tale of the little servant girl, pp. 221–22; the lament of the weaving rooms, 153; the satires of the trades, 188–89.

The Old Testament story of the fugitives under the flax is quoted from Joshua 2:6, while the twisting of flax is mentioned repeatedly in Exodus 35–39.

Two tombs from Beni Hasan, those of Baqt and Khety, picture the processes of spinning and weaving rather extensively. They were published by Percy E. Newberry, *Beni Hasan II* (London, 1894), pl. 4 and 13. For all such scenes and for the extant patterned textiles, see Barber 1991.

The quotation from Grace Crowfoot comes from her very lucid pamphlet *Methods of Hand Spinning in Egypt and the Sudan. Bankfield Museum Notes,* series 2, No. 12 (Halifax, 1931), p. 30.

The workmen's village at Amarna is published by T. E. Peet and Sir Leonard Woolley, *Tel el-Amarna, the City of Akhenaten* (London, 1923); further discussion of the weaving remains occurs in Barber 1991, 88–89.

Information on women's professions was gleaned from the titles listed and discussed by William A. Ward, *Essays on Feminine Titles of the Middle Kingdom and Related Subjects* (Beirut, 1986), 3–23. The quotation about the female gardener and winnower comes from p. 23. Further data on textile-related professions in the Middle Kingdom appear in William C. Hayes, *A Papyrus of the Late Middle Kingdom* (Brooklyn, 1955), especially 105–08.

The ceiling of Hepzefa's tomb and other data concerning tombs with Aegean textile motifs on the ceilings are collected, discussed, and illustrated in Barber 1991, 330–57.

The leather canopy was published by Emil Brugsch, *Le Tente funéraire de la Princesse Isimkheb* (Cairo, 1889).

Wah's tomb linens, which are at the Metropolitan Museum of Art in New York, are described by William C. Hayes in *The Scepter of Egypt* I (New York, 1953), 304. The quotation about the casket comes from p. 246, and that concerning Sit Snefru from p. 215.

The beaded dress of the Fifth Dynasty from Qau is illustrated and discussed, along with the leather-net dresses, by Rosalind Hall, "Fishing-Net Dresses in the Petrie Museum," *Gottinger Miszellen* 42 (1981), 37–43. The later ones from Kerma are described by George Reisner, *Excavations at Kerma* IV (Cambridge, Mass., 1923), 103–04, 300, 303.

CHAPTER 9: THE GOLDEN SPINDLE

The Alaca tombs were published by Hamit Z. Koşay in *Les Fouilles d'Alaca Höyük, 1937–1939* (Ankara, 1951). The silver spindle is mentioned on p. 168 as an object of unknown use; the tomb drawing is based on pl. 191. Data and illustrations of the other Anatolian spindles are collected in Barber 1991, 60–62.

The passage from *Ion* of Euripides is lines 1417–22.

The quotation from the *Iliad* about Helen weaving comes from Book 3, lines 125–27; about Chryseis, from Book 1, lines 366–69 and 29–31. The quotations from the *Odyssey* are as follows: the Taphian pirates, 15.427–29; Eurykleia and the servants, 22.422–23; the Phaiakians giving Odysseus clothes, 13.10 and 13.67; Helen giving Telemachus a robe, 15.105 and 15.126–28.

Heinrich Schliemann's accounts of his excavation of Troy can be found in *Troy and Its Remains* (London, 1875; reprinted, New York, 1968), and *Ilios: The City and Country of the Trojans* (London, 1880). The clay box containing beads is discussed and pictured in the latter book on pp. 360–61. The subsequent discovery of gold beads in the fill around a loom was published by Carl Blegen, John Caskey, Marion Rawson, and Jerome Sperling, *Troy: General Introduction: The First and Second Settlements* I (Princeton, 1950), 350–51. These and further finds of ancient beadwork are collected in Barber 1991, 171–73.

For the reexcavation of Troy, see Carl Blegen, John Caskey, Marion Rawson, and Jerome Sperling, *Troy* I (Princeton, 1950); for the loom and beads, see vol. I pp. 350–51 and fig. 461.

The analysis of the Linear B archives and of the economic reality represented is an ongoing process involving many scholars. The most comprehensive and readable treatment is that done by the decipherers of the script, Michael Ventris and John Chadwick, *Documents in Mycenaean Greek*, 2d ed. (Cambridge, England, 1973). Much of the synopsis given here can be gleaned from that source. See also John T. Killen, "The Knossos o-pi Tablets," *Atti e memorie del 1.o congresso internazionale di Micenologia* (Rome, 1968), 636–43. The drawing of Pylos tablet Ab 555 is based on Emmett L. Bennett Jr., *The Pylos Tablets* (Princeton, 1955), 57.

Details on fleece weights, flock sizes, and other technical aspects of the Mycenaean (and medieval English) wool industry were taken from John T. Killen, "The Wool Industry of Crete in the Late Bronze Age," *Annual of the British School at Athens 59* (1964), 1–15; John T. Killen, "Minoan Woolgathering: A Reply II," *Kadmos 8* (1969), 23–38; and J. P. Olivier, "La Série Dn de Cnossos," *Studia Micenei ed Egeo-Anatolici 2* (1967), 71–93. Work on the status of apprentices in particular is published by Killen in "Two Notes on the Knossos Ak Tablets," *Minos* 12 (1972), 423–40.

Considerable information on textile production in northwestern Europe in the Middle Ages occurs in Edouard Perroy, *Le travail dans les régions du nord du XIe au début du XIVe siècle* (Paris, 1963). The quotation concerning the Maltese textile industry came from H. Bowen-Jones, J. C. Dewdney, and W. B. Fischer, eds., *Malta, Background for Development* (Durham, England, 1961), 124.

The evidence for the evolution of sheep fleece is discussed fully in Michael Ryder's tome *Sheep and Man* (London, 1983). A much briefer account of it and of the role of shears can be found in Barber 1991, 20–30, along with an analysis of the associated archaic vocabulary on 260 ff.

The Etruscan pendant was published by Christiana Morigi Govi, "Il Tintinnabulo della 'Tomba degli ori' dell'arsenale militare di Bologna," *Archeologia Classica* 23 (1971), 211–35; the drawing is based on pl. 53–54. Marta Hoffmann's book *The Warp-Weighted Loom* (Oslo, 1974) contains her descriptions and pictures of the warp-weighted loom in use as well as of the warp found in the bog at Tegle, Norway (p. 169, fig. 81) and the Lappish woman weaving a heading band for her warp-weighted loom (p. 66, fig. 26).

E. C. Clark considers the problem of Turkish rug weavers in "The Emergence of Textile Manufacturing Entrepreneurs in Turkey, 1804–1968," Ph.D. thesis, Princeton University, 1969, 54. The development of textiles in Crete is discussed at length in Barber 1991, 311–57, and (Iron Age) 371–72.

Concerning grave mounds: Patroklos' funeral is described in Book 23 of the *Iliad,* and Beowulf's mound in lines 3156 ff. of *Beowulf.* (See, for example *Beowulf,* tr. M. Alexander.[Harmondsworth, 1973], 151.) A brief account of Gordion appears in Seton Lloyd, *Early Highland Peoples of Anatolia* (London and New York, 1967), 124–35.

The story cloths from Kertch are discussed and illustrated (with Russian references) in Barber 1991, 206–09.

CHAPTER 10: BEHIND THE MYTHS

Ovid tells the story of Philomela and Prokne in his long poem, *Metamorphoses,* Book 6, lines 424–674, and that of Arachne's contest with Athena in Book 6, lines 1–145.

Realgar and the mineral called "dragon's blood" are discussed by H. Quiring, "Vorphonizischer Königspurpur und *uqnû*-Stein," *Forschung und Fortschritte* 21–23 (1945–47), 98–99.

For the archaeology and folklore of nettles, see Margrethe Hald, "The Nettle as a Culture Plant," *Folk-Liv* 6 (1942), 28–49. Perhaps the most famous tale involving nettles is that of Hans Christian Anderson called "The Wild Swans." But Hald also mentions Lithuanian and Hungarian tales.

An entire book has been written on the subject of *The Spinning Aphrodite* by Elmer G. Suhr (New York, 1969). The quotation concerning the magical effect of spinning comes from Grace M. Crowfoot, *Methods of Hand Spinning in Egypt and the Sudan. Bankfield Museum Notes,* series 2, No. 12 (Halifax, 1931), 11, and is attributed to C. G. and B. Z. Seligman.

Ariadne and the cult involving couvade are mentioned by Plutarch in section 20 of his *Life of Theseus.*

The short quotations from Hesiod come from *Works and Days,* lines 60–65, the longer one from *The Theogony,* lines 573–76.

For a fuller discussion of the nature of Athena, see Kenneth Atchity and E. J. W. Barber, "Greek Princes and Aegean Princesses," *Critical Essays on Homer,* ed. Kenneth Atchity (Boston, 1987), 15–36. For Greek weaving vocabulary, see Barber 1991.

The quotation concerning Mokosh is taken from Marija Gimbutas, *The Slavs* (London / New York, 1971), 168. The geographical differences in the *vily* are discussed by Linda J. Ivanits, *Russian Folk Belief* (Armonk / London, 1989), 75–76.

Many of the early representations of women dancing at the Rusalii festivals are reproduced by B. A. Rybakov, "The *Rusalii* and the God Simargl-Pereplut," *Soviet Anthropology and Archaeology* 6.4 (1968), 34–59.

The translated sections from the story of the Frog Princess are taken from the first of the three versions collected in the mid-nineteenth century by Aleksandr Afanasiev, published by him in *Narodnyje Russkije Skazki* ("Russian Folk Tales") as No. 267. This is also the version found in the abridged translation by N. Guterman in *Russian Fairy Tales* (New York, 1973). The third and longest version (No. 269) is close to the one used by the Russian artist I. A. Bilibin in his beautiful illustrated edition of the tale.

For scholarship about the "coat of many colors," see Rabbi J. H. Hertz, *The Pentateuch and the Haftorahs* (London, 1976), 142.

For the tomb paintings, see Percy E. Newberry, *Beni Hasan I* (London, 1893), pl. 28, 30–31.

The quotations from Exodus come from 35:25–26 and 36:8, that concerning Goliath's spear comes from 1 Samuel 17:7, and the passage from Revelation comes from 16:16.

Thutmose III's account of the captives and other booty from the battle of Megiddo is partly translated in James H. Breasted, *Ancient Records of Egypt* II (Chicago, 1906), 187–88.

CHAPTER 11: PLAIN AND FANCY, NEW OR TRIED AND TRUE

The story of the East Indian prints is collected with other such by Bette Hochberg in her booklet *Spin Span Spun: Fact and Folklore for Spinners* (Santa Cruz, Calif., 1979), 46 and 62.

Thutnofer's townhouse is pictured and discussed by Norman de Garis Davies, "The Townhouse in Ancient Egypt," *Metropolitan Museum Studies* I.2 (1929), 233–55. Neferronpet's titles are found in Alan Gardiner and A. E. P. Weigall, *A Topographical Catalogue of the Private Tombs of Thebes* (London, 1913), 28, Tomb No. 133, while Davies published drawings of the weaving scene in *Seven Private Tombs at Kurnah* (London, 1948), pl. 35 (on which the author's drawing is based). What can be gleaned about Neferhotep's weaving scene is brought together by Henry Ling Roth, *Ancient Egyptian and Greek Looms. Bankfield Museum Notes,* series 2, No. 2 (Halifax, 1913; 2d ed. 1951), 15–16, with illustration.

All the pieces of fancy Egyptian cloth from the Eighteenth Dynasty are discussed at length both by Barber 1991, 153–62 and by Elizabeth Riefstahl, *Patterned Textiles in Pharaonic Egypt* (Brooklyn, 1944). Both works contain extensive bibliographies. The Amarna weaver's waste and the Gurob spindle are also discussed in Barber 1991, 49, note 6, and 64–66, with references. The drawing of the Nine Bows and Captives tapestry fragments was based on the photograph in G. Daressy, *Fouilles de la Vallée des Rois* (Cairo, 1902), pl. LVII, no. 24987. The drawing of Kha's bedspread was based on E. Schiaparelli, *La Tomba intatta dell' Architetto Cha* (Turin, 1927), 131 fig. 114.

Howard Carter describes his discovery of Tutankhamon's tomb in vivid detail in his book with A. C. Mace, *The Discovery of the Tomb of Tutankhamen* (New York: Dover, 1970), a reprint of *The*

Tomb of Tut'Ankh'Amen . . . (London, 1923), vol. 1. The quotations come from pp. 95–96 of the reprint.

A brief account of the Mitanni princesses occurs in John A. Wilson, *The Culture of Ancient Egypt* (Chicago, 1951), 202, 230. The accusations against Paneb are published by Jaroslav Černý, "Papyrus Salt 124 (British Museum 10055)," *Journal of Egyptian Archaeology* 15 (1929), 243–58; the quotation is from p. 246. Other information about slaves and workers was drawn from J. J. Janssen, *Commodity Prices from the Ramessid Period* (Leiden, 1975), and about Deir el-Medinah in particular from Jaroslav Černý, *A Community of Workmen at Thebes in the Ramesside Period* (Cairo, 1973).

The trial of Erenofre was published by Alan Gardiner as "A Lawsuit Arising from the Purchase of Two Slaves," *Journal of Egyptian Archaeology* 21 (1935), 140–46.

Apollonia's loom is discussed by Diane Lee Carroll, *Looms and Textiles of the Copts* (Seattle, 1988), 42–44.

The quotation from Lysias' speech "On the Slaying of Eratosthenes" comes from sections 23–26 (Oxford ed.). Xenophon's story about Socrates and Isomachos occurs in his *Economics,* Book 7; the quotations are from sections 5–6, 32–34, 35–36, and 41, respectively. The story of Aristarchos and his female relatives is told in his *Memorabilia,* Book 2; the quotations are from sections 2, 3–5, and 12.

The material for studying professional textile work in Athens is to be found in Wesley Thompson, "Weaving: A Man's Work," *Classical World* 75 (1982), 217–22, and in A. W. Gomme, *The Population of Athens in the Fifth and Fourth Centuries B.C.* (Oxford, England, 1933); the quotations are from pp. 42 and 21.

The Homeric quotation about the wool worker comes from the *Iliad,* 12.433–35.

Plutarch talks about "the Spartan life" at length in his *Life of Lykourgos;* the quotation is from section 14. The quotation from *Moralia* comes from section 241d.

Concerning the peplos of Athena, see John M. Mansfield, "The Robe of Athena and the Panathenaic Peplos" (Ph.D. thesis, University of California, 1985); Barber 1991, 361–82; and E. J. W. Barber, "The Peplos of Athena," in *Goddess and Polis: The Panathenaic Festival in Ancient Athens,* ed. Jenifer Neils

(Princeton, 1992), 103–18. For the festival more generally, see Erika Simon, *Festivals of Attica* (Madison, Wis., 1983).

CHAPTER 12: POSTSCRIPT: FINDING THE INVISIBLE

The story of Petrie and Amélineau is told more fully by Michael Hoffman in *Egypt before the Pharaohs* (New York, 1979), 268–69. The quotation is from W. M. F. Petrie, *The Royal Tombs of the Earliest Dynasties* (London, 1901), Part II 2.

The First Dynasty Egyptian shirt was published by Sheila Landi and Rosalind Hall, "The Discovery and Conservation of an Ancient Egyptian Linen Tunic," *Studies in Conservation* 24 (1979), 141–51.

Emmett Bennett Jr.'s work on the filing systems at Pylos appeared as "The Find-Spots of the Pylos Tablets" in *Mycenaean Studies: Proceedings of the 3rd International Colloquium* . . . , ed. E. L. Bennett Jr. (Madison, Wis., 1964), 241–52.

The Hallstatt cloth with lice in it was published as No. 34 (p. 141) by H.-J. Hundt in "Vorgeschichtliche Gewebe aus dem Hallstätter Salzberg," *Jahrbuch des römisch-germanischen Zentralmuseums Mainz* 7 (1960), 126–50.

For linguistic analyses of Greek (including Mycenaean) textile terms, see Barber 1991, 260–84.

The loom weight experiment was described by Avigail Sheffer in "The Use of Perforated Clay Balls on the Warp-weighted Loom," *Tel Aviv* 8 (1981), 81–83. The quotation is from p. 82.

The basic book on applying symmetry analysis to cultural material is Dorothy K. Washburn and Donald W. Crowe, *Symmetries of Culture* (Seattle, 1988). The application to Cretan motifs appears briefly in E. Barber, "Reconstructing the Ancient Aegean / Egyptian Textile Trade," *Textiles in Trade: Proceedings of the Textile Society of America, Biennial Symposium* (Washington, D.C., 1990), 104–11.

Index

d = definition, i = illustration, m = map, t = table / chart